# MEN,
# POWER,
# and MYTHS

# Men, Power, and Myths

## The Quest for Male Identity

Allan Guggenbühl

*Translated by Gary V. Hartman*

CONTINUUM • NEW YORK

1997
The Continuum Publishing Company
370 Lexington Avenue
New York, NY 10017

This translation has been supported by a grant from The Ann and Erlo
van Waveren Foundation.

Printed in the United States of America

**Library of Congress Cataloging-in-Publication Data**

Guggenbühl, Allan.
   [Männer, Mythen, Mächte. English]
   Men, power, and myths : the quest for male identity / Allan
Guggenbühl ; translated by Gary V. Hartman.
     p.   cm.
   ISBN 0-8264-0781-1 (hardcover : alk. paper)
   1. Masculinity.  2. Men—Psychology.  3. Mythology—Psychological
aspects.  4. Jungian psychology.  I. Title.
BF692.5.G8413   1997
155.3′32—DC21
                                                97-2431
                                                 CIP

# Contents

4
## MEN AND THEIR GRANDIOSITY

5
## THE SHADOW OF GRANDIOSITY

6
## THE TENSION BETWEEN ARCHAIC SAVAGERY AND OVERCIVILIZATION

# 1

## MEN—
## Deficient Beings?

♂

## Psychology's Neglect
## of Men

"Men," claims psychology, "must learn to think differently." "They must learn to show their feelings, to take personal issues more seriously, to do without power, to talk about themselves, to become aware of their aggressive tendencies, and to think less rationally." There is no room for difference, continues the litany. The two genders are psychologically the same. I could not agree more if "thinking differently" means giving up male supremacy, preferential treatment, and a fixed division of labor. If, however, "thinking differently" means that I thereby lose my freedom to be a man, then I feel my resistance stirring. Such demands from psychology reveal themselves as the arguments of an attitude that only partially corresponds to a man's soul. In this chapter I describe how, until now, psychology has failed to develop an understanding that does justice to a man's true being.

*I find it difficult to talk to my husband. He hasn't learned to express his feelings. He carries on monologues about the slump in the construction industry, complains about federal and local politicians, or explains why the Dallas Cowboys are leading their NFL division. A lot of times I can't even talk to him. He buries himself in the newspaper, stares at the boob tube, or just putters around the house. It never occurs to him to reflect on himself. If I complain, he just looks at me dumb-founded and asks why I am not happy: I have everything I need! Putting his feelings, sensations, or what he thinks about our relationship into words is completely foreign to him.*

We have all heard similar opinions about men. A man is speech-less, when he has to talk about himself. He is a deficient being, shutting off the inner realms of his personality. Apparently, he dedicates his energies to work, to delivering lectures, developing projects, seeking solutions or fighting for ideals. Yet, in relation-ships and when it is a question of feelings, he remains strangely dumb. "A man is a human being without language, the one who keeps silent," notes one psychologist. His superiority is a fallacy for, when he turns his gaze to himself, his vision becomes clouded and his mood irritated. His helplessness in terms of his own psy-chology results in others' perceiving him as a male chauvinist, as patriarchal, as a Peter Pan, Don Juan, Casanova, or an urban cow-boy. The average male strains mightily to live down the epithets. He tries desperately to express his personal feelings and impres-sions, to listen and to engage in relationships. *Is* the male a speechless being? *Is* he simply underdeveloped?

Men are constantly confronted with these kinds of state-ments, these questions. A flood of psychological books on the sub-ject emphasizes how important it is that we men stand up for our feelings, control our tendency to violence, work through our per-sonal biography, show emotion, and not shy away from what is personal. Have several thousand years of the patriarchy left such scars on men that they are innerly crippled, that they are inca-pable of developing these qualities? In contrast to women, men are less interested in questions of relationship, of personal needs and sensitivities. Even when he tries to compensate for these shortcomings through work, prestige, adventure, or new relation-ships, a man's inner life remains nonetheless psychologically underdeveloped. Naturally, this description does not apply to all men. Most men, however, feel helpless when it comes to personal matters and the areas of feeling and relationship.

Our culture demands of men that they strip off the rational-istic, impersonal, superficial, and boastful affectations of past eras. They must lay aside their uniform mask, to allow men conscious of themselves to emerge. The hypocrisy of relationship is passé. Men should let go their hard won roles that have made it possible for them to overlook the personal aspects of their existence. "Yes, it is completely clear that I have become more demanding with time. A man like myself must be in a position to show his feelings. I can no longer tolerate these up-tight types . . ." It is no longer accept-able for one man to work side by side with another for years and know practically nothing about that colleague's personal life. It is no longer acceptable for a man to fail to notice that his cubicle-mate is upset over something.

Beginners in relationship need not apply! Our culture demands a man who is sensitive and feeling, who does not hide his moods, and is also capable of being personal. Our culture demands a man who, following the terminology of Jung's Analytical Psychology, is also oriented to his feminine side, to his anima. Such an anima man does not judge the world one-sidedly according to logic and reason, but has the capacity to register subtleties and to admit his own, personal weaknesses. He can do without competition, aggression, and the desire for greatness, control, position, and dominance. He can open himself to his fellow human beings and act with greater consideration for his environment in general. The ambitious man, who dreams of safaris in Kenya or his own computer company, without realizing his wife's unhappiness, has been outstripped. Our culture has openings only for the sensitive, considerate man, who reflects on his relationships and his personal life.

Like the majority of my acquaintances, I am largely in agreement with these demands. I, myself, get angry at friends who can only talk about sports, business, or the economy—or who believe they can impress me with their cars, their careers, the women they date, or their corporate positions. I get upset at the man who plays the big boss at work, designating authority importantly while rocking back and forth on his heels. He fails to notice that his subordinates suffer under his self-importance and consider him a laughable figure. I, too, become angry at men who think only of themselves, of their careers, and their hobbies and take it for granted that their wives support their grandiosity. I do believe that we, as men, must work on ourselves. It is up to us to attend to our shadow aspects. It is up to us to be or to become more sensitive, related, considerate, and feeling oriented and, at the same time, less prone to violence.

## MEN'S RELUCTANCE TO ACCEPT HELP

We are a long way from this goal and, correspondingly, the "anima man" is still a rare species. One reason for both of these factors lies in the stubborn refusal of most men to accept help.

Going into therapy or seeing a counselor because of a personal
crisis is alien to many men. Even when they are struggling with
severe problems, men avoid the office of psychologists or psychotherapists like the devil the baptismal water. How come? "I will
solve my problems, myself!" While the advice of a specialist concerning employment possibilities is within the realm of the tolerable, the idea that a stranger might root around in one's psyche
remains a horror. Women are the ones who fill the offices of psychotherapists, marriage and family counselors, and psychiatrists.
Men keep their distance and show up in such places only in emer-
gencies or under extreme personal pressure.

Men often hesitate even to admit that they might need help.
"I am doing fine!" comes the laconic response, even when they are
suffering from tremendous tension in their marriage and have
immense professional difficulties. Many women are capable of
articulating their problems within the framework of their relationships, of expressing their wishes, hopes, and expectations to
their spouses or partners. With men silence reigns. They have
fewer friends they can call on to discuss personal issues and the
subject of feelings is taboo. "They are brought up to function without feelings," remarks one commentator.

In doing marriage therapy, it has been my experience that
men are less conscious of personal problems than women. When
they are dragged in by their wife or partner, many seem awkward
or defensive: "She is the one with the problem. She is unhappy
with the relationship. I think everything is fine." "How we met?
You had better ask my wife, she remembers all that better than I
do." "I know I am no good. That's just how it is." Or, "The problem is simple: *she* wants to move out and make chaos in the family!" Men prefer to carry their suffering themselves, to keep it
separate from their relationships. They have difficulty formulating anxiety, feelings, and personal desires. They may talk briefly
about themselves to an unknown cocktail waitress after a couple
of martinis or to someone in the next seat on an airplane. They do
so seldom as part of their everyday routine. There are exceptions.

When a man is attracted to a woman or even in love with her
or when he is talking with someone who is not part of his immediate circle of acquaintances, he often revels in his feelings and
perceptions and considers the most banal psychological idea a
profound insight. Such sporadic eruptions do not affect his basic
attitude. In his everyday life and work, he continues to ignore psy-

chology. He continues to be unreceptive to any personal insights: "It is not true that I could not separate from my parents. There were all kinds of financial reasons for my living at home until I was thirty."

Naturally, I have somewhat exaggerated this picture of men. There are many men who are capable of reflecting about themselves, who know their own dependence and neediness, and who attend to their relationships. Most of my friends and colleagues take great pains not to live according to the image of men I have just described. Men today are allowed, even encouraged, to express their feelings and to be receptive to others' feelings. They are supposed to stand up for their individual perceptions and fantasies. They remain a minority. Most men are curiously timid when it comes to discussions of relationship. They experience difficulty in formulating personal feelings and view the psychologizing of their being as a threat. In management courses they cursorily register the discussions of psychology and discard the information as unimportant. "It is all well and good to talk about mutual understanding. I have to see to it, however, that my company survives the competition in today's market."

I understand the demands of psychology and feminism and partially agree with them. At the same time, I ask myself whether we are not barking up the wrong tree by ultimately demanding of men that they change, that they become more psychological? Does such a demand truly do justice to a man's being? Is it not possible that, behind men's resistance, there lies a fundamental, an essential difference? Is it not also possible that the real failure is not that of men? Could it not be that psychology has failed, that psychology has not yet been capable of grasping what it means to be male?

I am reminded of one session in my own psychoanalysis in which I discussed a very meaningful dream. In the dream I was an inmate of the Dachau concentration camp. I was somehow able to escape this inhuman situation. After an odyssey over numerous passes in the Alps and overcoming various impediments, I was finally captured again. I was to be shot, but first the Nazi executioners forced me to eat wood. At the end of the dream I was freed by the Allies and released in a mountain meadow.

How did my therapist react? She nodded and began asking about my personal associations. I thought of news photographs from World War II, the fate of the Jews, and the role my native

Switzerland played. My therapist is not satisfied. Apparently she
wants me to be more personal. Straining, I try to connect the
dream with my everyday life situation. Why am I resisting? Finally,
I make a connection to tensions in one of my relationships. The
discussion with my therapist is admittedly revealing and worthwhile, but at the same time I have a curious, stale feeling at the
end of the hour. The session did not satisfy me. The dream col-
lapsed and became banal. Something was taken away from me.
Was this kind of psychological work really the right way to reflect
about my dream?

Perhaps we need to change our perspective, to seek out other
theoretical tools. It is not that men are soul cripples, but that a psychology that places emphasis on relationship, feeling, and the
personal, only partially captures what it means to be a man. To
understand men, we need another pair of soul glasses than the
ones psychology offers.

Perhaps our current psychological thinking corresponds
most directly with the feminine soul, while the language of the
masculine soul has not even been discovered. Psychology
demands of a man that he become aware of his feelings, understand himself out of himself, and attend to the personal. These
demands become an attempt to repress the masculine, as long as
psychology does not correspond to the primary quality of the masculine soul. The psychological approach directs itself to an underdeveloped side of a man and fails to consider the mythical
orientation of the masculine, as I will discuss in chapter 2. Since a
man lives primarily from mythical images, relational psychology
always remains a secondary plot.

What about psychology's neglect of men? We might first
briefly consider the history of psychology from the perspective of
the influence of the feminine. We might ask whether psychology
has "feminized" men. At first glance the idea seems absurd. Didn't
men establish most of the great concepts in psychology?
Compared with the large number of well-known male psychologists like Sigmund Freud, C. G. Jung, Alfred Adler, Gregory
Bateson, Cyril Burt, or Jean Piaget, the number of women who
have made significant contributions to the field is extremely
sparse. Men have conceived many of the fundamental axioms of
psychology: the collective unconscious, repression, sublimation,
complex, transference and counter-transference, projection,
dream theory, and the theory of neurosis. They have also elabo-

rated the significance of cognition, the locus of control, the learning process, and the therapeutic dialogue. Is it not audacious to maintain that psychology does not do justice to the male psyche? Generally, psychology is accused of just the opposite tendency, of being patriarchal and underestimating the position of women!

## THE INSIDIOUS POWER OF THE CONSULTING ROOM

I have posed the question of whether psychology has failed to grasp what is essentially male. To answer this question, we need to examine the manner and style of psychotherapeutic work. Where, how, and with whom the men of psychology did their work influenced the conclusions they drew.

Psychotherapy occurs for the most part in the consulting room. The patient enters the office, possibly waiting until the hour begins, greets the therapist, looking him or her in the eye, lays her- or himself on the couch, or takes his or her place opposite the therapist. The door is closed; the outer world is shut away. No one may know what is discussed in the consultation room. Secrecy reigns. The patient knows that he has put himself in the hands of someone who is prepared not to reveal the content of their exchange. The general public may know nothing about his fears, weaknesses, and experiences.

We have to take into account the nature of this place where the analytic work occurs. The setting influences the thinking and contributes to how the soul manifests itself. We have to relate Freud's and Jung's insights as well as those of psychotherapy in general with this place of meeting. Next to the secrets of the unconscious, intimacy is the subject of the consultation room exploration. What the founding fathers of depth psychology observed was colored by the place and the ritual that they chose for their work. The personal encounter of two human beings in a closed room served as their medium for the investigation of the soul.

Behind a closed door the patient and therapist sit opposite one another or the patient lies on the couch while the analyst sits behind him on a chair. The therapist directs his attention to his patient, listens to his problems, and tries to feel his way into the patient's situation. The therapist attempts to understand the patient and to empathize with him and explores with his under-

standing and empathy the background of the patient's problems
and difficulties. Why does he suffer from self doubt? What do the
anxiety attacks or sense of alienation mean? Together they arrive
at conclusions. Usually, they seek a consensus and develop,
thereby, a story that is true for both of them. Through his personal contact with the patient, the psychotherapist discovers the
source of the patient's suffering and guides him to healing.

What unfolds before the therapist in this setting, however, is
one-sided. Psychotherapy has selected a specific ritual for itself to
explore the soul. This ritual produces corresponding soul images.
When in the seclusion of the consulting room therapist and
patient explore biographical connections or decipher dreams or
when the patient gives the therapist her trust and secrets are
aired, they create a psychological landscape. In such privacy and
in such a dyadic situation, only part of the human soul reveals
itself. When the emphasis falls on relationship, contact with others, intimacy, and the importance of human beings as individuals,
the landscape of the soul that opens up is a very specific one. It
would look quite different if the exploration of the soul were carried on outside in a field, at work, or in a public situation. Only *a
part of the human soul* reveals itself in the consulting room.

What reveals itself in the setting of the consulting room is
*psychology.* Just as in a house of prostitution erotic desire or moral
indignation manifests itself or as in the presence of violence our
own aggression or fear comes to the fore, so the consulting room
evokes the psychological part of our personality. (I will differentiate the psychological part of our personality from the mythological one in chapter 2.) Since the psychotherapist devotes
herself to the patient as an individual and offers herself for relationship, the patient also has to mobilize his psychology in order
to come to terms with the situation. The interpersonal dialogue,
the interpretation of dreams, the reflection about personal feelings and life circumstances, the investigation of unconscious
motives—all these fundamentals of therapeutic work—turn out
to be psychological tools that do not do justice to the mythical
need of human beings.

Myths require another ritual, another setting for their manifestation. In traditional forms of psychotherapy, they are readily
overlooked. Psychotherapy shuts out the world of myths that for
men is their life's blood. In its place the psychological world holds
sway, a world more familiar to women. The discoveries of Freud

and Jung would probably have looked much different had they carried out their investigations of the soul on the battlefield, in corporate offices, in men's clubs, or in the halls of government.

The therapeutic setting does not address a man's soul, since the basic conditions for therapy derive from psychology, a field foreign to myth. The atmosphere is too personal and private, too centered on the individual to speak to the mythical side. Psychology directs its gaze toward the individual and overlooks the great mythical themes that shape the world outside. Even when he does touch upon the mythical, the psychologist usually rejects it hurriedly: the personal dimension takes priority. It was this emphasis upon the personal that bothered me in the discussion with my analyst about the Dachau concentration camp. Her personal interpretation ignored the power of the mythical images that the dream contained. She addressed the dream within a psychological context and did not consider it from a mythological perspective.

I would like to mention a further point regarding psychology's failure to do justice to men's souls. We need to consider who it was who first entered the psychotherapeutic consulting room and for whom this setting was immediately conducive. Both Freud and Jung gained their most important knowledge in dealing with *female patients*; they discovered the meaning of psychology through working with *women*. Freud developed his theories of hysteria and neurosis from his experience with Anna O, Emmy von N., Miss Lucy, Katharina, and Elizabeth von R. and transferred his understanding to men by diagnosing hysteria in men as well as women. Women showed Freud the way to the meaning of the unconscious and of personal trauma. Of Jung we know that his thinking was stimulated all during his life by his work with women patients and that Toni Wolff, Jolande Jacobi, Marie-Louise von Franz, and Aniela Jaffé were important collaborators.

In other words, the discoveries of these great psychologists might be only the expression of their confrontation with the feminine soul. Through working with women, Freud and Jung discovered psychology, a perspective that women had long taken for granted. What they declared to be objective discoveries about human nature, might in reality be but the results of their attempts to understand the female soul. As investigators, they directed their attention to what was alien and unfamiliar. In doing so, they would of necessity have turned to the psychic orientation opposite their own. They selected a ritual that seemed unusual to them and followed their fascination for the female, something they experienced as a powerful counter-position to their masculinity. They thus expanded the unconscious by an added, mysterious dimension. What they considered to apply in general to the soul of human beings, turns out under more critical observation to be the language of the feminine soul.

Naturally, I do not mean by this that they conceived a psychology that does justice to the feminine psyche either. Although Freud and Jung moved in a feminine environment, they directed their attention as *men* to the psyche of women. Their masculine perspective colored what and how they saw. We can assume that they used their masculine system of reference to orient themselves in an arena unknown to them. While they looked into the souls of women, they did so with the eyes of men. Their masculine background inevitably intruded in producing what they took as valid answers.

In the context of his Oedipal theory, Freud described the psychic differences between boys and girls as well as those between men and women. During the Oedipal phase, children become aware of the genital differences between males and females. During this phase of life, a boy has to come to terms with his erotic expectations of his mother. Because mother already belongs to father, she cannot meet his expectations. The overpowering figure of father forces the boy to an inner denial of his needs: he has to give up mother as a sexual object. The boy senses father as a rival and even fears the fatherly revenge for his fantasies and expectations.

Since he knows the genital difference between the sexes, the boy concludes that girls have experienced the terrible punishment of castration because of similar sexual needs. The shock stemming from this recognition leads to the formation of the super ego, a process through which a boy develops "conscience and morality." According to Freud, "characteristics that critics have since time immemorial attributed to women find extensive substantiation in the . . . modifications of super ego formation. Women show less sense of justice than men, less of a tendency to submit to the great necessities of life, and allow themselves to be led more often by tender and aggressive emotions in their decisions."

Freud recognized the essential differences between men and women even though he was of the opinion that "pure masculinity

and femininity remain constructions with uncertain contents."
According to Freud, a boy's super ego has a different quality and
developmental history that that of a girl. In a boy, the super ego
forms to ward off the danger of merger with the feminine. By
identifying with the contents of the super ego, the boy saves himself from a complicated triangulation. He thereby directs his
energy to "the great necessities of life" and through them to the
outer world.

There is another way we can understand the conflict that
Freud attempted to grasp theoretically. Instead of his psycho-
dynamic interpretation, we could chose a mythological approach.
While from a psychological perspective the super ego results from
fear of the father's revenge and of insurmountable instinctual
drives, the reverse is the case from a mythical view. The super ego
does not result from a developmental conflict, rather the soul of
the individual man "arranges" situations to guide it to the myth.
According to this way of seeing, the "great necessities of life," the
myths, are the goal of the process and not simply the results of the
boy's development.

Without realizing it, Freud described a boy's budding mythical orientation. In its yearning to be one with the great necessities
of life, a boy's soul seeks a way out of the personal labyrinth to the
world outside. It tries to turn away from the personal and toward
the mythical. Castration anxiety expresses not only the fear of the
father's revenge, but also the boy's real anxiety over losing his
mythical potency. From this perspective, castration means to be
cut off from the myth. Like Parcifal, the boy has to fight his way to
the level of mythical experience in the world while being continually threatened by the danger of succumbing to the personal.

A boy is castrated when he allows himself to be "psychologized." By orienting himself only through relational psychology,
he loses his specifically masculine aptitude for the mythical. He
assumes the psychological perspective when he understands himself only as an individual being and allows himself to be defined
from his relationship to his mother. He thus remains cut off from
the outer reaches of his soul. The boy must, therefore, stave off
the feminine symbolized for him by the mother, who further represents a particular psychological orientation. Castration anxiety
is justified from a male point of view: men would become "feminized" were they to follow the fantasy of merger with mother and
psychology. They would no longer find their way to the myths

were they to place their own, personal needs in the foreground and orient themselves exclusively to "mother."

According to the current understanding in developmental psychology, the Oedipal phase does not apply to all children. Not all girls are in love with their fathers and not all boys see father as a rival. Freud, however, considered his discoveries to be objectively valid. To establish and verify his theory, he cited the Greek myths or supported his position with the ethnological theories of his time. Freud's thinking was masculine. His theory and support for that theory derived from his own mythological orientation to life. While he, himself, believed he was establishing a universally valid psychological theory, in reality he was recounting myths. The immense success of Freud's Oedipal theory stems from its mythical background and Freud's assuming the role of a narrator of myths. Freud clearly answered a popular need. The general public demands myths in order to understand the mystery of the soul and to be able to master the recurring challenges of life.

Within the discipline of psychology, though, Freud thought mythically. Freud viewed myths as a collective dream, the deposit of human challenges met within this phase of development. He reduced myths to psychomythologies, to constellations reflecting different varieties of relationship. Believing in psychology, he applied mythological images as a means of representing his clinical experience. His focus on the personal and biographical as the foundation for personality, however, insufficiently reflected the power of the myths and their significance for masculine development.

Freud's position and that of other investigators has had a lasting effect. More than a generation of psychologists and psychotherapists have elevated the insights won in the intimacy of the consulting room to the position of the sole legitimate source for the soul's exploration. According to this view, we only gain access to the truth about human beings in a dialogue. Any chance for recognition of the mythical orientation of the masculine soul has been lost.

Men's grandiose fantasies, their collective plans and strivings, are the sublimated expression of their psychic biographies and are not recognized as forms of psychic reality in their own right. A man establishes himself in his profession, makes plans, fights, strives for position, carries out conquests, or accumulates possessions because he sublimates his sexual drive or has not worked out his biographical material. According to such a reduced view, he continues to overcome the father or he retreats into the outer world to compensate for early childhood losses. The theory fails to acknowledge a man's genuine fascination for myths, the unique field of his soul. When psychoanalysis reduces masculine ambition to individual development though, it disregards a crucial part of the male soul.

I am convinced that a man's soul expresses itself in mythical images and that of a woman more readily in psychological images. The fundamental concepts of depth psychology developed by Freud, Jung, and others are, therefore, one-sided and make men's resistance to psychotherapy understandable. Men sense that through psychotherapy they subordinate themselves to a system and a ritual that does not correspond to the primary language of their souls.

## THE SEDUCTIVE NOTION OF PSYCHOLOGICAL WHOLENESS

*"The Anima as a feminine component is exclusively a figure compensating masculine consciousness."*

*"I designate the outer attitude . . . persona, the inner attitude I designate anima, soul."*
— C. G. Jung

According to Analytical Psychology, the anima confronts a man with his soul. By anima, C. G. Jung means the feminine side of a man, which he contrasts with the animus, the masculine side of a woman. The anima is the personification of the unconscious. She is a psychopomp, a soul guide, and the archetype of life, connecting a man to the depths of the collective unconscious. Through the dialogue with the feminine, which he projects on the outside world or experiences as autonomous stirrings in his psyche, a man learns about the reality of his soul. This process comprises one of the greatest challenges a man meets in his life. He achieves psychic maturity only through the encounter with the feminine part of his soul.

The anima, however, shows different faces. She reveals her power through projection, a seductive woman, or irrational, unruly feelings, emotions, or moods. She fascinates, excites, threatens, or bewitches. A man lives in a tension field, never simply man or woman, but both, confronted at every turn by the numinous power of the anima. The "eternal feminine" attracts him, enlivens him, and also casts him into the abyss.

Some Jungian analysts go a step further. For them the anima is not only the underdeveloped part of a man's soul, but represents the archetype of life itself. The anima symbolizes soul, the unconscious, and life and does not depend on biological gender. According to these theorists, the archetype of the anima affects women as well as men. They see the anima's gender-specific characteristics as sociocultural conditioning.

Although society may see us as men or women, the soul sees us as both. Culture identifies what it accepts as masculine or feminine characteristics. Whether we see ourselves as male or female depends upon the end of the spectrum with which we identify. In most individuals, the conscious sexual orientation corresponds to physical gender. At the same time, a man always has his anima that he is supposed to integrate, while a woman has to come to terms with her animus, her masculine side.

Jung's conceptualizing these polarities contributed greatly to mutual understanding between the sexes. His concepts helped to depoliticize the issues and to avoid the establishment of social roles or claims to superiority based on gender differences. They have helped to make the walls separating men and women more porous. Men and women encounter each other not as alien beings, but perceive the other as an opportunity to learn something about their own psyche.

Thanks to the anima/animus concept, we do not base our identity one-sidedly on biological gender, but men can admit feminine behavior and characteristics and women can enter areas of living seen as masculine. There are characteristics concealed within the masculine personality that our culture considers feminine and the other way around. The anima/animus concept has led to a more differentiated assessment of the experiential and behavioral patterns of human beings. It has also opened our eyes to areas of the psyche that heretofore had been closed due to our fixation on gender.

Although I find this perspective convincing, at the same time I see a danger in it: the threat of obscuring our sense of difference between the souls of men and women. For fear of being considered reactionary or opposed to the emancipation of women, we take refuge in wonderful discussions about femininity and masculinity, as such. We thereby shirk the task of helping individuals to cope with the differences they experience. Psychology thus becomes aesthetic talk and distances itself from life's reality.

For my own part, I must say that I do *not* feel like a woman to myself. I can perhaps empathize with women, but I sense that women do not share many of my reactions, interests, feelings, or preferences. As long as we only carry on the discussion of gender difference on a lofty, philosophical plane and ignore everyday reality, I feel betrayed. We do not reflect on men and their personalities, but only about the masculine and feminine in general, and how they manifest different expressions in both sexes. In therapy a man focuses on his anima, and a woman attempts to develop her animus. We only reluctantly consider the ways in which their souls differ due to varied biology and historical traditions. Here psychology shows its fundamental tendency to give socially volatile issues a wide berth and to limit itself to the personal.

The equality myth governs Analytical Psychology as much as other psychologies. Analytical Psychology joined the legitimate collective trend in calling for equal rights for women in society. Psychology presents itself as a science for the emancipation of women. The time has come, however, for us to free ourselves of this myth of equality and to reflect seriously on the differences. If we regard the characteristics of gender only as metaphors for various aspects of existence, then emancipation, too, will stagnate. If we continue to blur gender differences, those anthropological realities shaping our being, we will miss the chance to develop social structures that would make emancipation possible in spite of clear gender identities. Without a sense of difference, we could succumb to the seductive idea of psychic equality and neglect the need to conceive a language for the male soul.

## THE DOWNFALL OF MYTH

The archetypes of the collective unconscious dispose us to particular psychic experiences. As the master plan for our souls, these fundamental patterns direct our behavior and experience. Through the concept of archetypes, C. G. Jung sought to express the collective determinants behind seemingly individual behavioral patterns. The CEO who feels responsible for the entire company and demands competence everywhere, who attends to the well-being of his subordinates, while being both accessible to them and raging at them, lives out the archetype of the All Father. His behavior derives not only from his personality, but from a fundamental pattern. He will experience his subordinates becoming dependent on him, admiring him, or rebelling against him. They will turn into children, in other words. This archetype provides him energy and motivates him to pursue his profession.

As I noted earlier, archetypes are the universal and fundamental patterns of the psyche and, according to Jung, are recognizable in myths and fairy tales. The hero, the trickster, the devouring mother, the punitive father, the warrior, the outcast son, the eternal daughter, the nymph, and the high priestess are a few of the possible archetypal figures that we encounter in these stories. We also find archetypal messages and patterns in the products of civilization: in a baroque church, a high-rise office, an art deco lamp, or in a pompous school building from the 1920s. We cannot separate what we construct, invent, think, or discover from the psychic environment in which we live, for the soul's expressions manifest themselves everywhere that man actively places something in the world.

With the concepts of the archetype and the collective unconscious, Jung sharpened our eye for the psychic forces manifesting themselves in the impersonal environment. He gave us cognitive instruments with which to understand the realms of the soul beyond individual and personal life situations. The pyramids of Ramses the Second were not built solely from the pharaoh's personal ambition, but because an archetypal energy was at work in the population and found expression in the corresponding symbols. The pyramids evidence the power of the myth that ruled the Egyptians at the time: setting out for new levels of consciousness and the corresponding development of the will. Jung's brilliant achievement lies in his having acknowledged the deeper impersonal and collective layer in human beings. Man lives from this deeper, archetypal layer and cannot be understood exclusively from individual, personal history. Instead, man lives from the myths that the archetypes relate over and over.

At the same time, Jung emphasized that those things outside ourselves that fascinate, move, or frighten us are the representations of our inner reality. We project our soul onto the outer world and, in turn, our soul fills the world with meaning. The source of this psychic process is the archetypes. As Jung comments, "All myth evoking natural processes are . . . symbolic expressions of the inner and unconscious drama of the soul, a drama that natural occurrences reflect back to us by means of our projections — that is, become understandable for our human consciousness."

While it was probably not Jung's intention, combining the concepts of projection and archetype resulted in a devaluation of the importance of the outer world. The archetypes became psychologized through being relegated to the interior of individual human beings. The outer world was colonized in the name of psychology: the world became *only* a mirror of the soul. This separation of subject and object threatens to destroy man's mythical unity with the world. Instead of mythical participation with objects outside, man is becoming a being that ensouls the world out of himself. The world is turning into a convenience market for our personal, psychic realities. In the resulting egocentric arrogance, we believe that the outer world only works on us and not the other way around, because we give it meaning. We lose respect for the autonomy of the world's power.

A man becomes a pilot, because as a *puer*, the archetype of the eternal youth, he flies from life and has difficulty committing himself personally. According to this interpretation, he projects his psychic needs onto his profession as a pilot. His motivation is all internal. From a mythical perspective, however, the situation is reversed. By flying he participates in a myth. Flying appeals to him, ensouls him, and awakens new strength in him. The deciding factors are not solely motives derived from his personal life. He has, rather, been infected by the mythical substance concealed within the aircraft, landing fields, and images of the wide world have infected him. He feels called to serve a myth—for him "one of the great necessities of life."

Psychoanalysis traces myths back to inner realities and overlooks their power "out there," as well. Again, the experience of the unity and subject and object is lost. Psychoanalysis does not consider sharing in the beauty of a landscape, the participation in newfound strength in a group, or the emotion at the sight of a Gothic cathedral to be psychic reality in its own right. Instead, it reduces the world to an epiphenomenon. Our environment, society, and culture turn into a gigantic backdrop for images of our own, personal issues. Are we then to free ourselves from the world and its myths and indulge ourselves in navel gazing? If psychology is the exclusive activity of the consulting room's seclusion, we readily overlook the demonic power and fascination of myths that continue to work on us unconsciously through our dependence upon society and the environment.

The emphasis on projection also obstructs our seeing the qualities of the male soul. Men have, themselves, been psychologized, their role in the psychic functioning of society overlooked. Going into psychotherapy could mean psychic castration for a man. Should he submit to the intimacy and seclusion of a psychologically oriented therapy, he runs the risk of losing his contact to the outside world of myth. He gives himself up to his interiority and no longer allows himself to be animated by the "great necessities of life."

A male-oriented therapy must not succumb to the illusion of healing through one-on-one relationship and the therapeutic setting, but must keep an eye out for the mythical forces in which the patient participates in the outer world. I experienced the influence of such forces with one of my own patients.

As a nurse, this man suffered from the inability to assert himself in his profession. Again and again he was "outfoxed" by physicians or taken advantage of by the female nurses. At work he was generally misused and considered a good-natured fool. In therapy we reflected over the background of this inability to assert himself. We discovered that even as a child he had the feeling that everything had to be adjusted to meet his needs. As mother's little darling, his parents assumed all responsibility for dealing with the outer world. In addition, his mother treated him like an intimate companion, while his father remained a shadowy figure. I might have derived the patient's lack of self-assertion from these biographical factors, factors that had to be worked through if we were to make any progress. We spent hour on hour discussing his role as a mother's son, his relationship to women, and some of his specific experiences.

One day my patient seemed suddenly different. His gaze was clearer, he seemed more determined and self-certain. He had joined his company's union representatives and began to advocate actively the rights of the nurses. By working with this organization he sensed new energy, which animated him and gave him a feeling of meaning. All of a sudden he decided to take on his problems at work. His lack of self-assertion had vanished.

*Power of myth in his man's life*

Thanks to the company's union representatives he came into contact with a myth, the myth of the workers who look to each other for solidarity and thereby form a serious counterbalance to their employers. While our psychological work had been important, it had not taken into consideration the entirety of his soul. Since psychology and mythology comprise two separate worlds, my patient found real help only by participating in a current and living myth. He had to connect with a myth in order to individuate.

I have explained that Freud as well as Jung sensed the significance of myths. Freud, himself, functioned as a grandiose teller of myths, while Jung sought to uncover the interactions between myths and the human psyche. Where Freud elevated natural forces to the level of the actual myths playing out in the psychology of individuals, Jung diverged from this perspective with his theory of the archetypes. The setting or the methodology, however, which both recommended for analytic work, shifted the central focus onto psychology and lost the sense of the mythological. Since then, the psychological perspective has increased in influence and crowded out the mythical way of thinking.

Through this development that goes back to Freud and Jung, we have also lost the sense for a man's soul qualities. Men avoid consultation rooms, get bored quickly with extended reflections about personal history, and grow nervous when the talk centers only around harmony and consensus. As long as conceptions of empathy and wholeness or the unity of soul and body dominate, men will not feel completely at home with psychology, an approach that corresponds only partially to their psychic reality.

Men live less from psychology and realize more an important part of their soul in myth. Our understanding of men can not be based only on psychological ideas, but must take into consideration their longing for mythical participation. One part of a man's soul lives in the myths manifesting themselves in groups, in society, in public life, or in collective events. An emphasis on the individual comes closer to the feminine psyche. For this reason psychology corresponds more nearly to women than to men and, additionally, women are better able to reflect on themselves. Women possess a sense for psychology; men, on the other hand, are attracted by myths.

# 2

## MYTHS:
## Vessels for Nation, Culture, Profession, and Family

♂

## The Tension between Mythology and Psychology

Any discussion by men of psychological gender differences is taboo. Should a man point out such differences he invites suspicion: his opinions are merely psychological platitudes aimed at restoring men's privileged position. Equality is the slogan of the day. Anything else threatens the emancipation of women. Nevertheless, I would plead for genuine reflection about psychological gender differences. I would do so not to put obstacles in the way of women's emancipation, but because I am convinced that any progress toward emancipation must be based on a recognition of the differing perceptions, reactions, and feelings of both men and women.

Equality as a concept has served an important purpose: it has allowed women to rally themselves. It has enabled them to claim positions traditionally allotted to men, while neutralizing men's arguments against them. Women's emancipation, though, has moved into a second phase. We will only realize true gender equality when we acknowledge the differing psychic orientations, when men can fulfill themselves based on their psychic orientation, and when we can accept the language of soul particular to women. In this chapter I show that there are two identifiable positions of the human soul: on one hand the psychological, on the other the mythological. While women derive their fundamental orientation from psychology, the central focus for men is the forms of mythology.

We human beings are creatures of discord. We live in the opposing tension of psychic forces. On one side, the psyche, as an
autonomous power, influences our being, desires, and fantasies
from inside. On the other side, myths rule the outer world and
draw us into their orbit. We can understand human nature based
on psychology, resting our conclusions about environment and
behavior on an interior perspective. Or, we can take our perspective from the outer world by considering the myths to which individuals feel themselves drawn.

The human soul expresses itself both in the psychological,
personal realm as well as on the mythological stage. I am applying
the term, "psychology," to the individual aspect of soul, that part
of the personality centered in private life situations, personal history, and relationship. By myth or mythological, I mean the soul
force which exercises its power over the collective, public life, and
the value structure of our civilization. Psychology and myth. How
can we differentiate these fundamental tendencies of the human
soul? How do these two soul forces express themselves? What are
their specific and respective characteristics?

As a starting point for my discussion, I will describe a curious
experience that has not left my mind. It had to do with a friend's
relative in a remote part of Switzerland. My friend drove me to
visit his parents and his uncle, the latter a farmer and the propri-
etor of a small electronics shop. We had been invited to have a
bite to eat with them. We all sat, along with a second uncle, in the
small, dark living room of a traditional, Swiss farmhouse. Over the
radio, we heard an announcement from the local representative,
someone like a local congressman in the United States. He
appealed urgently for a "yes" vote in the upcoming election in
favor of affiliation with the European Community. "I would mark
a 'no' on my ballot," the forty-year-old businessman commented
brusquely. "Europe can wait!" The others nodded.

According to the arguments of the government, the political
parties, and the unions, peripheral regions such as the Swiss interior stood to profit from affiliation through compensation pay-
ments and subsidies. Should the electorate, should the people,
not vote in favor of affiliation, it would mean economic catastrophe, warned newspapers and television. It was clear to everyone
that there was no real alternative. In spite of the threats, this rural
Swiss inhabitant remained unimpressed: he was not so easily
swayed. He perhaps thought that, if everyone else shared the same

opinion, something was not right. Something in him resisted. The government, the political parties, and the experts all emphasized that affiliation with the European Community was unavoidable and economically sound. "If those guys upstairs think for a minute that they can tell us how to vote," this man announced defiantly, "they have another thing coming."

We might ask why this man reacted so irrationally and non-sensically? What was going on with him? His determined behavior took me aback. I sensed that his opinion was not based on logic, but that other forces were working on him. I could not get his reaction out of my head. Was his behavior an expression of his character? Would I need to search his childhood, his background, and his personal history to find an explanation for this defiant behavior? According to comments my friend made, this man was a lovable and gregarious boy in his childhood. A devoted and dutiful son, he never was much of a problem for his parents.

His stubbornness, however, was surprising, a defiance which surfaced particularly toward authorities. When a teacher in elementary school ordered him to return home to fetch a missing textbook, he ignored the teacher and spent the day playing hooky. Although the teacher had threatened him with harsh punishment, the nine-year-old boy chose to spend the day at a nearby pond. The teacher's authoritarian demeanor displeased the boy profoundly. In his eyes the teacher's assignment was unjustified, the tone of voice inappropriate. As an adult, he seems to react in a similar manner. Should the powers that be grow arrogant, it is up to him to defy them. The feeling he had as a boy, that he had to look out for "those up there," has remained with him to this day. If authorities appear too self-certain or make demands without offering any alternatives, he reacts with opposition. He seems to sense the danger of being treated as a spineless object. In such cases, the instructions from those in power have to be ignored, even when they make sense.

For my part, I would like to get to the bottom of such defiant behavior. Why can this man not react in a level-headed and objective way and comply with the government's recommendation as long as it is logical and plausible? As a psychologist and psychoanalyst, I was taught that childhood shapes our individual personalities. In order, then, to learn more about the causes for this man's behavior and character, I will need to examine his personal history. According to my friend, this man suffered as a child under a strict and unapproachable father, who spent little time with his children. Instead, tending his yard, community politics, the church choir, and the Saturday evening drinking circle were important. The father was incapable of being open and sharing his feelings and emotions with his son. Of course, he was proud of his son, but he was nevertheless emotionally distant.

Was this man's defiant reaction over the European Community vote an expression of his problematic relationship with his father? Was he avenging himself on the State and the government instead of on his father? Perhaps, as an adult, he still carried the bitterness about his father's absence, reacting according to the script which the father co-authored? Based on this kind of psychological analysis, I could now make a diagnosis of an authority complex and mild psychosocial stressors.

Tracing a political attitude back to an individual's childhood and education has its precedents. According to Lloyd de Mause, Alice Miller, and A. Mitscherlich, a harmonic, unproblematic childhood will prevent dictatorships and authoritarian governmental systems. Miller, for example, locates the causes for Adolf Hitler's National Socialism in his childhood. Could this theory apply to the rural Swiss man of our discussion? I do not find the above analysis satisfying. Have I really understood this man by knowing about his childhood, his relationship to his parents, and the remainder of his personal biography? How about other men? Are their attitudes, strivings, and goals simply a mirror of their childhood experiences?

I am reminded of the comment of an acquaintance. As director of an important cultural institution, he was questioned by a journalist about his desires for his professional activity. He answered, "I have an image of the countryside where I grew up that lives in me. In front of me, I see its hills and woods. As a boy, I rummaged around in them, experienced them as being endless, and felt that they animated me and gave me the feeling of endless possibilities. I still have that feeling today. I find myself in an environment where it is difficult to get any perspective, where I will have to orient myself, yet where I know that there is much that I can do." This acquaintance conjured up the landscape of his childhood to explain the motivation for his work.

I should, therefore, consider the character of the first man from a vantage point other than that of a psychological analysis. Maybe the key to his personality also lies, like that of my acquaintance, in his geographic origins.

When I walk out the door of the house in which the discussion on the European Community took place, I am presented with an incredible landscape. Steep, towering walls of rock shoot up from behind the village. In the distance the road over a pass curves and snakes its way up a mountain. Halfway up the mountain a little hamlet stands defiantly on a small plateau. The countryside takes my breath away. In this landscape the man was born; he grew up in just such a village. Could this be the explanation for his behavior? Turning from his personal history, I focus on his environment. Maybe I will understand his reaction better if I take in the surrounding region from which he is descended. The valley, the village, the mountains, the houses, and their respective history contain messages from the soul that had an impact on the boy. They are the stuff of the myths into which he was born. The towering peaks stretching to the sky and the tiny village communities mercifully tolerated by nature in their small clearings must have become symbols for the local populace. To live here is to defy the adverse conditions of nature and its powerful forces. Such a defiant posture shows up in the stories of the valley.

Two hundred years ago, a government representative was thrown without hesitation into the village well when he demanded higher taxes. Everyone around knows the story. Three hundred years ago, soldiers from this region returned home in spite of threats of punishment from their officers, because they no longer saw the point of the battles. Up until then they had fought valiantly for the country. So goes another story of the region. The mildly anarchistic attitude toward the State and authorities runs like a theme through the tales of the area. Instinctively the inhabitants of this valley have defended themselves against attempts by the ruling powers to take anything from them. This characteristic shows itself clearly in the landscape.

If we bear in mind the region from which he came, the man's reaction over the European Community vote takes on a very different coloration. There self-determination becomes a central value. The people have always resisted slavery, arbitrary commands, and official mandates. They will have nothing to do with "superior" or "better people." It is not the problematic relationship with his father that stands behind this man's defiant "no," but the mind-set of his entire region. Perhaps, the ancient Swiss will to independence revives in him when he refuses the demands of the administration. He senses a nationalistic arrogance and moves to block it expeditiously. Depending on our perspective, the same behavior acquires a very different significance.

Maybe I should not attempt to understand this man with psychology, but need to see him through very different lenses to grasp the nature of his soul. It is not psychology that enables me to illumine the underlying motivation for his point of view, but a soul language, a language that incorporates the collective atmosphere into which he was born. This man is not an isolated being: the soul of his land lives in and speaks through him.

Two psychic forces are at work in every human being: on one hand the *psychological* and on the other the *mythological.* Each of these forces acquires specific images and symbols and creates its own stories with which to express and assert itself. Psychological symbols are different from mythological ones. Psychology finds its symbols in the realm of the personal. Our individual history, our personal life situations, and our circle of acquaintances shape us as psychological beings. At the same time, however, we are the product of the life and tradition of a given region and its spirit. The impetus toward civilization, the attempt to come to grips with a wider field of action, has its effect on us. It is this energy I have called "mythological."

We experience ourselves as warriors in the metropolitan jungle of New York, citizens of the world in the port city of San Francisco, gregarious Angelinos, or reticent midwesterners with a sense for the essential in life. Myth is the representation of this outer, psychic field. We are, therefore, also mythological beings, living from the energies and information that our environment and the public sphere direct our way. As mythological beings we are not the product of personal origins, of our family, but an expression of the spirit, the symbols, and the rituals of the community and region in which we grew up. Our character, then, is shaped by psychological forces on one side and directed by mythological ones on the other.

This dual nature characterizes the male as well as the female soul. Gender difference lies in the degree of mythological and psychological predominance: men strive to realize themselves as mythological beings, while women take their orientation from the psychological. This fundamental difference in the soul's direction leads to men's preference for living in terms of myths, while women relate to life through the psychological dimension.

## THE PSYCHOLOGICAL DIMENSION

To understand the actions, comments, reactions, and thought processes of ourselves and others, we look for some kind of explanation. We look for an image, a theory, or a cause to give meaning to the brusque demeanor of a colleague or the dissatisfaction of a spouse. We try to connect what we see, feel, or sense with a background. Why was my friend so sarcastic? Why do I shake when I play my guitar for visitors? We want to understand ourselves and our fellow human beings to be able to accept ourselves and others on the one hand and, on the other, to be able to rectify any problems.

A glance behind an individual's facade throw's light on hidden motivation. An acquaintance boasts to compensate his inferiority feelings or a friend is continually aggressive and critical to relativize her admiration and overvaluation of others. We try to find images, metaphors, fantasies, and narratives that cast a different light on the our behavior and characteristics and that of strangers, friends, and partners. We hope thereby to make the contact with others easier. We are more likely to accept bizarre and irritating character traits if we can recognize the underlying dynamics.

Psychology begins with the premise that human beings affect their environment out of an inner dynamic. Psychologists track down decisive events in an individual's life, point out connections between experiences, and describe images from the past to make human behavior comprehensible. Women, for example, would have difficulty relating to men if their fathers mistreated them as children. From a psychological perspective, our personality consists of both life experiences and our inherent nature. Our past produces a lasting effect on us and also pushes toward its own expression. Women marry men like their fathers. Men avenge themselves on their boss instead of their fathers or take on the anxiety of their mothers.

If we want to understand ourselves or other human beings, we have to begin with the personal, with a familial anamnesis, and an analysis of the network of relationships. Perhaps we will expose typical patterns or secret programming acquired through our childhood. "My mother carried on a running battle with my father and me," remembers a thirty-year-old woman during a therapy session. "I later realized, that I nagged my husband the same way. My mother still affects me."

Depth psychology places this personal dimension very much in the foreground: in psychoanalysis the key to the personality lies in the experiences of childhood. Father, mother, and siblings are the formative influences of personal development and live on in adult life through our complexes. An unresolved Oedipal conflict makes it difficult for a thirty-year-old woman to find the right man, or a symbiotic relationship to mother holds a man back from entering into a genuine relationship with a woman. Thanks to psychological understanding, we have learned to regard human beings as products of their childhood and the effects of their parents. We, therefore, operate with concepts such as "mother image," "father imago," "trauma," "transference," "resistance," "defense," and "projection," and thereby trace human essence back to personal life history.

With psychology's array of conceptual instruments, we identify *core experiences* in an individual's personal past. Persistent anxiety attacks might be late manifestations of a traumatizing encounter with fire, of sexual abuse, or of the parents' difficult divorce. With the help of these identifiable occurrences, psychologists lay out a *psychography*, which serves individuals as a guideline. Whether the formative events and relationships took place in the recent past or—as Melanie Klein, Miller, or Bowlby postulate—were barely sensed in the twilight of early childhood, is immaterial. A mother's inability to offer adequate resistance to the child, double-bind situations, or the emotional waiting period of early childhood are considered justifiable causes for suffering or neurotic behavior. Psychologists hunt out trauma, inappropriate relationships, abuse, problematic parents, and difficult life circumstances to identify events that clarify psychological disturbances.

One woman told me that, as a young girl, she often missed her father. Since he was frequently away on business, weeks went by without her seeing him. In his absence, she would imagine how he would greet her. One time when he returned after having been gone a long time, she burst out of the house and ran toward him. Her father remained strangely cool and did not even open his arms to receive her. This experience made a considerable impression on her. She still has the feeling today that, in spite of everything she does, men will never take her in their arms and accept her. The image from her childhood corresponds to a feeling in her everyday life.

According to Hillman, the psyche creates stories of the soul, narratives that help us to bear our problematic qualities, to accept our limitations, and to recognize our strengths. Such a psychological attitude comes from a specific image of humanity. It is based in the notion that human beings live from and in *relationships* and that we survive because of these relationships. According to psychologists, we attempt to adapt to the world of our concepts and desires. Dialogue and a good relationship are the most important access to other people. Contact with our fellow human beings is central, something we need to compensate for our existential helplessness. The attention, dedication, and love of father and mother introduce a child to the world. The influence and emotional concern of other people determine the strength of our feeling of self-worth. Relationships are the elixir of life for us, for only through relationship can we be aware of and develop ourselves.

All this is certainly accurate, yet it applies to only a part of the human soul. If we understand the soul exclusively from the perspective of psychology, we overlook a significant part of the human personality. We are not exclusively psychological beings. We also think, experience, and act out of the mythical part of the personality. This mythical side, however, does not fit the picture of human beings that psychology portrays. If we seek to grasp the individual only out of a personal dynamic, only out of his or her personal relationships, an important side remains hidden. An individual biography is incomplete when we exclude the mythical context.

Human beings do not only live out of their psychic reality, but realize themselves in the myths which shape their larger environment. If we want to learn something about an individual's goals and motivation, we have to couple mythic considerations to any psychological analysis. Just as our *psychography* reveals motives from our personal history, a mythological consideration describes the mythical identifications of that same individual. We can never derive an understanding of how we behave, what we strive for, and what comprises our suffering solely from our psychology. Instead, these aspects may well be the expression of the myth in which we participate. The human personality expresses that *mythical canon* which each of us confesses.

## THE MYTHICAL PERSPECTIVE

> *"In the beginning God created the heaven and the earth. And the earth was without form, and void, and darkness was upon the face of the deep. And the Spirit of God moved upon the face of the waters."*
> — Genesis

*"I will never forget my visit to the hydroelectric plant that lay above a
blue lake mirroring the fantastic Armenian heaven. When a
journalist asked me how I liked the time-honored Armenian churches
and monasteries, I answered: "The church that I like the best is that
hydroelectric plant, a temple by a marvelous lake.'"*
— Pablo Neruda

When we hear the word *myth*, we think of a fiction, something that
is not true, or of a product of fantasy. A myth is supposed to be a
belief or a perspective that one holds to, even though one knows
better. For example, women are worse drivers than men; coffee is
harmful to one's health; men are less fearful than women; or,
blacks possess greater rhythmic abilities. Myths, therefore, are
ideas that cannot prevail in the face of rational analysis. When we
label an opinion a "myth," we rob it of any power. Myths are not
valid arguments in a discussion: "just a myth" means the same as
"meaningless."

We further associate the word myth with the activity of the
gods, with mythologies. Myth reminds us of Hermes, who stole
Apollo's cattle; Aphrodite, born of the sea's foam; or the revelry of
Dionysius. We think of stories of the Greek gods, of the Germanic
tribes, or of the Indian subcontinent; of the Aesir of Germanic
mythology, who live in Asgard, the home of the gods, and fight the
Vanen; or of Vishnu, who drove off Kaliya, the snake king. The
word, myth, also evokes associations of calamitous proportions.
We may be reminded of how the National Socialists appropriated
the Germanic myths during the Third Reich or of how the Nazi's
chief ideologist Alfred Rosenberg (1893–1946) sought to prove
the racial superiority of the Germans with the "myth of the twen-
tieth century." We might recall Mussolini's claim before his march
on Rome, "We have created our own myth. Myth is belief, a noble
enthusiasm. It is not necessary for it to be reality. . . ."

When I speak of myth, I refer to none of the above meanings.
For me myths are neither flimsy rationalizations for a given ideology nor stories of the gods nor another word for superstition.
Rather, they are numinous, archetypal patterns of meaning from
which human beings derive their orientation. I am talking about
myths in their significance for the souls of individuals, about stories that are neither recorded nor consciously reflected upon. I
consider myths to be the most powerful reality in the psyche, to be
revelations of a part of the soul. I see myths as collective patterns
that we carry in us, that we find manifested in societies, and by

means of which we attempt to understand and come to terms with our lives.

A friend of mine took a two-week trip to the island of Bali. Enthusiastically, he reported to me how a sense of peacefulness radiated from the faces of the Balinese. In contrast to Westerners, this island people know neither anxiety nor stress and, in addition, display an unbelievable sensitivity. While listening to the report of his impressions, I asked myself whether he was not simply recounting a myth, the marvelous story of paradise in which he had submerged himself during his island visit. One of the patterns of meaning that our society, our collective, provides had made his vacation possible.

Such living myths are vital for the human soul. In spite of the fact that we generally are neither aware of them nor find them in written form, these omnipresent narratives exercise their influence over us from the unconscious. They provide specific lenses for our perception of the world around us. The myths that possess us condition how we see and how we interpret experience. We need these patterns, these stories. We need these powerful, psychic realities to order the new and unfamiliar. We need them for our day-to-day orientation in the world. We live in them, carry them around with us, and invoke them when we feel threatened or challenged.

Characteristic of these stories is that they are not something we make, but something that we can only *experience*. A story becomes a myth when it grips us completely, when it directs our feelings and perceptions. According to the myth, the inhabitants of Bali, for instance, are completely without aggression. Such a story, such a myth, controls us from inside as well as from outside. Human beings need such myths. We "seek out another reality, for the world of experience provides only conditional answers, humiliations, but no existential orientation, direction, and meaning," as one mythologist puts it.

Myths are foundational. As axiomatic patterns, the collective considers them to be reality. They are tales which try to explain phenomena, to illuminate mysteries, or to eliminate dangers. They form the basis for the activity and the orientation of nations, peoples, regions, professions, or larger groups of human beings with a common connection or relationship. Myths are the means by which these various human groupings respond to existential challenges and threats. They define the unconscious conditions for behavior and reaction at the disposal of any group. Myth represents the ways that the soul behaves on a collective level. Myth mediates the symbols that give a human collective, a country, or a region the strength to master the challenges that must be met. A collective finds its common image in myth, an image that engenders the spirit of togetherness. It thereby strengthens the collective's attitude and provides courage and energy for individual members to strive toward common goals.

"Whether a product is successful," a friend declared to me decidedly, "is solely a question of design." Based on his opinion, industry must concentrate on external form, since the qualitative differences of manufactured goods is no longer an issue. Design is everything. My friend is not alone in his perspective. Numerous entrepreneurs and advertising firms have adopted this new philosophy that is supposed to bring new life to the economy. I ask myself, though, whether this philosophy is not a myth, a creation story aimed at coming to terms with the economic uncertainties?

Myths do not result from conscious thought processes or rational decisions. We do not bring myths into existence by decree, rather they come into being independent of our intention and consciousness. It is a collective process; the psychology of a social group, of a political system, or of the media that creates myths. At the same time, the selection of a myth does not result on the basis of a decision-making process; rather, myths select us. Actually, we are seized by myths, by those myths with which our collective identity, individual past, and personal characteristics confront us. As autonomous forces, they seize us and force their reality upon us. Witness the stories of the peaceful island inhabitants of Bali or of the omnipotence of design.

Thanks to myths we act and think in accord with our environment. Therein lies their value and importance. Man cannot live without myths, since they make possible his orientation to the world "outside." Myth is a narrative that attempts to substantiate social reality through natural representations. They do so in such a way that the human being is embedded in both nature and culture in his feeling and thinking.

Participation in myth conveys to us a feeling of meaning. An energy flows over us, enlivens us, and gives us the feeling that engaging in something or fighting against something is worthwhile. Through our respective myths, we are bound to a collective spiritual reality in which we feel contained and which, at the same

time, energizes us. The phenomena of "out there" become understandable and comprehensible. Myths structure our environment.

## HIDDEN MYTHS

Generalized opinion holds that, at most, only less developed peoples believe in myths. We in the civilized world have exchanged
them for scientifically verifiable experience and the capacity of
sober, objective observation. Myths have served their purpose for
us, since we no longer direct our lives by diffuse stories, but orient
ourselves by empirical knowledge and logic. Peoples like the
Aborigines, the indigenous inhabitants of Australia, however, continue to explain the world through myths. The primitive mentality
does not *invent* myths, it *experiences* them. Confronted with the
question of the meaning of death, Aborigines tell their children
about the conversation between the spider, Adambara, and the
insect, Artapudapuda. In the breath-taking natural landscape of
Ayers Rock, Aborigines see the outcome of the struggle between
the light powers, Mala, and the dark powers, Kunia. Following
generalized opinion, we have no need to tell fantastic stories to
understand or explain something.

We reject the notion of a belief in myths out of hand: we have
freed ourselves from myth. Nonetheless, Karl Jaspers has pointed
out that, in addition to his scientific perspective, modern man also
thinks mythically. Logic and science do not replace myth, they
merely provide other ways of looking at reality. With logic, with rational thought, we analyze the world; with myth we participate in it.

We deceive ourselves in believing we have demythologized the
world—our myths have only changed form and are, therefore,
more difficult for us to recognize. We encounter them behind supposedly objective facts, behind collective opinions and logical convictions. They exert their influence over us without our realizing it.
While we believe we are functioning logically and rationally, we
really are "thinking" mythically! At times we insist on the superiority
of our thought processes and the irrefutable nature of facts. We fail
to notice that myths, those fundamental stories of the soul we carry
around with us, have conditioned our perceptions beforehand.

The difficulty is that when a myth seizes us, we become part of
it. The narrative takes us over, interprets and connects us with the
world around us. The businessman from the Swiss interior suspects

his government of devious intentions, my friend senses the peacefulness of the Balinese, and the advertising executive sees the influence that presentation has on the sale of a product line. The world
presents itself to our perception mythically. We see, feel, and sense
our environment based on the mythical reality in which we stand.
Because we do not clearly ritualize most of our myths, because we
lack the ceremonial observances to present myths, most of us overlook the mythical element. We fail to notice that we are immersed
in a myth, since our myths are not embodied in an identifiable, collective activity like those of the Aborigines already mentioned.
While the Aboriginal manhood rituals introduce the Rukutas, the
initiates, to the world through specific songs and chants, our myths
exercise their influence in secret. Through our collective we participate constantly in myths. At the same time, we see ourselves as
completely independent individuals.

I, myself, registered the conflict between my Swiss and my
Scottish mythical legacies on the occasion of a visit to Glasgow. My
hotel lay somewhat outside the main part of town. Having flown in
from Zurich, I tried to ascertain which bus line would take me to
the area I sought. I tried to decipher the bus routes on the little map
at the bus stop. The routes listed were a total chaos and the schedules consisted entirely of exceptions. The buses I wanted to board
stopped either a hundred feet up the street or a hundred feet down
the street. I felt frustrated and longed for logical, written information and a straightforward graphic representation of the bus routes.

Only after some time did it dawn on me that I had committed
a mental error: I was dealing with the situation out of a Swiss/
German myth. In me lived the notion that a trip should be
planned and predictable, something to be laid out in writing in
advance. Following this notion, we control a trip by means of maps
and schedules. Given my impression, people in Celtic Scotland
approach the matter of travel rather differently. Schedules and
maps are not of primary importance for orientation. What is decisive is the spoken and the personal. In Scotland I find my way by
turning to other people. They are the ones who know directions,
not the maps. Timetables do not contain information, rather information is passed on by word of mouth. Behind this fact lies a Celtic
myth, a myth for how people in Scotland derive their orientation.
The spoken word is more important than the written one! It makes
me think of the ancient clan law of the Scottish highlands, which
was retained in oral tradition and passed on as such.

Our myths do not only shine through behavioral patterns such as this, but diverse objects of our civilization point to the myths by which we orient ourselves. We form our cities, villages, institutions, schools, and work places according to mythical patterns. Correspondingly, we react to the mythical messages which these places exude. When a truck driver carefully cleans and polishes his vehicle, dreams about it, and sees to it that no stranger comes near it, a myth expresses itself just as much as it does with the factory worker, who feels responsible for the machine he works on and allows no one else to touch it.

Pablo Neruda waxed poetical about a hydroelectric plant in Armenia. The mythical quality of that installation evoked his enthusiasm: in his perception it was a "temple." Possibly what Neruda responded to was the myth of progress, one which requires no special ceremonies or rituals, because the power plant so graphically represents it. The hydroelectric station that Neruda described carries a double significance. On one hand, it serves to produce electric energy and performs a function in the economy. On the other hand, its whining turbines, towering facade, and imposing structure fulfill a psychic function: the plant evokes a story. It also symbolizes a myth which inspires and stimulates or against which we struggle. It symbolizes the myth of progress, which plays such a central role in our civilization.

Naturally, we do not encounter evidence of this central myth only in distant Armenia. We can get excited about a new CD player or the latest video camera and are always convinced that the new model has immense advantages. We hear the myth of progress through a variety of new products, for it expresses itself in the surround-sound of a home theater, the anti-lock brakes of this year's car model, or the digital readout on a washing machine. The belief in progress is a myth. It makes us feel that the newest is also the best.

Another central myth of our culture is the notion of cleanliness or the myth of harmonic existence, in which human beings live in total accord with themselves and their environment. After a visit to a Soviet factory, Waldo Frank wrote,

> The mechanic . . . is a true Soviet proletarian. His face, stamped by his work, carries fine, noble, and sensitive characteristics . . . All the men in the warehouse work with intensity and concentration, yet at the same time give one the impression of polite reserve while they labor. Their movements are not carried out mechanically, with no connection, like American workers. . .

if the supervisor stops a group of the men in their task to ask them something, the men seem to surface from a distant world, like poets, who suddenly find themselves in a prosaic world . . .

In this enlightening description of the Soviet industrial
worker as the essence of purity, we can recognize a variation of
Rousseau's myth of the noble savage. Frank was not fantasizing; he
actually *experienced* these workers in this way. In his perception, the
facial features of these proletarians expressed detachment and
enthusiasm. What Frank wrote was not false, even though it later
developed that many of these men were doing forced labor and
had suffered terribly under Stalin's reign of terror. Frank was participating in a myth that had employed these workers to carry its
message. His mythical thinking expresses itself in these people
and things without his being aware of it.

Pablo Neruda was gripped by the myth of progress. Frank
lived the myth of purity or of the noble worker. Myths affected
both of them and strengthened their critical position over and
against Western society. They lived a myth, perceived the world
through the myth, and due to their respective psychic backgrounds, became politically active.

How do myths come into being? We know that they are constellated by life transitions, by fear in the face of natural disasters,
death, or disease, or by the primeval longing for salvation from
our dark and problematic side. Myths are constellated when we
are confronted with a repetitive problem or when we sense the
limits of our own abilities. Birth, danger, war, hate, catastrophe,
disease, and separation, but also love, happiness, and the experience of bliss, the great mysteries of our being, birth myths.

We react mythically when our existence is threatened or we
are severely challenged by difficulty. At those times we require a
*mythos*, a story that keeps us going. Without the powerful under-
girding of myth's stories we would not survive these kinds of existential challenges. We submerge ourselves in myth when we do
not have the answers, when we are fighting for our lives, or when
we are overwhelmed by emotions. They free us from the unconsciousness and uncertainty of human existence by narrating a
story which gives us strength and the feeling of meaning.

"I believe that free enterprise is the only meaningful activity,"
declared an economist after giving up a lucrative position for the
second time. His situation had become unbearable due to diffi-

culties with the company's owner. Now he is trying to build something himself, to make his way easier by adopting a new myth, by shifting his perception of his situation and his failure mythically.

The central patterns of activity in our lives rest on myths: education, nourishment, profession, as well as relationship to death and disease or our reaction to crime. The answers we give to these vital questions of our lives grow from mythical ground.

There is little agreement regarding what is effective in education and how our children should be integrated into social life. In the 1960s and the early 1970s, we took our orientation from an antiauthoritarian perspective. Children should have the opportunity to acquire learning experiences on their own, should not be forced into adaptation, and the teacher and educator should take a back seat. "Life according to one's own law is the right of the child to free development, without external authority in matters of mind and body." The belief in the autonomy of the child held dominion, and in colleges of education students waxed enthusiastic over the ideas of Summerhill.

These days, another mythology is making its appearance: we are to engage children with values. By so doing, we enable them to cope in a complex, pluralistic world. Our activity is now determined by the myth of values. Today, when we deal with children, the notion of the importance of communicating a sense of worth is what motivates us.

Myths are psychic realities and should not be confused with "reality." The empty whiskey glass in front of me, the clatter of a passing train, or the fact that the Hudson River flows through New York, are things that others can confirm. The information that presents itself to our sense organs as irrefutable fact is "real." Reality, however, is not always that which has an effect on us. We register the shell of a burned building without reflecting further on it or we gaze at a painting without being stirred by any great emotion. Only when information acquires psychic significance, does it become elevated to the level of reality. In the burned building an architect sees the undeniable proof for the fallacy of restrictive building codes, a politician the speculative madness of profit-hungry developers, and a city manager an example of poor planning. Depending on the narrative we hear, the world reveals itself in different ways. Myths are the psychic patterns that correspond to the outer world, gigantic collective narratives that direct the life of our soul.

"This here is my dream. I tend the earth, but I do not exploit it . . . This piece of land is our Garden of Eden," confesses Hans Lehr, a German who emigrated to New Zealand in 1987. He thinks of Germany only as a place of gray buildings, rainy weather, foolish political wrangling, and frustrated faces. The notion of being able to find something like a garden of paradise, where he could live in harmony with nature, gave him the strength to leave his homeland.

The major decisions of our lives we make with the help of the myths in which we participate. While, as a rule, we arrive at everyday decisions based on rational reflection, greater existential challenges quickly overwhelm us. We need additional energy to make such challenges manageable. Whether we are trying to decide to read a book, take a walk, or vacuum the living room, simple, cognitive reflection is our chief tool—unless, of course we get caught in our neurosis. But deciding which partner to marry, which profession to follow, even whether we should buy a house, move to another country, or start our own company are matters that we cannot master solely with rational criteria and thought processes. While rationality perhaps enables us to recognize the different possibilities theoretically, it cannot provide the inner motivation necessary to select one of the variants. Logical thinking by itself offers too weak a basis for major decisions; it does not possess the necessary force. As Freud noted, for major decisions, we have to "also allow the unconscious to speak." I would say that we have to be gripped by a myth in order to have the feeling that we are doing the right thing. Our psyche needs the connection to a larger reality to master such problems. A student enrolled in a degree program in education states, "I decided on the teaching profession, because youth is the most valuable asset our culture has. The future belongs to the children." He chose education as a profession even though there is a surplus of teachers and his chances of getting a job are less than rosy. He followed a myth related to the divine child, a fundamental myth of Christianity that we all know from the Bible accounts. On closer inspection, this student's choice of profession reveals the immense psychic power of mythology.

While we carry psychology around inside of us, mythology reveals its power on the far side of personal limitations. When we are gripped by a myth, we no longer behave according to our personal stories, but according to what the myth demands. Myth calls to us, entangles us so that we focus our attention on motifs beyond the sphere of the personal. The dedication to myths depersonalizes.

In the following sections I introduce three categories of myths. Starting with national myths, I then turn to myths of profession and finally to the myths that rule the family.

## NATIONAL AND REGIONAL MYTHS

I will try to identify the myths that hide behind our activities, institutions, ambitions, and societal values, to uncover the mythical bases of our lives. To begin with, I will examine national myths, those axiomatic explanations that provide an orientation for a people. This orientation generally derives from a story or narrative contaminated by myth. The story must be one that resonates for the people in question and they spontaneously relate. It need not correspond to actual occurrences, but must serve to answer a people's psychic need for a sense of origins and ancestors, to legitimize contemporary values, and to provide the quality of uniqueness. The story mirrors the mythologies that carry meaning for a particular nation or ethnic group. Times of crisis and existential trials often give birth to these collective motifs on which a people rests its identity. The national psyche extracts significant events from the past, interprets or corrects them and, according to their archetypal needs, fashions a myth. Frequently, these collective motifs contradict the discoveries of historians: their primary function is mythological, not factual. They serve the needs of the psyche.

After the First World War, the belief spread among the Germans that the defeat could have been avoided had the country's leaders not failed. Hindenburg's and Ludendorff's perception in September 1918 that the war could not be won, the abdication of the Kaiser on November 9, 1918, and the founding of the Republic led to the legend of "the stab in the back." The German people did not experience a defeat directly and, therefore, the factual events could be reinterpreted. Out of a need for greatness and the desire to preserve their sense of superiority, the Germans produced the "November myth," we could have won had we not been betrayed! The German leaders' decision in favor of life and against a "Nibelungen finale" was later regarded as an act of cowardice.

A similar myth arose around the German defeat on the Russian front during the Second World War. The Germans would have won a military victory, according to the myth, if the decision-making power had been in the hands of the German army; the failure belonged to the political leadership with its idiotic ideas. According to this myth, the German army was also not responsible for the atrocities in Poland and Russia. These were attributed to the SS. Although the first part of the myth is extremely doubtful and the second has been clearly disproved, this is how collective narratives come into being. We can only shake our heads at this dissembling and at the naiveté necessary to believe these narratives. We would be well advised, though, to study the psychic origins of such popular stories. What is the deeper background of this kind of presentation of the past, that many take as rock-solid fact?

Germany's collective, psychic situation is a difficult one. The catastrophe of the Second World War and the crimes of National Socialism weigh heavily on the German people. How can Germany develop a positive, grandiose myth after the national myths of the last war led to such total disaster? Germany's striving for "a place in the sun" and for more *Lebensraum* ended in the horrors of Auschwitz and the Nuremberg Trials. If we take a closer look at the existing myth of the time, we recognize that it was a mixture of an expectation of salvation and a belief in superiority. Germans looked for redemption and greatness in the fulfillment of duty. To attain salvation according to this myth, the country had to be capable of criminal acts on one hand and of sustaining suffering on the other. Germany had to stoop to what was horrific and unspeakable in its striving toward a higher destiny. Germans considered the annihilation of the Jews an heroic act, carried as they were by the conviction of eliminating one of the world's burdens. We can see this in the way the National Socialists recorded and filmed the murder of the Jews in the Warsaw Ghetto. They wanted future generations to know what atrocities they were capable of in the name of the Reich. They offered the world a dramatization of redemption through hell.

A further mythic theme for Germany was that of the *Führer* principle, an orienting image for the Germans before Adolf Hitler appeared on the scene. "The best thing in the world," wrote one German commentator in 1932, "is a command," thereby giving expression to the myth that only strict obedience makes a nation great. "Not happiness, but fulfilling one's duty is of greatest importance."

The horrifying "guiding fictions" of World War II have departed. The national myths behind them, however, surface at regular intervals, albeit in completely different costumes. The initial sympathy and interest aroused by the Baader-Meinhof terrorists was noteworthy in this regard. Authors like Heinrich Böll and other intellectuals focused their attention on the group, which received wide coverage in the media. The argument that lofty goals legitimize terrorist acts touched an old, national myth: violence is "necessary" in the context of political struggle.

A broadcast on German television reminded me that the belief in authority remains very pronounced. A satire mimicking a press conference of the German chancellor several years in the future was the setting. The chancellor was completely shielded from the people who would have furiously reminded him of his promises of reunification with East Germany and blamed him for the nation's economic desolation. The program moved me in a strange way. The extreme criticism was directed rather one-sidedly at the person of the chancellor. It was this *Führer's* fault that the economy was not improving. To me it seemed like the reverse side of the belief in authority, that notoriously critical attitude toward authority figures by which we can remove ourselves from all political responsibility.

Every country needs a national myth to make sense of its historical past and to provide the means for coming to terms with future challenges. Germany needs a *new myth* to give it the strength to join with other countries as a nation in its own right. It requires a new myth to integrate the population of the one-time German Democratic Republic, to come to terms with existing internal tension, to prevent extremist groups from exercising a disproportionate influence, and to give the nation a constructive direction for the future. Germany needs a myth that will leave behind the crimes of redemption and the blind belief in authority. The German people require a common history and a common image, enabling them to see themselves as a nation.

The new myth must also project an image that leaves behind the one of the "ugly German," that is so troublesome to many German citizens. It should be a myth that does not hide behind the reputation for quality of German goods. Instead it would give the nation history and meaning without evoking arrogance and without increasing or splitting off the demonic.

Let us take a look at another country: Scotland. The nature of the psyche of this nation in the northern part of Great Britain is

fundamentally different from that of Germany. In contrast to
Germany, Scotland is not independent in its own right, but is a
country that united with England and Wales to form Great
Britain. The Scots, though, consider themselves an autonomous
people. This rather complex national situation leads to special
myths, stories that represent the Scots' desire for autonomy and
the fact of their unification with England. The Scots have reacted
to their military defeats against the English in a very different
manner than the Germans did to their defeat in World War I.

In 1745 Charles Stuart, the "Bonnie Prince," landed at
Moidart in the north of Scotland and invited the leaders of the
Scottish clans to join the struggle against the English. Unselfishly,
Charles had disposed of his fortune and given up the easy life in
the courts of France and Italy, because the liberation of his homeland was of more importance. Scotland, he claimed, ought not to
be ruled by Englishmen. The prince's goal was an independent
Scotland. On April 16, 1746, however, his undertaking ended in
disaster. More than a thousand Highlanders lost their lives at the
Battle of Culloden, while the remainder were forced into disas-
trous retreat and hunted down for years.

According to reliable historical sources, the Bonnie Prince
mismanaged the organization of the battle, dreamed of having his
own kingdom, and felt little interest for the Scots themselves.
Scotland really did not matter to him, but was only a means to an
end. Only with the greatest reluctance did he ally himself with the
wild, primitive Highlanders. According to these same sources, the
"Bonnie Prince" was, in addition, extraordinarily ugly. The final
revolt of the Scots against English domination, though, gave birth
to a myth. Scots extol the heroic deeds of Bonnie Prince Charlie
to the present day. They are even narrated in many of Scotland's
history books. Scotland needs this myth for its collective orientation, to overcome the disgrace of not being its own nation. The
Scots' deep-seated desire for national autonomy lives on in the
Bonnie Prince.

The Scots romanticize the Highlands as part of their collective image, cherishing the myth of the Highlander to support
their sense of national identity. The myth carries a lingering
effect, making it possible to be a Scot.

The myth's effect came to my attention at a congress of British
psychologists in York, in the north of England. The purpose of
the congress was the exchange of information among British

psychologists working in different institutions. The lectures of the various presenters carried sensible titles such as "The Concept of Social Dissonance and Therapeutic Stipulations" or "The Tasks of Social Micro-Units in the Field of Health Management." One Scottish psychologist, however, entitled his paper with the single word *Porridge*. He chose this national dish to highlight his demands for more planning freedom for Scottish school psychologists. His reference to this Highland image gave weight to his argument, though he, himself, lived in the Glasgow metropolitan area and only knew the Highlands from occasional vacation trips. To the proper English participants, he presented himself as the wild, rebellious Highlander.

Every country has its myths that bolster national identity. In Switzerland we have the myth of Arnold Winkelried. In 1386, at the battle of Sempach, he is said to have thrown himself on the lances of Leopold III's soldiers with the words, "Look to my child and my wife and I will do you some daring deed." Thanks to his selfless action, the Swiss succeeded in breaking through the Hapsburg lines and repulsing their attack. Even though, in all likelihood, no man named Arnold Winkelried ever existed, his heroism was officially recorded in 1533. His action is a "fundamental image" and appears again in similar form at the battle of Bicocca in 1522.

The figure of Winkelried is not a historical character, but a "mythic form," devised by the "freely creating popular fantasy." Winkelried's image expressed the wish to counter the self-sacrificing feats of the knights with a heroic figure from the common people. The collective unconscious traced down the legend and elevated it to a myth as a way of strengthening the Swiss national identity. Winkelried became the symbol for a collective orientation and gave expression to a value that the nation cherished. Like the mythic William Tell, Winkelried emphasized that the individual citizen can be effective in a national context. His deed, historical or not, is vital for the national well-being. In Switzerland it is not the leaders who are honored and emphasized, but the simple, unknown citizen.

In the course of time, myths can change or be replaced by new myths. In Switzerland today, the myths of Tell and Winkelried have faded. People argue over whether the nation came into being in 1291, at the time of the first confederation, or in 1815, at the conclusion of the Napoleonic Wars. They question whether

Switzerland is a nation by choice or simply a group of self-serving individuals who live together for the sake of financial profit. Different mythologies clash against one another, background narratives to attitudes constellated in the population at large. The myth of the Rutli Oath of 1291 or that of Winkelried evokes the image of Switzerland as a fundamental democracy defining itself against outside powers. In the myth of a Switzerland dating from 1815, another image asserts itself: a country stamped by European forces, shaped through outer influences, and making no claim to special status. Both myths are as false as they are accurate. It is irrelevant which myth can be proven from a historical perspective. What is decisive is which story wins out and is recognized as myth.

Both myths, that of 1291 as well as that of 1815, are apparent in Switzerland today. My grandfather, Adolf Guggenbühl-Huber (1896–1971), already described the Swiss citizen as characterized by a resistance to authority figures. Anyone behaving too overtly like an authority figure determining how things should be, quickly meets with rejection. As in the myth of Winkelried, the average citizen is of greatest importance.

I experienced this aspect of my Swiss heritage during a continuing education course for psychotherapists in Wiesbaden. Two Swiss colleagues and I signed up for a training seminar with a recognized American Family Therapist. We were extremely fortunate to be accepted for the seminar, since the participants were limited and the interest was great. The therapist was considered to be the leading authority in her area and her presentations were correspondingly intensive. At the end of the second morning, she informed the participants that we would only take one hour for lunch, since she had to catch an early train and wanted to complete her material. During lunch, we realized that an hour was not enough time to eat, so the three of us decided to take an extra half-hour. We were certain that the others in the seminar would come to a similar conclusion and decision. Of the sixty participants, however, we three were the only ones who returned thirty minutes late. The others had accepted the abbreviated lunch break without protest and had not dared to incur the anger of this famous American.

The cosmopolitan nature of the Swiss shows itself in their dedication to language study (there are more language schools in Zurich than there are churches) and in their readiness to criticize national peculiarities. They use the expression, "typically Swiss," to mean rigid and simple-minded, while in England, the expression, "how very un–British" means primitive and uncivilized. This denigration of their own characteristics, releases energy in the Swiss and makes them receptive to the qualities of other nationalities.

Although the story of the United States began considerably earlier than the first immigrants, American history scarcely mentions the Native Americans, who had populated the continent for centuries previously. The majority of Americans are not interested in either the Native American religion or their specific ways of life. History, for European Americans, begins with the *Mayflower's* sailing from Plymouth to a land where a life of freedom and justice would be possible. This little band of daring Englishmen formed the kernel of the American myth. The kernel was elaborated with images of stern, deeply religious individuals, ready to forge into the wilderness with their families and take fate in their own hands. This myth formed the foundation of America.

In the last twenty years, this story has been rewritten. In the minds of contemporary Americans, the United States came into being not only thanks to the spirit of the *Mayflower* and other immigrants, but also through the contributions of slaves from east Africa and through coming to terms with the way of life of the indigenous peoples. Native Americans and African Americans have been incorporated into the story. In the history of the United States, it is not just valiant whites who play a role, but other ethnic groups are beginning to receive the recognition they deserve. The nation no longer identifies itself one-sidedly with the myth of the Pilgrim Fathers, but is developing a multicultural myth. A changing American self-image is finding expression through recognizing the indigenous peoples and other groups.

Bonnie Prince Charlie and the Pilgrim Fathers, as well as Winkelried and William Tell, are mythical figures that serve as points of reference for their respective nations. They are figures that release and arouse an emotional response, that evoke anger or intentional rejection. Usually, the individual response to such mythic figures is immaterial. Whether we are for or against William Tell, Joan of Arc, or the sentimental folksongs to Bonnie Prince Charlie is not really important. What is decisive is whether the figure in question is thought of and accepted as mythic by the respective nationality.

Our identification with myths takes place on different levels. In addition to the national myths, there are also regional and local

myths in which we participate. The Basques or the Catalans in
Spain, the Bretons or Corsicans in France, the South Tirolers or
the Langobards in Italy, the Berners or Vallisers in Switzerland all
have their own history, traditions, language or dialect. They consider themselves self-sufficient entities, distinct one from another.
While a myth inspires a region and a way of life, it does not find
expression merely in folklore, but animates other aspects of existence, even political institutions. Special myths exist in all regions
and serve the population as the basis for their local identity.

As a Zuricher, working in Bern, I am repeatedly confronted
with the specifically Bernese myths. I have noticed that if I want to
convince someone of something, I have to go about it differently
in Switzerland's capital. While in Zurich we expect a person to
make his argument straight out with a dose of aggressiveness, in
Bern such a thing is improper. One must first welcome the other
person with conversation, an exchange of small talk or over a cup
of coffee. Before one comes to the business at hand, enough time
must be spent to get to know one's opposite number. From where
does he or she come? What is his or her family background? Who
are his or her acquaintances? At the beginning of an encounter,
the main agenda is very much in the background, since it is important to know with whom you have to deal. Social position and family origins play an important role. In small details like these, the
more formal conventions of Bern make themselves known in con-
tradistinction to Zurich, a city influenced more by myths of business and industry.

Outsiders usually do not notice these regional myths until
they reveal themselves in corresponding situations. In the example at the beginning of this chapter, the man from Switzerland's
interior reacted out of his regional myth. I was only aware of his
perspective, however, when the conversation turned to the coming election. To decide whether to vote for or against membership in the European Community, he turned to his local myth.
The myth gave him a point of reference for his decision, one that
was too important to be arrived at rationally.


## PROFESSIONAL MYTHS

I would now like us to turn our attention to myths of different
professions. All kinds of professions or professional categories

legitimize themselves with myths. By way of their respective activities, various professions participate in a psychic reality that mediates their tasks and duties. By working in a clinic, physicians participate in the "myth of hospitals" with its special "liturgy." While doing patient rounds, physicians must "vest" themselves in white coats and intersperse their comments with Latin phrases as a first step in the struggle against the demons of disease. Teachers write down grades and talk about the deplorable state of education that can only be improved through great dedication and devotion on their parts. Bank tellers serve notice by their impeccable dress and impersonal manner, that they see themselves as servants of their customers and, in no way, entertain any personal fantasies or notions about the money changing hands.

Such external details and activities are often indicators of the myths in which a particular profession participates. For a profession or a company to convey certainty and competence, and to win the trust of clients, it must have access to a multitude of assurances. Professions need to draw on the psychic foundation of myth to obtain the energy and the feeling of certainty for themselves and those they serve. Usually there is but one myth that supports a given profession.

"In the drug scene I have experienced many more genuine, human encounters than anywhere else in our society. There, despite all the misery, there reigns a camaraderie and a sense of mutual dependence," was the opinion of one social worker to a meeting of those working with substance abusers. He received thunderous applause.

This comment points to the myth in which the social work profession participates. The claim that "genuine camaraderie" still reigns on the streets will certainly be disputed by many outsiders. Not that the claim is false, but that it points to the myth from which this profession draws sustenance. When social workers recognize value in misery, when they see meaning in marginal figures of our society, or when they consider themselves the bearers of some divine message, they are unconsciously referring to a myth. One example of this myth is the story of the rich man and poor Lazarus in the Gospel of Luke (16:19–31). This social worker's comment is a reference to the stories of meaning and origin that enable this profession to deal with its challenges. The myth colors the perception, the thinking, and the action of the profession's members. The applause from the

audience acknowledged that the social worker's statement fit
within the professional myth. (The applause demonstrated that,
in this professional group, only those explanations are convincing that fit within this myth.)

Such common truths are not mediated through consensus or
identified by way of discussion. Rather, they are *constellated*. By that
I mean that unconscious processes help a certain myth to manifest
itself. These collective, psychic mechanisms stand aloof from our
direct intervention. They occur through the collective process of
coming to terms with the *Zeitgeist*, with the "spirit of the times,"
without any individual being able to influence them. For this reason, a new myth cannot consciously be introduced by a single
human being.

A given collective, a group or a profession, lives *in* a myth to
have the strength and conviction necessary to fulfill its obliga-
tions. Social workers align themselves with the romantic myth of
the rejected divine messenger to be able to bear the deplorable
reality of their daily activities. Some years ago, the myth that
served this purpose for social work was that of the lost children,
for whom the caring father or nurturing mother provided with
a home.

As an image of profession, the railroad seems especially
important. Men in particular are often fascinated by trains.
They study schedules, identify different types of locomotives,
and fall into ecstasies when they finally get the chance to experience a famous locomotive like the Santa Fe Chief or a train
like the Orient Express. Again, a unique myth supports the railroad profession. Railroaders carry the image of mastering the
chaos in the world and the tumultuous instinctual forces in and
around us through technology and rational planning. Railroaders live in the myth of the one who overcomes nature, of the
hero shaping natural forces through his action and will, thereby
establishing the laws of civilization. They cope with chaos by
means of a well-ordered system. The route is planned, predetermined, and the times are set. Nothing is left to chance; relationships are predictable.

Central in the myth of the railroader are on-time departures
and handling periods of peak travel—"Five additional trains
have to be scheduled after Memorial Day for vacationers." Acts
of sabotage or natural catastrophes feed the fantasy of railroaders even more. When the gigantic system of plans is endangered,

the myth mobilizes new energies. Those who work for the rail-road speak in hushed tones of near catastrophes, bridges flooded out, devastating storms, or other interruptions in the scheduled routines. These events animate railroaders, who cele-brate over and over again the myth of their struggle with the unpredictability of nature.

When we claim that railroaders take their life from accidents and catastrophes, we are also talking about the reality and experi-ence of their everyday work. Those who work for the railroad are also motivated by the notion that they are responsible for con-necting the most widely differing areas. The railroad brings together hamlets, separated from each other by distance and geography. Thanks to the rails, the movement of goods and pas-sengers is accomplished. The tracks symbolize a route known in advance, a view into the future.

The myth from which the railroad and its workers live is a mixture of Hermes and Hephaistos. Hermes, the mercurial, shim-mering, clever god of travel and border crossings, binds himself with the practical and gifted god of the smithy's art. Thanks to Hephaistos and his inventions, nature's powers serve human beings. Both archetypes are represented in the myth of the rail-roaders, where the journey of incredible volumes of material and people is only possible due to ingenious technology.

Every living profession has its own myth, a story that grounds the profession's activity. The teaching profession lives partly from the myth of the divine child. Many teachers and educators see children as the carriers of hope for a better world. Unconsciously, they make the child into the "savior of the world." This child has to be protected against the corrupting influences of our civiliza-tion. As adults, we are already corrupted and, therefore, can only learn from the children. To become ourselves like children is the first requirement for educating children. Teachers who identify with this myth unconsciously cherish the hope of renewing the world through their pupils or of receiving some profound wisdom through the children. With sparkling eye, one of my teaching col-leagues said, to me, "Do you know what one little boy told me today? As he watched two other boys in a fight, from which neither would walk away, he said, 'If we cannot solve problems among our-selves, how will we be able to solve the other people's problems?' " The philosopher Rousseau was inspired by this myth of the divine child. His goal was to preserve the uniqueness of the child in the face of civilization's corrupting influence. The pedagogues, Neil and Mallet, and the psychologist, Alice Miller, likewise derive their perspectives from this myth.

Should an educator identify exclusively with the myth of the divine child, he will always feel as though he has too little time for his work. Everywhere, he sees the contaminating influences of modernity and would somehow like to reserve a special, protected place in the world for children. Often, too, he will believe himself to be the only one who truly understands "his children." When children are violent or unruly, he lays the blame one-sidedly on the behavior of their parents or the influence of the media. The child remains immaculate.

## FAMILY MYTHS

Families, too, live in myths. Closer inspection of the values and goals of a family often brings to light stories that serve to legitimize the family's behavior, unquestioned truths shared by all the family members. Family myths often revolve around specific periods in the family history that all recall, prosperous or difficult times when seen in retrospect, that give the family its sense of identity. The myth can spur family members to extraordinary efforts—living up to one's heritage—or lead to a conscious distancing. The myth contains energy, challenging the family to react. A colleague told me this story. "In my family of origin, we held high the value of physical labor. Sitting all day at a desk did not count as real work. My family believes they knew what it meant to work. My grandmother's father was killed by a falling tree when she was eight years old. With her mother, she had to care for her brothers and sisters. Thanks to an iron will, great effort, and a profound belief in God, she was able to survive this time of deprivation. She was a woman who knew that perseverance and hard work were the only remedies for hard times." My colleague's family mythologized his grandmother's life. Her myth hovered over his family, reminding them that while life is difficult and trying, it can be mastered through the right attitude.

In many ways the extraordinary, even mysterious, clings to family myths. They proclaim heroic deeds from earlier times and marvelous feats of forefathers: "Uncle Albert emigrated to America, bought an old Volkswagen, and drove from the East

Coast to the West, finally arriving in California. There he started an artichoke farm and became a millionaire."

The other side of marvelous family myths is that they make failure more likely. The stories support axioms that are not reflected upon, but that family members feel obliged to present as justification for the group's attitude. One's own achievements quickly pale before the gallery of glorious ancestors. Of what importance is a career as an architectural draftsman, when grandfather was a senator or Aunt Mildred a well-known author?

In contrast to a family's psychology, the power of a family myth often affects outsiders. Myths are impersonal and other human beings can, therefore, take part in them. Others can sense the fascination with earlier deeds, can identify with a collection of beliefs. They can be either infected by the power of the family's myth or distance themselves completely from the family's axiomatic justifications. Outsiders may emulate the successes of ancestors other than their own or use another family's myth to support their own perspective.

As a well-known journalist and writer, my grandfather advocated particular political positions and a general attitude toward 'ife in no uncertain terms. His perspectives and activities congealed into the family myth that has been described in the novel *All in All* by Willy Guggenheim. Various outsiders unconsciously emulated my grandfather or thought like he did. Even today many go on at length about the "good old days" when the Guggenbühl-Huber family allowed a group of artists and writers to take part in its myth.

Family myths come into being against the backdrop of a broadened sense of family. Not only does the nuclear family belong together, but the grandparents and other close relatives are psychologically bound to each other. According to this notion, the various individuals comprise a single unit, even when there is relatively little contact among them. Relatives and forebears make up the psychic field, from which myths arise. The specific nature of the myth often permeates family gatherings or celebrations, or reveals itself in family members' professional activities. If a health-care myth animates members of a given family, they become physicians, nurses, or pharmacists, while another family may orient itself more by a social myth. Members of the latter chose the ministry as a profession, go into private practice as psychologists, or become social workers.

It is my experience that many couples and parents attempt to escape the mythical significance of the family. They, therefore, consider a wedding, for example, to be a personal experience, not a mythical, public occasion. One must not provide too wide a stage for Aunt Mildred's caustic remarks or Uncle Fred's drinking. Ceremonies become correspondingly boring and dull. Instead of experiencing the tensions, the battles of personalities, and values that surface in a confrontation of differing family myths, couples plan small, "intimate" receptions, where they can just enjoy the fact that John has found Mary.

In immigrant families, the family myth often blends with national myths of the old country. Even when the myths are not present in the outer world, they live on within the family's traditions. Seen from the immigrant perspective, the alien environment, lacking mythical animation, denies national or regional myths a place in society. Often the myths that immigrants keep alive have little to do with actual myths in their homelands. They are much more reminiscences or caricatures of earlier myths.

A Turkish woman, who had lived for more than fifteen years in Switzerland, commented, "In my country hospitality is very important. If a stranger comes to my town, the inhabitants greet him, make him welcome, and invite him to eat with them." What she fails to realize is that, since her departure, television arrived in her hometown. Now the inhabitants have little interest for strangers, filling their need for contact with the world at large with American adventure movies on Channel 5!

I would like to recapitulate briefly the difference between psychology and mythology. A myth is an axiomatic narrative of meaning that enables us to come to terms with fundamental experiences and to master existential challenges. We base our convictions on these axioms. A myth is a story that resonates in our souls thanks to the power of its images and symbols. Myths bring us new sources of psychic energy. A myth is not the product of individual psychology, but constellates itself autonomously through psychic processes in the collective. Myths, therefore, are not private narratives, but collective stories of the psyche. They are created by the archetypal forces of the psyche, forces that we sense in the depths of the unconscious.

Myths animate life's outer world, the "not personal." They provide the mortar for a nation or a region, for a manufacturing plant, a profession, or an extended family. The corresponding

*[Handwritten margin note at top: Do myths' prominence in the lives of men explain why more men are pastors? Why patriarchs led their family? Why tribal leaders were men?]*

myth provides energy to members of the group—mythical substance—allowing them to see meaning in their activity. Myth does not replace conscious thought or empirical observation, but supplies energy for our reasoning, making conclusions and confrontations possible. The logical reflection by which we resolve problems only becomes effective when it is embedded in a mythical context, for myths are the only thing that we are ready or willing to fight for.

*[Handwritten margin note: This is why I (and others) cling to the Bible – it is the myth that guides our life]*

Developing a relationship with our own myths is difficult, since they control us and not the other way around. We are inspired, ensouled, by them. We are immersed in them, so that we can only see ourselves and our environment through the lenses of myth. We experience myths as reality in life's outer world, not as projections, but as *autonomous forces* that cannot be reduced to individual psychology.

*[Handwritten margin note: Myths are almost a wv of sorts]*

From the perspective of psychology, the outer world only takes on meaning through individual human beings. Mythology rejects this egocentric view. The world does not only have meaning because of what we bring to it, rather the world outside is an autonomous reality in itself. We colonize the world with our personal complexes when we assume that objects only have importance from our ascribing meaning to them. With myths we speak of the *identity between subject and object.* We human beings do not transfer inner psychic content onto the outer, rather the outer corresponds with an inner, archetypal readiness in us. Myths appear in the situation, the ritual, or the existential task that correspond with them. They are autonomous forces, that reveal themselves in the outer world or in collectives and invite us to share in them.

We can surrender ourselves to myth without having any relationship to it personally. Visiting a museum of the labor movement or reading a book like Upton Sinclair's, *The Jungle* (a novel of workers in the Chicago stockyards), the myth of that collective struggle may well seize us, even though we, ourselves, do not come from working-class backgrounds. We feel as though we can sense what work meant for those people, and we suffer with them their exploitation by the capitalist system. We can be gripped by this myth, even when we come from the upper middle class, in the same way that the American intellectual, Waldo Frank, was gripped by the myth of the proletariat during his visit to the USSR.

## ARENAS OF MYTH

Myths affect us in particular mythical situations, the arenas of myth or *temenoi*. In antiquity, a *temenos* was a sacred space. One classicist describes it as "a circumscribed, enclosed, and consecrated place in which a deity was present. More generally, though, any place in which a god dwells is a *temenos*. It can be a spring, a grotto, a mountain, a grove, a meadow . . . Even house and property, to the extent that they are endowed with mythical substance, can be such sacred places." *Temenoi* are areas where the power of the gods is perceptible, a place where Apollo, Aphrodite, or Poseidon lingers. A *temenos* is dedicated to a deity, who selects it as a place to appear and display his or her power. The rituals and images that symbolize the deity predominate in these sacred spaces.

A deity, on the other hand, symbolizes an *arché*, a fundamental pattern of human perception and behavior. In a *temenos,* we participate in the numinous emanations of a god or an archetype. We tremble, we are terrified or fascinated, we rejoice or are frightened. *Temenoi* demonstrate the transcendent quality of the archetypes, that through their effects seek to influence human beings. In these "holy" places, mythical substance is transferred to us, for they invite us to participate in myth. In the arenas of myth we come into contact with the gods. The Greeks located Zeus, Hera, and the other gods, for instance, on Olympus. In the Bible, Moses speaks with God on Mount Sinai.

Human hands, however, can also shape and form sacred spaces, permeated by their respective myths. The Aztecs built two gigantic pyramids, dedicated to Tlaloc, the god of rain, at Tenochtitlan. In front of the pyramids, they planted an artificial forest, in the middle of which stood a special tree. Once a year, the tree was felled as part of a ceremony and an eight-year-old girl was sacrificed. This brutal ritual served the god who was responsible for rain. According to the Aztecs' myth, human beings must play a part in promoting fertility. They have to sacrifice someone to ensure a good harvest and thus come closer to paradise on earth.

Every group of individuals erects temples to their myths or reserves special areas for them. In this way the group can experience psychic renewal and receive some of the power of the myth through the appropriate ritual. Stonehenge, the megalithic monument in England, which was build ca. 3500 B.C.E., probably served this purpose. The same holds true for the Neolithic temple complex of Tarxien in Malta (ca. 3000 B.C.E.), the stones in the Teutoburg Forest, or the conical hillock near Glastonbury, England. After the coming of Christianity, pilgrimage sites and cathedrals became the arenas of myth, Santiago de Compostela in Spain or Chartres in northern France, for example. Later, even the smallest village parishes erected churches to honor God. These churches became the place of myth. Villagers were invited to participate in the great Christian myths portrayed in frescoes on walls and ceiling.

In Europe today, the churches are still the largest and most conspicuous structures. They symbolize the Christian myths that comprise the foundation of the community's life. In petitionary processions, all the members of the parish move through the village in two columns, praying for favorable weather and a rich harvest. Like the Aztecs, these Christian communities seek to come to terms with an existential task through their participation in myth.

As moderns we know no consecrated mountains like the Aborigines' Ayers Rock or temple cities like the Mayas' Palenque in Central America. Even the importance of churches as mythical arenas has decreased. The significance of mythical places has not decreased for us, though. We have simply relocated them, blended them into *prominent objects of our civilization*. We want myths to continue to possess us: our souls need the tension and the challenges that myths provide us. Today, mythical fascination penetrates our world through apparently profane objects. Architectural, technological, or cultural works contain mythical substance, even if we, ourselves, only perceive their functional significance. Pablo Neruda was smitten by an Armenian hydroelectric plant because he found in it the myth by which he oriented himself. We encounter mythical arenas in hospitals, airports, train stations, stadiums, malls, or restaurants. They carry a dual meaning. On the one hand, they fulfill a specific, utilitarian function. On the other, they serve to engage us in the myth that shapes our civilization.

As a young man, freighters, passenger liners, cruisers, and aircraft carriers fascinated me. On a two-day sea voyage to the Shetland Islands in the North of Scotland, I had the fortune to experience a storm on the North Sea. The waves broke heavily over the bow, and the impact of the ship reverberated dully over the storm-lashed ocean. Transfixed we gazed at the giant swells that towered again and again in front of us. All the hatches on the freighter were bolted shut and loose objects secured in anticipation of the waves that would pour over the ship. During the storm I watched out the upper window, saw the water running down, heard the creaking of the ship and the raging of the ocean. Naturally I was afraid. Yet, I enjoyed the storm as the most magnificent moment of the trip. I was ensouled!

The ship represented symbolically a myth that was important for me. Through that ocean voyage, I participated in a mythical arena. Our civilization knows many such objects and activities through which we can take part in our myths. The activities connected to corresponding objects, institutions, or tasks fulfill a predetermined goal. At the same time, however, they are often ritual activities of the myth on which they are based. Seen superficially, a ship serves to transport passengers and goods across the water's surface. Seen mythologically, a ship carries a psychic meaning. This is true of many of our activities. If we watch a broker, for example, on the floor of the stock exchange, he is not just buying and selling, gauging supply and demand, but participating in a myth. The cries on the floor from the jobbers testify to the divine sparks that have infused them. Profit means more energy, more life and meaning. The myth of success has been constellated.

Money, too has a mythical quality. We are energized, angered, or depressed by changes in our bank accounts; we develop fantasies of happiness and power when we think of wealth. "Money makes everything possible," "everything has a price," say some people. Others stress that "wealth by itself does not make us happy."

The discrete manner and the conservative dress of bank employees communicates that they will not succumb to the magnetism of money. Numbers, statistics, graphic illustrations, and elaborate calculations assert that money is a rock-solid value, something we can completely control. But money continuously eludes us, is iridescent, changes in size, and works magic. In banks we get a sense of respect for the incomprehensible quality of money: the imposing buildings, the computers, the hierarchy of management, the precisely determined procedures and regulations. Banks must have rituals to offset the quicksilver, Hermes-like aspect of money. Money is uncannily transitory; it is too unpredictable to be let loose. Banks identify with the myth of the magic potion, a powerful spirit, about which no one can predict exactly what it might do. In a certain sense, bank employees are magicians, who must submit to strict laws so that the spirit they attempt to control does not wreak havoc. Banks are *temenoi*, temples, designed to make the mercurial quality of money useful.

The arenas of myth are impersonal, places where each one of us is invited to let ourselves be addressed by myth. Whether we *hear* a myth does not depend on our personal psychology, but on whether a particular myth speaks to us or leaves us cold. Since myths are forces that influence us from the outside, we can participate in myths regardless of our origin, race, or socioeconomic status. This "outside" constellates an inner, archetypal disposition in us. The outer situation, the mythical arena, exerts its influence on us, joining with our inner patterning. We take part in myth without any particular preparation or personal background. A farmer's son can be ensouled by the myth of banks or a salesman's daughter can be caught up in the myth of a mission to save the world.

Often dedication to a myth shows itself through the passion of our attachment to this or that outer situation. The *temenos* lies hidden in the passion. One example is the "monster chasers" of Scotland. Between Fort Augustus and Dochgarroch near Inverness stretches an extensive lake, Loch Ness. In the depths of these dark, mostly cold waters, a prehistoric monster supposedly makes its home, the Loch Ness Monster. The local populace has sighted this unidentifiable being on numerous occasions—something the locals seldom tell curious tourists, since the latter just laugh at the reports. Unfortunately, the Loch Ness Monster has seldom been photographed or filmed.

Nonetheless, there are constantly men who feel called upon to pursue the secret of this creature. They wait patiently for months, alone in a house trailer or a shepherd's hut, staring at the surface of the lake in the hope of deciphering the mystery. At great personal sacrifice—the "monster chaser," Steve Feltham, sold his house and quit his job for the purpose—such men continue looking for "Nessie." Their engagement is complete.

These men are participating in a myth just as do dedicated bankers, enthusiastic pilots, or motivated physicians. Loch Ness is an arena of myth that ensouls the "chasers." The men are not simply living out a romantic hero fantasy: they are entering the myth of the dragon-slayer, the dragon-finder. Their searching points them to the underworld, where chthonic beings have their homes. They are ensouled by a myth, according to which there is more in the world than we see at first glance. The world contains uncanny regions that we can only penetrate with the help of courage, strength, much patience, and a fighting spirit. Without the Loch Ness Monster, without the animation of this myth, these men would hardly spend months waiting patiently in the wilderness!

The monster chasers are following an archetype, like anyone else who is dedicated to a cause or a profession. These archetypes, these fundamental patterns of human perception and behavior, lie in the depths of the human soul as dispositions or tendencies. We recognize archetypal behavior as much in psychology as we do in mythology. These basic dispositions of human behavior express themselves, however, differently. In the realm of psychology, the archetypes manifest themselves through personal history and individual symbols, while in mythology they express themselves through the collective and the arenas of myth.

When someone lives a myth, he will be moved by the hidden mythical forces or a corresponding mythical arena. The librarian, who sits for hours behind her desk, puts in overtime, and devotedly registers each new book, is gripped as much by a myth as the employee of the city sanitation department, who maintains the sewer system. Through their professional activities, both participate in myth. We can understand both individuals from a psychological perspective as well as from a mythological one.

In my department, we have had a great deal of difficulty finding someone to fill the librarian's position. Twice, a newly hired librarian quit the job after only a few months. Their reasons were not convincing: they had too little contact with the students or their integration in the department was not satisfactory or the work was too monotonous. A third librarian was hired. In contrast to his predecessors, he developed a great deal of enthusiasm for his work. He spent hours thinking up new cataloging possibilities, pondered about the proper keywords for ordering the books, and devised plans to improve how books were exhibited. His relationship to the job was not psychological. For him being a librarian was an arena of myth, an opportunity to serve and participate in the greater drama of the human spirit.

A hobby can also conceal a mythical *temenos*. Often these hobbies are rather eccentric. Some men make military paraphernalia their pastime. They spend hours of their spare time studying books on uniforms and insignia of rank, collect posters illustrating the various insignia, and discuss their knowledge with others at military club meetings. We might consider this unusual hobby useless or possibly pathological, even though it corresponds to a genuine interest. The very intensity and pleasure these men experience testifies to the *temenos*, to an arena of myth. Clearly, they are moved at a profound level. Perhaps in their fantasies, they become part of a worldwide group of men, identified with the various armies around the globe, working their way through the ranks in their imaginations.

For others a fascination with geography, with different makes of cars or airplanes, or with all the islands on the map can unlock a myth. Any intense, burning interest can serve as a bridge to one of the myths that is alive and active in our civilization.

Psychology approaches human beings as individuals. It attempts to understand human behavior based on the individual's primary relationships, social environment, and personal history. The individual is the primary focus, not his or her mythical context. Psychology places the emphasis upon the personal. The mythical environment in which we are born and participate is seldom of interest. Psychology has no sense of the collective forces of the soul. Since individuals and relationship between individuals are of primary importance, psychology refers questions of mythical participation back to the personal.

Of course, we can approach the character, behavior, and activity of an individual from the perspective of psychology as well as from that of mythology. Depending on the focus, a different part of the personality reveals itself. A mythological consideration of human beings does not exclude a psychological analysis, since in our everyday lives, the mythological is frequently mixed with the psychological. A man may read the newspaper both to avoid doing housework and, simultaneously, because he wants contact with the myths of his culture celebrated by the media. Separation from myth, the feeling of not having a task in life, can cause a depression. At the same time, the depression may stem from a trauma in a relationship like the death of a spouse. The unconscious speaks to us individually as well as collectively. While psychology explores the realm of our private lives, mythology connects us with collective forces of the soul through its mythical arenas.

Let us call to mind once more the man from the rural part of Switzerland, whom I described at the beginning of this chapter. He had decided to vote against Switzerland's membership in the European Economic Community. With his decision, he was participating in one of the myths of the region in which he lived. The man identified the subject of the election with the myth reflected in many stories of his part of the country: resistance as a means for gaining respect from authority figures. This unsophisticated man remained true to a myth, which is reflected in stories, architecture, political assemblies, and thousands of everyday conversations. The matter appears in a different light, when seen psychologically. Here we have a negative father complex, feelings of impotence, generalized anxiety, or a lack of self-worth generating the man's attitude.

*Ex. Contrasting the way psych vs. myth attrib. it core*

## CORE EVENTS OF THE SOUL

All of us sense the mythological and the psychological as dimensions of life. The importance of psychology in relationship to mythology varies from personality to personality. [Core events of our souls inform us whether we take our orientation more from psychology or from mythology. When I speak of "core events," I mean experiences or encounters through which we are moved in the depths of our souls and to which, in retrospect, we ascribe great importance. [They are events that influence the direction of our souls and determine our attitude toward life and our goals. We can experience core events of the soul psychologically and mythologically; we can be shaken by a myth or touched through our psyche. [The places where we experience core events psychologically usually have to do with significant experiences within our personal biography.

*ex. of psych. core event*

A thirty-two-year-old woman tells the following story:

> I can still remember how, when I was fourteen, my father forcibly cut off my hair. There was a terrible struggle. I cried, wriggled, and protested. My father, however, was unrelenting. With active help from my mother, he brutally removed my long, dark hair, of which I was extremely proud, from my head. For my parents, long hair was indecent and led to a loose way of life. This experience has followed me. It is an important image that expresses my relationship to my parents. While my father feared my attempts at autonomy, my mother saw me as a rival, whom she had to combat.

Whether this incident took place in this way or was dramatized later, is secondary. For this woman, her experience from childhood is a key event that helped her understand much about herself and her parents. The incident is a reflection of her childhood. Her father's act of violence and her mother's complicity have become important factors of the woman's personal history. The memory images, however, also express this woman's great striving for self-sufficiency and her desire to hold her own against father figures.

The memory further reflects a strongly moralizing super-ego, an inner authority, that combats her irrational and erotic sides. In other words, the image represents an inner struggle in which the woman again finds herself. A self-sufficient, autonomous woman with a good relationship to the unconscious and a well-developed Eros, wrestles with a strong rational side demanding adaptation. The hair-cutting scene is a psychological core event, something that happened within the framework of her personal life and relationships. Her parents have their part to play and her childhood serves as the setting. That she has selected this occurrence as a core event indicates that this woman orients herself in life psychologically.

Mythical core events have a different quality. In contrast to psychological ones, they do not appear in the realm of personal life, but in the outer world, in the mythical arenas. In such places, a location, a group of people, or a situation, we experience the way a power grips us, how a myth takes hold of us from outside. We register this kind of core event as fantastic, fascinating, terrifying, or sacred. They challenge us and present us with a task. The arenas of mythology are located beyond the landscape of the personal soul in the temples of our civilization.

As part of a conference at the university, several of my classmates and I visited a school for special education. One teacher presented examples of his work. He beat a rhythm on the floor for a group of handicapped children. I noticed a girl who was deaf and blind placing both hands flat on the floor. When she felt the rhythm, she suddenly began to beam and to dance in a circle. The experience touched me deeply. Among other things, it convinced me to follow the profession of a child psychologist.

Unlike the hair-cutting scene of the thirty-two-year-old woman, my personal situation, actual relationships, and my wishes and motivations played no part in this core event. The event

occurred even though I, personally, had no relationship whatso-
ever to special education or to deaf and blind children.⌉

My father remembers this experience of his:

> During the war, when I was eighteen years old, we continually heard of the
> atrocities being committed in the Third Reich. I learned that Hitler was sys-
> tematically eradicating the Jews. I felt helpless and irate that I could do
> nothing for these poor people. Finally, I decided to study Hebrew so that,
> at the very least, I could help keep their language alive.

⌈ Politically significant situations and social eruptions frequently trigger mythical core events.⌉The uprisings of 1968 stick in
the memories of many of us. The general strike in France, Rudi
Dutschke in Berlin, the anti-Vietnam demonstrations, and the students killed at Kent State are landmarks of a generation's past. It
is pointless to argue whether the events of 1968 really changed
anything. The fact is, the year became the foundation of a myth
that provides thousands with their orientation. The practice used
by student groups like the SDS of placing a brick on the professor's lectern, symbolized the intention of not forgetting the past.
1968 was a mythical core event in which millions participated,
although at the time many were unaware that they were sharing in
an extraordinary experience.

Today, the myth of a better world inspired by youth crowds out
memories of the student revolts, Hyde Park, or Haight Ashbury.
The myth of 1968 finds expression in the music and pictures of that
time, in highly stylized images we preserve in our memory as
*temenoi.* These temenoi, through which the myth radiates, include
grass-roots democratic assemblies, protest marches, musical com-
positions, political manifestos, and the first rock festivals.

A typical example is the New York realtor who exhibits his
unused ticket for the Woodstock Concert in a frame on the wall. He
proudly tells every client how he climbed over the fence to hear the
Who; Arlo Guthrie; Crosby, Stills, Nash, and Young; John Sebastian;
Richie Havens; Jimi Hendrix; Joan Baez; Janis Joplin; The Grateful
Dead; and Joe Cocker. In his memory, the concert was a core event
through which he became incorporated in the myth of his time and
generation. "Woodstock was . . . the confusing, chaotic establishment of something new, of something that our world will now have
to learn to deal with," reported *Rolling Stone* in 1969. Through memories and images like these, later generations are introduced to the
myth of 1968 and profit from its power.

A journalist writes in retrospect:

> The good news of Woodstock reached me in 1978. At the time I was a suspicious, fourteen-year-old rock-music enthusiast. Flower power music, radio stations specializing in the history of rock music, and teen-age, devotional reading anchored the notion of Woodstock, together with a diffuse utopianism, in my adolescent emotional economy. The saga of harmonious collectivity, of the Hippie life-style, long hair, and prospects for a peaceful, better world took possession of me . . . Woodstock represents a cultural and mental dynamic, that Western society produced to an extent that would have been unthinkable at the beginning of the sixties.

Here is another example. A thirty-year-old addict reported an overwhelming experience he had at a political rally.

> For a number of years I suffered continually from phases in which I completely wilted. I lost my inner orientation, took drugs, and did not know what to do with my life. When the Gulf War broke out, I took part in a demonstration. I heard a conscientious objector speak against the military solutions of the Western nations. I felt something: this confrontation was powerful. Unbelievable forces were being unleashed in the Middle East. The question of how to proceed against such a power-hungry dictator without recourse to violence would not let go of me. I was healed.

This man took part in a mythical, collective challenge, that forced his individual situation into the background. For him, the Gulf War demonstration served as a core event.

Unlike psychological *temenoi*, mythological *temenoi* involve challenge and confrontation. In the myth of 1968, challenge and confrontation took the form of a rejection of society, the Vietnam War, and the Establishment. Since myths are shaped by existential challenges, we encounter core events when something is demanded of us, when we are fundamentally threatened, or when we meet with the extremes of life's experiences. Political upheavals and natural catastrophes, but also peak experiences and sports activities like bungee jumping or the Iditarod sled race are some examples of extreme experiences. The activities or their images express the myth or the other way around. The myth seeks out an image or activity inviting human beings to participate mythologically.

In earlier times, mythical core events were concentrated in experiences in churches or in conjunction with religion. The power of the Christian myths revealed itself in church, during a worship service or in the study of the Bible. An outer, transcendent power gripped the believers and made them see the world differently. Something in the liturgy, the sermon, the grandeur of the choir, the pictures of the saints or other Christian symbols spoke to them and made them aware of a power within that place. They were participating in a mythical *temenos*. Those individuals were moved in the depths of their souls, without any personal reference to what was happening.

Naturally, I can turn to church or religion out of personal motives. If I do, it is not so much myth I am seeking as it is reassurance and consolation and contemplation. The church then becomes a container for my personal religiosity, becomes converted to a domain of psychology or the carrier of projections for psychological issues. It thus loses its mythological power and effect.

Core events help determine whether we are more oriented toward psychology or toward mythology. They lead us either toward the mythological or the psychological, since either one can be the basis for the personality. The core events of the corresponding *temenoi* are the "switch points" determining whether I will allow myself to be gripped by a myth or will take my orientation more from psychology.

## MYTH, THE LANGUAGE OF MEN'S SOULS

Mythology is the language of men's souls. They hear and are moved by myths more readily than are women. As children they sense the mythical power emanating from the *temenoi*. Because myths correspond to men's being, men turn to myth for their self-realization, while women tend to turn to psychology.

Men are ensouled by a "spiritual potential" that is transmitted to them by situations and objects. They experience their souls in public life, in movements, crusades, and causes. When they pour themselves into their work, become excited about political issues, or wax enthusiastic on sports, they are engaging the fascination, the fear, and the power of the myth represented by the subject in question. Work, politics, or sports are ways of mastering existential challenges and produce corresponding collective myths. In those myths, men see soul images inviting them to participate.

Myths hide themselves behind the various traditional fields of men's activities. The armed services, for instance, do not just offer the chance to operate weapons of war, but give men a sense of the myth of good and evil. Like the images from Greek mythology, things military give men the opportunity to encounter Ares, the god of war, who not only attempts to ward off the evil threatening society, but also takes delight in violence.

When men devote hours upon hours to their business, to their company, when they get excited or upset over the closing numbers for the stock market or the latest economic indicators, they are participating in the myth of Hermes, the god of merchants. The transactions fascinate men as much as does the notion of directing and controlling them over the telephone or through the computer. It is not always the striving for personal enrichment that motivates men to apply their energy to economics and business, but Hermes' myth and the energy it brings. Myth fills professional activities and social movements. Politics, economics, business, education, research, the military, and technology all offer spiritual constructs through which men can come into contact with myths. Myth is what serves to justify any profession and its activities.

# 3

## GANGS, VIOLENCE, AND LONGING

♂

## Why Modern Education Fails with Boys

The whole neighborhood talked about the air rifle a friend of mine left me when he moved away. I was proud and a hero in my gang. In spite of this experience, I had terrible inhibitions about firing a rifle when, years later, I did my basic military training. What was the meaning of my earlier interest in guns? My enthusiasm for fire engines, for cars and airplanes, and my dedication to the gang that I shared with my friends, points to a fundamental masculine fascination.

Boys interact with the world in a different way from girls. They are noisier, more violent, wilder, more expansive, less adapted outwardly, and seek out contact with symbols of our civilization. In this chapter, I throw some light on this behavior. I point out that, during their childhood, males try to establish a connection to the primary myths of our time and, in the process, have to overcome various obstacles and fears. The demand of education, that girls and boys be treated equally, leads to neglect of these masculine needs for confrontation, tension, and participation in the existential challenges of our time.

*Overview of chapter*

I am in conversation with a mother. She seems young, emancipated, and belongs to a generation that does not rear children according to traditional role models.

My son and my daughter always got the same toys and my husband and I always tried to give the same amount of attention to both children. My

husband and I share the housework and the discipline of the children. For
us the idea that boys shouldn't cry, need to be brave, and be more interested in technical things is outdated. But what does my son do at the age
of four? He is fascinated by anything that has wheels, he loves war games
and, in contrast to our daughter, has to climb everything. He borrows toy
cars from all the neighbors and uses sticks of wood for guns.

I hear comments like this over and over. Mothers and
fathers realize how their children develop gender-specific behavior, even though they as parents set other priorities. Typically
male behavior patterns show up in their male children: a drive
for expansiveness, the search for challenges, pleasure in struggles, interest in technology, attempts toward autonomy, and fascination for objects.

According to the credo of the social sciences, the greater part
of male behavior is acquired. Biological gender differences are
not of "inner psychological significance for the child." Instead,
typical male behavior is said to result from role expectations that
boys in our society have to emulate. Theorists trace male and
female characteristics back to social conditioning. In other words,
boys and girls acquire characteristics they do not have naturally.
We evaluate children's spontaneous behavior based on gender
and, subtly and without being conscious of doing so, exert influence on them to conform.

In spite of everything, the gender stereotypes exert their
effect—we could say to the woman mentioned above—and make
typical boys of male children and typical girls of the females. This
woman's concept of child development leads to the demand that
children not be exposed to the pressure of society's gender models, but should grow up gender neutral. According to this perspective, we must prevent children from taking their gender
orientation from the gender clichés demonstrated on television,
in movies, and in advertising. Children's books are, therefore, sanitized from sexist comments and classes exclusively for boys or for
girls removed from school curricula. An entire generation of parents and teachers have made an effort to convince boys that they,
too, are allowed to cry and play with dolls, but not to shoot up the
neighborhood with makeshift AK-47s.

The result of such enlightened attempts, however, is dismal.
In spite of educational efforts toward a neutral attitude, male
behavior patterns persist in most boys. Boys continue to be mani-
festly more aggressive, tend to more dangerous activities, have

more accidents, and prefer problem-oriented projects. Even when boys occupy themselves with gender neutral or so-called "girls'" toys, they play with them differently. "If you give dolls to girls, they tend to mother them; boys are more likely to transform them into dive bombers or super heroes," an educator notes. Classes in sewing and cooking have had to be changed since being opened to boys. In some schools, there has been pressure from parents of girls to reinstate the traditional gender separation. Are all characteristics truly acquired? Have we failed? Have we educators and psychologists followed an image of sexual equality down the primrose path?

Gender neutrality is a fiction, an idea we have derived from the demand for equal rights for men and women. In the reality of everyday education, the idea of equality is absurd. *Clear differences* exist between boys and girls, whether in the developmental process, in recreational behavior, in relationships, in ethics, or in self-understanding. The idea of equality is important. Girls as well as boys should have the opportunity to pursue atypical interests. Girls should have the opportunity to follow an interest in computers or mathematics and boys might choose to stay home to sew and cook. The notion of equal treatment becomes questionable when the male or female qualities that naturally manifest in children are no longer taken into account. It becomes questionable when boys and girls are allowed no room to experience themselves as typically male and female. It becomes questionable when, because of the dogma of equality, boys are no longer allowed to celebrate male interests and characteristics. I consider it important to also promote the female or male qualities of the respective children. If what is typically male or typically female is overlooked or, worse, pathologized as the result of false influences, then we have gone too far. Childhood and education have then become the arena for an ideological struggle.

To return to men the freedom to become men, we have to consider the themes and the challenges that are important in the formation of male identity. I would, therefore, refer to the areas of experience in which the differences in men and women show up. Boys have a different childhood than girls: they behave differently and come into the world in a different manner. These characteristics of boys provide grounding for what is essential in men and cannot simply be explained away as the result of incorrect education, gender expectations, or societal stereotypes.

If we remain fixated on the ideal of equality and ignore or devalue the differences between males and females, we run the danger of having the educational reality catch up with us. The postulates of education will become empty phrases and parents, teachers, and educators will have no one but themselves to blame. My attempt to describe the direction of male development and to differentiate it from female qualities does not mean that I am advocating new standards, with which boys will have to conform. Naturally, there are also boys who develop a feminine ethic or girls who come into the world in a masculine way. For this reason, sexual stereotypes may not be forced upon children as norms or become the basis for education. If I advocate consideration of male needs during childhood, it also does not mean that I am promoting a return to one-sided development or that I believe male development to be better. I only want to point out the differences in being that persist beyond the culturally determined patterns and that form the basis for men's self-understanding.

Before entering the world of boys, however, I would like to respond to several counter-arguments. Naturally, the fact that the efforts of "emancipated" parents have not been fruitful, proves nothing. The gender role clichés could be so deeply anchored in us, that we *unconsciously* comply with them. Of our own accord, there is nothing at all that we can do to free ourselves of these pre-feminist era stereotypes. Thus, parents deceive themselves if they believe they are treating their children the same. They give son and daughter thousands of small, unintentional signals that let them know how they are to behave. Equal treatment remains an empty phrase, runs the objection, if a father instinctively plays rough and tumble games with the son and reacts with embarrassment when the son cries, or if a mother talks with a daughter more about feelings and emotions.

While contemporary parents may believe they are living up to the ideal of gender neutrality, in reality they are at the mercy of the gender roles anchored in their unconscious. They carry the images of male and female behavior inside them. Mothers experience their sons as polar opposites and daughters as a natural continuation of themselves. Gender roles are part of us. According to this line of reasoning, it will take generations before we can free ourselves from these stereotypes. Thousands of years of the patriarchy have consolidated themselves in us and we cannot simply shake off their influence. Carrying, as we do, the history of the

human race as a part of ourselves, we cannot separate ourselves
from the experiences of our ancestors.

Accordingly, we must work intensively on ourselves, change
our inner reality, so that equality in rearing our children becomes
a reality. Boys must "feel the harshness of reality" to finally learn
not to dominate girls. With an iron will we must strive for this goal
until all influences that give rise to gender-specific behavior are
eliminated.

If we insist on this approach, there exists a grave danger that we
will sacrifice children to the myth of equality. Education should formulate its fundamental principles through on-going interaction
with reality and force neither parents nor children into a utopian
ideal. In addition, the question arises whether identical developmental processes in boys and girls are really that necessary as a
means of realizing equal rights for men and women? Can we not
have equal rights that allow for differences of gender? Emancipation
of the sexes has to be possible without standing the nature of men
on its head or without desperately trying to talk boys out of their
more violent, more expansive, and more group-oriented behavior.

Men are not determined by their culture, rather culture
develops as part of the dialogue with men's gender-specific behavior. If men are identified with specific areas of life, it is not the
result of men's having established a monopoly of control and
power, but the expression of the characteristics of men's souls.
Male behavior is not solely the result of acculturation: culture also
reflects men's being.

We cannot give a definitive answer to the question of why a
boy's behavior, perception, and thinking differs from that of a
girl. We have to consider many male behavioral patterns in conjunction with hormonal/biological differences. The greater
secretion of testosterone might be responsible for greater aggression among men, and neurological research has shown that the
brain functions differently in boys than in girls. In men the faculty
of speech is concentrated in a particular area of the left hemi-
sphere, while in women it is spread throughout the brain.
Additionally, the areas of speech and feeling in women are joined
by additional nerve pathways and the corpus collosum, the connection between the brain's hemispheres, is thicker. Perhaps, this
is one reason women more readily express feelings.

It is probable, however, that genetic predisposition manifests
differently depending on the type of behavior and the individual.

While temperament may be genetically determined in one individual, it is strongly influenced by the environment in another. Depending on the personality trait and the individual, the factor of predisposition is more or less determining. We should not, therefore, elevate the question of predisposition versus environment into a doctrinal issue. Whether our predisposition determines our character or whether we are shaped by our environment cannot be finally answered, as the twin studies of Thomas Bouchard at the University of Minnesota have shown. The question I address in this book, though, is not why these differences manifest the way they do, *but how we react to those differences.*

*[handwritten marginalia]: G is not trying to explain why boys & girls are different. That is a fact. Now we must determine what this means for us. What's next?*

## MALE EXPANSIVE BEHAVIOR

> When I used to visit the playground with my daughter, I could sit on a bench and read a book. Brief glances were enough to reassure me that I could still see her. With my son, reading is impossible. Again and again he disappears, leaves the swing set, climbs, clambers over the fences, or decides to explore the street running past the playground!

We notice a clear drive to expansiveness even with very small boys. Spontaneously, they expand the radius of play or activity prescribed by mother, father, or teacher. Familiar environments seem not to suffice for them: they have to be on conquests or forays, bursting the limits of their world. The house seems too small for them, the school yard too narrow, the playground too boring.

Not only do boys try to expand their *Lebensraum,* they also seek out challenges. They want to experience their physical limits. Often they are driven by a desire for movement, making it difficult for them to sit still. They do not use the bookcase for books the way sister does: they transform it into a ladder or mountain to be climbed. They jump in front of cars, fall down stairs, or cut their fingers. Groups of boys are noticeably more difficult to discipline. They are noisier and less cooperative with teachers. They are dominated by centripetal forces. They leap away from and charge toward. Vastness invites them. During a quiet class picnic in the woods, they throw hot dogs in the coals, trample the fire, and turn companionable togetherness into an opportunity for duels with stick swords or rolled up towels. Especially in groups, boys are more unruly than girls. What explains this expansiveness and this unruliness?

## SYMBOLS OF CIVILIZATION

My family and I are visiting friends in the south of France. The mood is relaxed and we chat about old times. My oldest son lies next to me on the floor and draws. Finally, he shows me his picture that I immediately and discretely conceal from our French hosts. The picture shows the Swiss National soccer team winning a match against the French by a score of 383 to 0. Swiss flags wave everywhere, the white cross on its red background can be clearly recognized on the jerseys of the Swiss players, while the French lie on the playing field, small and ugly. Why did my son not just tell me that he did not like being here?

We can better understand the motif of an outward drivenness if we think of it in conjunction with a further characteristic of boys. I mean here their fascination for *symbols of civilization.* According to Jung, a symbol represents "in visible form a thought, that is not consciously thought, but is only present potentially, that is in non-visible form, in the unconscious." A symbol does not embrace and not explain, but "points beyond itself to a still other-worldly, ungraspable, darkly sensed meaning that no single word in our language can sufficiently express." Private symbols, images that we encounter in our dreams or in everyday life, point to the presence of a personal complex or issue.

A thirty-year-old woman dreamed repeatedly about a cherry tree, a memory from her parent's home that was surrounded by cherry trees. Cherry trees were a private symbol for her, representing childhood feelings and harmony, her desire for a family, but also a regression, a return to the past. Collective symbols carry a general message and point to issues, themes, or complexes of our culture.

We know collective symbols from religion. The cross, for instance, expresses Christianity's theme of death and rebirth or the rainbow symbolizes forgiveness and promise. When I speak of symbols of our civilization, I also mean prevailing images or figures that characterize contemporary life, present-day images that express the contents, issues, and values of our civilization. An atomic reactor's cooling tower is a modern, collective symbol that conceals a variety of explosive meanings. It points to our belief in the practicality of energy, the dangers of technology, the possibilities of the human spirit, and to humanity's fantasies of omnipotence. A gun is another collective symbol of our civilization and represents aggression, assertiveness, fear, and security. The automobile symbolizes our need for mobility; flags express our need to be anchored in a region or nation.

Such symbols fascinate boys. They fantasize about cars, the army, the police, canal systems, the fire department, caves, bunkers, skyscrapers, He Man, the Teenage Mutant Ninja Turtles, or computers. It often seems that something had preprogrammed them for these products of our society. Little boys turn their heads when a plane roars overhead or listen intently at the sound of a siren.

The spectrum of toys to which boys respond is considerable and very different from girls. According to a survey one educator carried out, boys play primarily with cars, Lego blocks, Indian figures, marbles, trains, and construction or chemistry sets. Outdoors, they build castles, dams, caves, or, in sandboxes, sharp curves for their cars.

"I built, I don't know how many, miles of streets . . . in my sandbox and when it looked like rain, I nagged at my father until he covered my sandbox with a plastic sheet so that the rain would not destroy the artistry of my construction," reports a man I know.

The symbols of our civilization have an impersonal quality. The policeman as an individual is not of interest, but the police as such; not the single fireman, but the fire department catches our symbolic fantasy. These prevailing figures do not need to be present in our everyday life. Our eagle-eyed imagination will pick them out of the immediate or the wider environment, out of the media, books, or stories. A boy vacationing in the mountains, who fantasizes about deep-sea diving or hunting sharks, is as typical as the urban boy imagining himself an Oklahoma cowboy or an explorer in the Congo. Often the symbols are purely technical in nature: helicopters, tanks, rockets, or battleships surface in fantasy and inspire further fantasy.

The spontaneous drawings of many boys mirror, too, their fascination with symbols of our civilization. The first, hesitant lines are not dedicated to father, mother, friends, or other individuals, but to bridges, railroads, automobiles, bombers, soldiers, or at best groups of individuals. Boys chose significantly fewer scenes from the area of family or personal experience as subjects. In their drawings, boys express their attachment to another world, to the life outside.

What soul messages conceal themselves behind the wish for greater *Lebensraum*, the search for challenges, and the fascination with symbols of our civilization? I would like to trace the significance of these characteristics and take the mythological or psychological orientation I described in the previous chapter as the starting point for my reflections.

## THE LONGING FOR MYTHS

The symbols of civilization contain *mythical substance.* Boys have a premonition that through the objects representing these symbols, they can participate in a sacred realm, a *temenos.* Through these objects they can penetrate to the existential challenges that their civilization has to master. Boys want to feel those challenges, want to experience them in their own being. Their enthusiasm for technical objects, for supra-regional images or institutions belongs to the myth they sense behind the symbol. Their interest does not belong to the fire engine, sports car, or train engine, individually, but to the myth expressing itself by way of the corresponding symbol.

Unconsciously, they chose the symbols whose myth attracts them. The symbols of civilization are for them indicators of the myths they sense in our society and in which they would like to take part. When boys expand their territory or turn their heads at the sound of a fire engine, they are responding to parts of the world outside that carry a message for them. They intuit that there are mythic *temenoi* that correspond to the orientation of their souls.

## SEPARATION FROM THE MOTHER

Boys are born of woman. As a rule, their relationship to mother is the most important one during the first months and years of their lives. Mother protects, nourishes, cares for, loves, and encourages her child. Mother is the first human being with whom a child bonds. A child's survival is fully dependent upon the behavior of the adult in this first relationship.

Seen from the perspective of soul, children are born into a psychological realm: relationship, contact, empathy, and security are of primary importance for the development of a healthy child. Those caring for a child strive to fulfill its personal needs and provide an atmosphere of harmony. The child experiences the ways in which its well-being depends upon another human being, namely mother or father. Through relationship, the child enters the world, seeking out the gaze or the smile of mother or father to orient itself. For boys, the emphasis on relationship means that they find themselves initially in an area of soul that does not correspond to their primary mode of orientation. They experience themselves as psychological beings: myths remain in the distant future. For girls, this realm of soul will become more familiar. They will grow into it, while boys will strive to leave it.

In the course of their development, boys will attempt to break out of this personal/familiar realm. They will search out a confrontation with myth instead. As they develop a fascination for automobiles, draw trains and engines, group together in gangs with other boys, and explore the neighbor's yard, they express their longing for the myth-filled world outside. Their drive for expansion is their attempt to participate in myth. Boys sense the forces outside that speak to them and, therefore, go in search of them. They experience civilization as an immense space ruled by powerful myths that encloses the more limited space of their private lives. They begin to distance themselves from the only-personal and the psychological and to search for a myth that will bind them to life. In this myth they are masculine beings: there is a place for that part of their personality they could not live in the mother's realm. The psychologist, Heinz Kohut, talks about a "bipolar self." One pole of this self is the "mother as a self-object," the other pole the "masculine ideals." A boy experiences the latter as the demands of society and the outer world, calling him to himself.

Naturally, this does not mean that boys change completely in the course of their childhood and end up as adults with no need for psychology. They continue to carry the psychological orientation and their memory of the past with them as a shadow function. Most men, however, draw their primary orientation from myths. This is a further reason why therapeutic sessions, as I describe them in the first chapter, are threatening for men. Men experience therapy as regression, as a reversion to the time when psychology dominated their lives and the myths of the outside world were still unknown.

Curiosity about the outer world is not only a characteristic of boys. Girls are fascinated by what they sense in the world outside as well and also long to step out of the private/personal realm. Their curiosity has another quality, though. In contrast to boys, psychological connections attract girls' interest: community life, relationships, and individual human beings and their fate. How do the neighbors live? What is my girl friend's father like? Although they strive to leave the private/personal realm, girls look for alternative psychological patterns. Boys, on the other hand, want to discover the impersonal realm of myth.

Men must fight for masculinity. By struggling and coming to terms with myths, boys discover their masculine personality. They have to hear the stories of the outer world and allow themselves to enter the field of mythic tension to become men. For this reason, most cultures demand perseverance, daring, self-discipline, courage, and broad-mindedness from boys. Their gender identity does not result from natural development, but from the conditions set by their culture. Boys must actively engage the goals and requirements that their respective society expects men to fulfill. Masculine being is not inherited, it is acquired.

In many cultures, boys become men through special rituals, initiation rites that often include harsh trials. During the initiation rites of the Australian tribes, the first phase begins with a usually brutal separation from the mother. The novices' relationship to their mothers are abruptly severed, and they are separated from the world of women. The initiates now belong to the group of men. The second phase introduces the initiates to the laws of the tribe, and the tribe's myths are recited to them. During the initiation ceremonies of the Gunwinggu in Arnheim Land, Northern Australia, boys have to lie for hours in the sun after having had their bodies covered with insects. They have to suffer, experience torture, and carry out repulsive, loathsome tasks. In this way the tribe's leaders introduce the boys to the necessities of life.

We do not have these kind of rituals. We may well suspect, though, that qualitatively similar processes are taking place behind various patterns of behavior that manifest themselves in preadolescence and puberty. Separation, torture, and a coming to terms with the powers of the public sphere may well hide behind delinquent behavior. I remember how, as an eleven-year-old, I sneaked through department stores with a friend. We were on a raid, stealing little model airplanes and toy pistols. The store detective finally caught us. In an impersonal office with glaring neon lights, a furious man lectured us and made both of us squirm. We were degenerates, our future looked very black, and juvenile hall would certainly be our next stop. Although we suffered anguish, we still felt important and part of the happenings of the great, wide world.

The initiation of the aborigines and other tribal peoples ritualize boys' desire to come into the world as mythical beings. The
necessary separation from the private realm of mother takes place
in the context of initiatory acts. In our culture, boys have to find
other ways of expanding the scope of their lives, finding challenges to meet, and discovering the symbols of our civilization. It
is more difficult in our culture, since we no longer use specific initiation rites, for boys to become men.

## THE FASCINATION WITH VIOLENCE

When a group of boys is together, they are anything but still.
Without a watchful eye on them, they shove, box, wrestle, tussle,
or flail around on the floor. Fighting seems to be the elixir of life
for boys. Even with preschool boys, horrified parents are likely to
observe how their little son points his thumb and finger at
the neighbor's boy and "blows him away." On walks through the
woods, boys have no appreciation for the beauty of nature.
Instead, they hunt for wooden clubs and arm themselves with
tree branches as part of the reenactment of Stalingrad, the
Second World War, the Battle of the Ninja Turtles, or some other
fictitious struggle. Of course, girls, too, take part in such struggles, but their fascination for these encounters is significantly
less. They withdraw for the sake of social harmony or because
drawn out physical struggles bore them. Boys cannot get enough
of physical encounters. They seem drawn to fights as if by magic,
even though their parents and teachers continually remind them
that violence is not a responsible form of relationship or conflict
resolution.

The fascination with violence wears different faces. While
with some boys it is restricted to a Tarzan cry while jumping onto
a classmate, with others it degenerates into destructive rage. They
shatter windows, blow up mailboxes with cherry bombs, or throw
schoolbooks in the toilet. Little boys express the tendency to violence through their fantasy life.

A five-year-old boy, in full warpaint, provided me with this
information. "Robbers have hidden themselves behind the house.
There are a lot of them, three or eight. We saw them, and we are
going to fight them. They have already attacked one house and
destroyed it."

Boys' heads are filled with shootings, beatings, hangings, stabbings, or bombings. Whether imagined or real, violence is omnipresent. An eight-year-old boy, asked by his teacher about his wish for the New Year, answered brightly, "I want more fighting in school." Unimpressed by his suggestion, the teacher asked him if he could not think of something better, like peace on earth. The boy became a little embarrassed, thought a while, and then announced happily, "I would wish for more peaceful fights!"

Boys' inclination toward physical violence, destruction, and fighting is a real problem in schools. Teachers often despair at the amount of commotion this need stirs up. In the locker room before physical education classes, boys turn bath towels into bull whips or a classmate's gym shoes into projectiles. On the playground during recess, boys wrestle around, throwing those in disfavor into the bushes, an available fountain, or into a sweat box. In primary school, boys seem to live under the constant compulsion to stage a fight.

What is astonishing is that the same boys appear to be quite peaceable when I talk to them individually. They swear to avoid fights and to try and resolve conflicts by other means. No sooner are they in a group, however, but the resolutions dissolve into thin air. They beat up on disliked comrades, even when earlier, in a one-on-one conversation, they presented themselves as avowed messengers of peace. They have been gripped by another reality. The group presence changes them. The need for physical conflict constellates itself when boys are with other boys. For no particular reason, they will push, tussle, and hit.

## THE DESIRE FOR A GANG

I find it instructive to think about boys' tendency to violence in the context of the gang phenomenon. In elementary school, boys discover that they can belong to a community of others their same age. In the group, they sense the quality of social reality. This reality fascinates boys and gives them strength and a new feeling for life. They no longer experience themselves as individual beings, but as part of something greater. The feeling of "we" grips them. Clear hierarchies and unspoken membership criteria often prevail in these gangs. Whoever wants to be a member of the gang has to own a particular baseball cap, a skateboard, or specific athletic shoes.

Boys feel connected to the other gang members. Due to their sense of belonging, they forget that they are weak, insignificant members of society at large. The gang compensates for any feelings of powerlessness its members otherwise experience in their everyday lives and gives them a sense of strength. The boys no longer see themselves as individual beings, but thanks to the gang, feel they are participating in something greater than themselves. I remember three nine-year-olds, who provocatively announced that this afternoon they would make the city unsafe and I had better be careful. In their fantasies, they conferred greatness on themselves and, in this way, felt like they were a part of the greater society. By forming a gang, they had placed themselves in another social reality and acquired more powerful positions.

Often the primary focus is not the personal relationships with other members of the gang, but the common projects and ideas: the exploration of a cave, the construction of a tree-house, or the founding of a rock group. Boys primarily seek identification with a group theme, and personal, individual issues remain secondary.

With a gang, boys create a subworld in which other laws obtain. They no longer think and act as individuals, but orient themselves according to the dynamic of the gang. Their thinking no longer rests on individual reflection, but instead reflects the gang's reality. From the perspective of psychology, this relegating of the individual to a secondary position is a dangerous development.

Gang experience confronts boys with an extensive palette of masculine behavioral patterns: claims to power, intrigues, petty jealousies, friendships, arrangements, oaths of fidelity, and punishments. The attitude that reigns in a gang fosters micro-societies in which boys can discover and vary fundamental male behavior: the gang avenges betrayal of its hideout and demands allegiance for common undertakings. Membership in a gang allows the staging and rehearsing of both positive and negative behavioral patterns.

Gangs do not have to exist in everyday reality. Often the fantasy of a gang is enough for a boy to participate in a gang and its activities. An inner image motivates him as he races through the house as the Ninja Turtle Raphael or the Lone Ranger. He imagines himself a member of a gang, participating through the fantasy in the group reality, even when he remains the only member of the gang. In school he is a Home Boy, provoking the teacher by wearing his baseball cap in class. Without that cap, he reverts to being just Peter or John. These inner gang images are important for boys. In their minds, they see themselves as knights, activists for Greenpeace, or Sioux Indians. Whether reality or fiction, the group is a reference point for a boy's soul, one by which he orients himself.


## CONCEALED INITIATION

One side of the nascent man finds expression in a gang. For the first time, boys no longer experience themselves as individuals or as family members, but as part of a *supraordinate reality*. Through belonging to a gang, boys detach themselves from their psychological bonds and discover the meaning of a social body. They come closer to culture. Through the group experience, they identify with or struggle against the powers motivating our civilization. Boys sense that these powers define the reality of social groups and feel called to come to terms with that reality.

Peter, Daniel, and Hansjorg meet each other by accident. Peter, a French paratrooper, parachuted into the Malaysian jungle, while Daniel, an American infantryman, and Hansjorg, a Dutch sailor, are trying to survive in the same wilderness. Bathed in sweat, all three fight their way through the tropical vegetation, no relief in sight. The jungle is filled with danger. Japanese soldiers are everywhere. They agree that anyone they meet must be considered an enemy. Even to cross a road is too dangerous and so they stay in the canals. The three are eleven-year-old boys staging a heroic myth, in which they know the enemy and must overcome untold dangers.

Gangs initiate boys into the world of myth. Thanks to their emerging mythical side, they master the challenges with which the gang presents them. When they struggle for answers and solutions, when they attempt to bring order into social chaos, then they begin discovering the power of myth. Myths give voice to the themes that dominate gangs: friendship, enmity, intrigues, jealousy, and power. Gangs deal with these themes depending on the prevailing mythical images of a given society.

By experiencing the fascination emanating from the collective myths of our civilization, boys discover a fundamental need of their masculine souls. Their masculine side strives to bring boys into the *world*. While psychology predominates in individual relationships and the family, in groups boys encounter another reality of the soul. What seems like senseless activity or nerve-racking squabbling to an outsider, is really the desperate attempt to try to understand a *mythical context.* A part of their souls wants to penetrate the world of myth. Gangs or other groups bring boys' mythical orientation to light. The *abaissement du niveau mental,* the lowering of the level of consciousness, that takes place in groups reveals, upon closer inspection, the emergence of those forces carrying the fundamental values of our civilization. The lowering of consciousness means that differentiated consciousness departs, making room for the collective orientation of boys' souls. The basic perspectives of our society push their way through. What does one do in cases of betrayal, enmity, attack, or deceit? In gangs, boys experience as reality that a society does not live from the individual, from psychology, alone, but from the common generativity of myth.

## VIOLENCE: A FUNDAMENTAL FASCINATION FOR BOYS

We reach a different understanding of gang violence if we think of it within the domain of myth. Boys' tendency to aggressiveness, which decreases with increasing socialization, is related to the dynamic of collective systems. Boys feel existentially challenged by collective systems. They must be aggressive as a group for the mythical to prevail or, on the other hand, must resist should the group not accept a myth.

If a perspective constellates itself in the group, the individual members can either accept it or fight against it. This perspective, this myth, while it threatens to swallow up the individual, provides orientation for the group. When gangs fight, the real question is not who will win, but which concept of justice will prevail, whether a certain hierarchy will establish itself in a group or between groups, and how prestige will be distributed. The boys struggle with these collective questions, fight for them or against them. On one hand, they want to prevent the spread of the chaos that would occur without a myth. On the other, they need to come to terms with society's axiomatic explanations and position themselves in a mythical light. Their efforts, their "aggression," serve the myth that they sense within and beyond the various themes. Good should be preserved, evil rejected. To put it differently, values based on the corresponding myth should prevail.

I have observed this process in cases of prejudice. Ethnic mixing of any social group represents a challenge that is not easy to meet. Anxieties increase; expectations and fears arise. How one deals with outsiders depends on what and how the group thinks. If a group of adolescents orient themselves according to a positive model, it can provide valuable assistance in such situations. Unfortunately, even the most positive model can easily capsize and an outspokenly negative hostility toward outsiders can take its place. Strangers, foreigners, then become threatening and the source of all evil. Another myth takes over, in other words. When this happens, it is difficult for individual adolescents to stand in the face of collective force. If the group myth defines what one may think, it requires tremendous mental strength to hold another perspective.

The fundamental values by which we as human beings orient ourselves rest on myth. As I mention in chapter 2, fundamental values are axiomatic explanations that provide us security and collective orientation. A myth makes collective action possible. When we identify with a myth, we can take action in the world *without consideration* for circumstances and other interests. At the same time, because of the lowering of the conscious level involved in myths, it is difficult to talk about them. We use myths to create order and to channel our energy. The only way we can come into the world, can be active in the world, is on the basis of myth.

If, for instance, we identify with the myth of equality, we will combat any tendencies that promote or secure inequality. We will oppose the aristocracy, take a position against class privileges and the disparate treatment of the sexes, and demand equal educational opportunities for everyone. We will attempt to shape the world according to our myth of equality and will be convinced of our message. We will not look for compromise, but for the realization of the myth in which we participate.

The tendency to violence in boys and male adolescents is an expression of their need for change. They use violence since, in their subjective perception, it is a question of demands that must be met *unconditionally*. Only in this way can one assert oneself in the world of myths and give one's own existence meaning. Thus violence can be an expression of the ego strength boys mobilize in coming to terms with myths or it can be the sign of participation in a myth. Based on their soul orientation, boys and adolescents have to fight for a place in the world. As males they cannot support themselves internally through relationships and the personal world alone.

The tendency to violence is conspicuous in the youth movements that take place every decade. We might remember the Beat Generation of the fifties, the student uprisings of the sixties, the Home Boy scene of urban teenagers, and the racial outrages of the Neo-Nazi's. Adolescent males want to make history, to enter the world on the basis of myth. Failing the conflicts of open warfare that generally satisfy these needs, young men must create a myth worthy of fighting for.

Our recognition of the natural tendency to violence, however, should not go so far that we accept violence as a means of confrontation. It also does not mean that we must fold our hands in our laps and henceforth allow the brawling, scuffling, escapades, and destruction of school boys and teen-agers. Yet, we must examine the soul's reasons for violence in males before we begin discussing educational, therapeutic, or social measures. Boys can learn to renounce their direct, physical and destructive violence. They will do so if we as a society allow room for mental violence, a capability of immense importance for the later adult males.

## SECRET SCHOOL REVOLTS

To my question, "How are you," a ten-year-old boy replies, "Life would be a dream if I didn't have to go to school."

The task of introducing children into our society falls to some extent to our schools. They equip children with those social and cognitive abilities necessary for survival in our society. In most societies, school attendance is obligatory until about the age of sixteen. Schools do not only teach, mold, and educate, they also initiate. In schools, too, boys come to know what it means to be a man. If we want to understand how a boy becomes a man, we must consider the process children go through in their education.

Our schools have changed over the last several decades. Schools have largely disappeared in which students were expected to cram their heads with meaningless information, in which the threat of punishment, sometimes physical, discipline, and order played a large role. Thanks to more recent currents in education, schools generally place the accent upon *student-cen-*

*tered and experiential teaching.* The child is the central focus and the starting point of all educational efforts. In this "child-based education," individually centered classes, projects, and workshops have become the watchwords directed at improving the atmosphere of the schools. The students determine the tempo and the manner in which they learn the various subjects.

The basic principle of this approach is to reach students where they are. Gone are the times when students were expected to repeat the individual vowels of a text without knowing the meaning of the passage as a whole. Through everyday examples, instruction becomes experientially real. Textbooks, therefore, build on experiences that are familiar to the children: scenes on the playground, from the school bus, with siblings, with their families, or with friends. What students hear in class is supposed to reflect their everyday lives. Using concrete problems and questions, teachers promote the verbal and arithmetical capabilities of their students.

The relationship between teacher and students has also changed. Teachers are not supposed to appear as distanced educators, but as guides to learning, who enjoy the trust of their students. If students have problems, they should feel free to bring them to their teachers. The latter try to establish and understand where the difficulties lie. Teachers assume that *individual* problems lie behind classroom inhibitions, difficulties in concentrating, and passive or aggressive behavior. Does the child suffer from tensions at home? Is he or she not accepted by classmates? Is the child entering puberty? Based on this individual diagnosis, the teacher talks to the student, advises and supports him or her, or calls in the parents.

Teachers try to respect their students, to think of them as individuals, not as learning machines or inert masses. Teachers strive to foster a democratic, integrative style, to help form a consensus with the students. Teachers place value on a positive and personal learning environment. Thanks to this model of reformed education, many schools have become more human.

The piper has yet to be paid, however. Unfortunately, problems in the schools have increased. Despite the improvements, many boys do not feel that classroom instruction applies to them. Instead of readily and independently taking on the task of learning and applying it to themselves, they react with rejection, rebellion, and brawling. They feel overworked or restless if the teacher assigns them an essay to write or math problems to solve. School administrations frequently try to deal with these difficult students through the help of psychological or psychiatric services. There were twice as many boys registered for the therapy groups I led as there were girls. Almost all of the boys were those whose rebellious or aggressive behavior made their presence in class barely acceptable.

The efforts of educational reform have had little success with this kind of behavior. The majority of boys attend school unwillingly. While, naturally, there are also many girls who loathe school, the widespread rejection of education on the part of boys is almost a cliché. School attendance is a boring duty and anything but sheer pleasure. In spite of skillful instruction, in spite of committed teachers, well-supplied classrooms, and interesting subjects, schools seem to irritate boys more than anything else. It bores them to have to think of the names of objects in their mothers' kitchens or to fill out worksheets with appropriate vocabulary words. Their behavior is in marked contrast to the majority of girls, who are generally more receptive and more interested in learning than boys. In all-girl classes, girls perform better in language areas and invest more of themselves. The disengaged behavior of many boys results in teachers courting their attention. Classes are oriented toward boys, since teachers know that disturbances are most likely to come from them. While teaching efforts focus on the difficult boys, girls are left to their own devices. The message seems to be that girls have to fend for themselves.

What is wrong with boys? Why are they so much less adapted in school than girls? I believe that boys' restlessness points to a specifically male characteristic. I would, therefore, like to examine schools from the masculine, mythological perspective. I would question whether the initiation experience provided by schools truly corresponds to the orientation of boys' souls. Their disinterest and educational weariness might be the expression of an orientation that schools fail to incorporate.

## SCHOOLS—A DOMAIN OF PSYCHOLOGY?

If we examine the root metaphors of schools, we notice that they arise from a very specific *temenos*: the value of the individual. Schools place the greatest emphasis upon individual learning, arriving at consensus, inclusion of the everyday, consideration of personal experience, acts of mediation, and seeking answers or formulating solutions. If we observe schools from a mythological point of view, it becomes readily apparent that classroom instruction builds upon *psychological ideas.*

Psychology, with its emphasis upon relationship, has a firm hold on our schools. Since boys' interest belongs to mythology, too, and they are less interested in the personal, familiar world, schools place boys in a dilemma. The other, primary orientation of their souls is not taken into consideration! School addresses boys in their inferior, shadow function and, therefore, they have to mobilize their feminine side to survive in the classroom. When the reading exercises deal with Johnnie and Janie playing in the yard or mother doing her shopping or the family's Sunday outing, most boys will listen, but their souls are somewhere else.

The stories and examples leave them cold, since they do not address the realm of life that awakens boys' passion. They find it tiresome to only hear about themselves and the world of their everyday lives. On the one hand, what they miss are the great narratives of the world outside, stories out of the past, from other cultures and civilizations. On the other hand, they miss the tension, fear, distance, and hopeless situations. The man in them does not want to hear about answers and solutions, but about life crises and bizarre occurrences. Boys want to experience the existential challenges of humanity. Only when they sense these challenges will their interest be awakened.

Teachers observe this phenomenon when a boy suddenly becomes enthusiastic for a given topic and expends tremendous energy on a particularly challenging assignment. A boy can display unsuspected activity when he is assigned a report on hydroelectric dams or song birds. After napping for hours or outdoing his classmates in insolence, he now does research, collects photographs, reads all the books on his topic, paints pictures, studies encyclopedias on animal life, or gets up at five o'clock in the morning to record the songs of birds. Gone are the characteristic boredom and passivity in a flood of activity. He continues, however, to show only lukewarm interest for the remainder of his classwork.

## GOLD MINING ON THE AMAZON

We have to confront boys with the fundamental questions of human existence if we expect to awaken their passion. What does death mean? Why is there war? How did life begin? They want to take part in the world of myths. They want school to lead them to life's exis tential challenges the way their gangs did. They need to hear stories about individuals who struggled with such challenges. They need to hear about Fernando Cortes, who searched for gold in the South American jungles, or about Claus Stauffenberg, who was killed try ing to stop Hitler and the excesses of the Nazi's.

It is important that boys *feel* the existential challenge and not just be given *answers*. The question is what matters, not the presentation of a solution. Answers and solutions stem from the *temenos* of psychology. Boys do not want to hear examples from personal psychology, but stories and narratives from the mythical canon of their culture. Personal situations or the life of the shopkeeper around the corner are of secondary interest to them. The psychological world only serves to *supplement* their mythological orientation.

The myths these nascent men want to hear, must fulfill certain criteria. They cannot be "safe for children," purged of all anxiety-arousing passages, nor concluded with a lofty moral. It is important that they convey the *quality of the terrifying and sinister*. They must also fully communicate the fear of failure in the face of the respective challenge. Boys must be convinced that the stories reflect an attempt to master an existential challenge and could just as well end in terrible disaster. The myth must help to overcome one of the terrifying dimensions of life. In the history of medicine, they would hear about human suffering caused by chronic pain, about the fear of infection, and the grief at the premature loss of loved ones. In the history of architecture, they would hear about the drudgery of life in the open, the stench of the tiny huts in the Middle Ages, or the isolation of inhabitants in the impersonal city suburbs. The children should hear how the terror of wars has led to other attempts to resolve conflicts and our efforts to contain violence.

History is a valuable source of themes for boys interested in mythology. Not only the history of one's own region or nation carries importance, but also the founding stories of nations. It is the latter that give us the values and attitudes of our culture. Which story tells us about justice, social theory, or freedom? While the myth of the French Revolution represents the concept of justice, students could hear of the mill workers' suffering in Manchester during the last century as an instance of social theory.

They could also hear about the dream of freedom that moved hundreds of thousands of Europeans across the ocean to America. Stories like these would offer boys a possibility of locating their mythological interest.

A Swedish teacher told me about working through World War II with her class. As she described the shortage of men in Russia from which millions of women suffered following the war, the girls listened quietly and attentively. The girls wanted to know what a life without a husband was like and how women dealt with the death of a son. The boys were completely disinterested. A few hours later, the teacher described the Allied landing at Normandy. The problem of keeping plans for the undertaking secret from the Germans, the number of ships and planes, the scheduling of the landing operation, the number of the dead and wounded now interested the boys. The girls, though, found such descriptions rather boring. The theme of the first discussion was psychological, the second mythological.

## YELLING AND SWEARING: THE MALE CONFLICT CULTURE

Contemporary challenges can also introduce the mythic element into the classroom and not just stories from the past. Part of the responsibility of schools is to initiate children into the powerful myths by which our society orients itself. Since we live in a pluralistic society and different social groups live according to their respective myths, this is not an easy task. Nevertheless, it is important to come to terms with these different myths in school. To touch boys' souls and awaken genuine interest, teachers should not present these stories with lifeless facts and dates, but as plausible, convincing narratives.

Thousands of refugees wait at a border crossing, clamoring to be allowed through. They have come from the southern part of their warring country. They want into our country, since their homeland lies in rubble and ashes. Our government does not feel that we have sufficient room for all the refugees. Should we open our borders? Are we obliged to provide them with help? What might that help be?

By means of an actual situation like this, children get a sense of "the boat is full" mythology—one which served as orientation for part of the Swiss population during World War II—and can

set other myths like "the good Samaritan" against it. The boys
sense the existential problematic and feel challenged to respond
mythically. They have to formulate their own "founding" stories.
For younger boys, stories about good and bad knights, evil
and good deeds of human beings, or the doings of monsters and
dragons suffice. Their mythology is still simple and differentiates
clearly between good and evil. Older boys and male adolescents
require more differentiated and contemporary mythologies.
Should teachers succeed in enriching their classes with contemporary myths, they increase the attractiveness of school, especially for boys.

There is a problem in treating these myths, however. The
danger of undue influence by teachers is considerable. They
might be tempted to focus on their personal myths. Parents and
politicians are not indifferent to such topics. Parents will probably
not object to teachers discussing the need for safety on residential
streets, the importance of environmental protection, or the experiences of a close friend in Spain. They are more likely to express
reservations when teachers talk about the necessity of a national
army, the role of the United States in the United Nations, the
questions of euthanasia and abortion, and the place of illegal
aliens. We are much more sensitive about the latter challenges
and issues. All of us are searching for a motivating mythology that
will promote common activity and communication. We, therefore, object if political questions are treated from any particular
perspective in schools.

As adults, we wrestle with different myths, different possible
collective explanations, that might help us on with our own existential challenges. As long as this process is not complete, it seems
foolhardy to carry it into our schools. The emotions and aggression produced by the search for the appropriate myth would be
considerable in classrooms. Schools would then become arenas
for political battles. Because of the demand for political neutrality
in the schools, however, many boys and adolescents find class
work boring and irrelevant. Schools are split off from the outside
world and take no part in the most important of life's mythological conflicts. As a result, schools have become "demythologized"
and take their direction exclusively from the realm of psychology.

It is crucial that schools not withdraw from such political conflicts. Naturally, teachers should not take a particular standpoint
and thereby identify themselves with one myth, alone. At the same

time, teachers have to give children the possibility of taking part in mythological-political confrontations. The teacher's job is to chisel out the core issues and to lead children to the existential challenges that form the basis for mythological discussions. The students should develop the capacity to differentiate the mythic bases for the various political questions. In this way, schools allow space for confrontation, for a culture of confrontation, in which different positions collide resoundingly, in which participants scream and curse at each other—and thereby find themselves!

It is important for both genders to take part in our culture's axiomatic explanatory and foundational stories. We should also remember that the stories do not replace the psychological values governing personal relationships. With boys, though, the chances are greater of such mythological narratives evoking a *resonance in their souls*. The private, personal, and individual emphasis that education has declared the model for schools interests boys less. Because of their soul orientation, they hunt for mythological confrontations with the challenges of being. They want and need to hear the myths about human communities mastering life's great struggles. Schools must satisfy this need if they do not want to lose boys altogether. It is up to all of us to respond to this need if only to prevent boys from staging life's terrifying and existential side on their own.

## THE DOMESTICATED MAN

> My husband's behavior is ideal. He was able to reduce his time at work to two days a week. The rest of the time he spends at home, looks after the housekeeping, and minds the children. He cooks, attends to the chickens he raises, and supports my professional efforts. He is completely there for the children: he shares their hobbies and takes bicycle trips with them.

The new fathers are men who devote themselves to their families with a new understanding of traditional roles. No longer do they act like sultans expecting to be served by their wives or to have nothing to do with housework. These new fathers spend Saturday afternoons with strollers or child carriers at the playground, the zoo, or in the mall. They expend a considerable portion of their time and energy for their family. Not content to leave the routine details of child care to their wives, they take their turn at changing diapers, dressing, bathing, consoling, baby-sitting, and nurturing.

There exists some dispute as to how many fathers really live this ideal. "The new father" is probably more of a model limited to isolated groups, while the greater number of men continue to shine by their extensive absence from housework and child care. It is a demand women make of their husbands, when the former are not willing to dedicate their lives exclusively to home and family. Men, today, garner applause if they can describe how to run a vacuum cleaner, how to change a baby's diapers, and how they participate in the PTA. "Don't be macho," has become the current slogan.

It is self-evident that a husband and wife share in the chores of housekeeping and tending the children. There is also no question but that a father is important in a child's development. A father's involvement means more than just a good-night kiss or an occasional reprimand. Both parents have to bear the work of home and children, not just the wife. The welcome sharing of responsibilities for home and family, though, conceals certain dangers.

No matter how much a father spends time with his children, goes bicycling with them on weekends, or cleans the house, the real question is whether he is able to share with his wife and children those things that *move his soul*? Can he bring his masculine being into the family? When the children's school work, the family's weekend activities, the relationships with the neighbors, or Janie's lost doll dominate the family conversations, there is a good chance that the quality of masculine spirit will be lost. A man may devote himself psychologically to the family and yet neglect the duty of introducing his children to the world of mythology.

In an attempt to free themselves from patriarchal attitudes, fathers often repress their masculine orientation. They focus on the private and the individual and fail to bring collective themes into the family for fear they will thereby succumb to traditional masculine roles. Since the interest in myth does not receive the same importance in women's souls as in men's, "the new father" deprives his family of confrontation with "the great necessities of life." He withholds contact with a vital part of life from his children and limits the significance of the family to a psychological container. If a father places relationship, the individual, and what is private in the foreground, he misleads his children into believing that the family is the center of the world.

It is navel gazing to delude children into thinking that the personal is the only place, the only *temenos*, where the soul can be experienced. On their own, children do not notice the important territories in the world worth fighting for. Fathers should not only mediate the psychological aspect for their children and give them a sense of personal security. Fathers also mediate *the world outside.* A father is the mediator for the collective forces outside the family. He models for his children that a human being is not defined solely by the psychological, by the realm of individual life. He lives out ways the ensouling arenas of collective existence fascinate and direct individuals.

This means concretely that a father attempts to make a place for the interests children have for things and situations outside the family. He provides explanations rich in new vocabulary for the most recent findings in medical research, for the engineering techniques of the Roman Empire, for the administration of the District of Columbia, or for the coming weekend's baseball double-header. Important for him is not only his son's headache or finding a place in his daughter's room for a desk, but a vision of the nation or of the working of the city. The outside world contains autonomous forces and energies. It is not just a reflection of our personal condition. Fathers and mothers who take their children to political rallies or demonstrations, for example, burst the framework of the familiar/psychological. Participating in a demonstration is one way of developing a child's sensitivity for mythological significance.

Men have to share the ensoulment they discover in politics, sports, work, hobbies, or religion with their families. This is not to say that women are not interested in these areas. The core thesis of this book, however, is that the *primary* direction of a man's soul differs from the fundamental direction of a woman's soul. A man's soul selects other symbols with which to represent itself, symbols arising from mythology. Women tend to express themselves with images and symbols from the realm of psychology.

Although the respective systems of reference differ, both promote active engagement in the world. Men base their activity on myths, while women legitimize their behavior on the basis of psychological images. A woman politician advocates safety measures for residential streets, because she knows directly or from friends the difficulties of raising three children on a heavily traveled street. A male politician, on the other hand, may champion the same measures, but for different reasons. He takes issue with the myth of complete mobility and dreams, instead, of communal neighborhoods amid the facelessness of a metropolis.

Children certainly need male figures with whom they can identify as they develop their masculine side or masculine identity. The father's own liberation, however, has to happen first. Many men, today, are present in the family physically and psychologically, but have shut away their souls. They have yet to find a way to live out their souls' primary interests in the family setting. Confusing emancipation with a psychological orientation to life, they lose what is their proper masculine orientation. Their children experience them as dull and boring. Within the family, it is men's task to live out their mythological orientation. Only in this way can they enable their sons to find their way as males in the world.

## DAUGHTERS

To conclude this chapter, I would like to direct a few comments to the relationship between fathers and daughters. I emphasized earlier how a father provides the mythological connection to the world. He plays this role not only for his sons, but especially for his daughters. Just as a mother introduces her son to the world of psychology, a father helps his daughter to participate in the myths of our culture and society. By conveying his fascination for realms beyond the family, a father leads his daughter into the world of mythology, a world that would otherwise remain closed to her.

It is a father's job to introduce his daughter to the myths that he experiences in politics, history, his profession, and his national identity. He does so not in the expectation that the daughter will later orient herself by these mythologies. He hopes, rather, that she will acquire a sensitivity for the world of myth and thus fare better in the outside world. In this way, a seed is planted for girls, that later will bear fruit as their psychological contribution in a mythological arena. These women of the future are able to enter politics, business, or art and make a contribution from their female, psychological perspective. Girls, however, have to be shown the way to these extra-familial areas. Otherwise, the danger exists that they will absolutize the personal and reject the outer world as irrelevant. "The only thing that counts in business anyway is money!" or "All politicians are just con men and liars; I want nothing to do with government!"

# 4

# MEN AND THEIR GRANDIOSITY

♂

# The Suprapersonal as Orientation

As a boy, I imagined myself as a sea captain on a schooner. In my fantasy, I fought against pirates in the Caribbean. That was why I learned to swim. As an adolescent, I fantasized how I filled entire stadiums as a rock singer: thousands of fans came to hear and applaud my group. That was why I learned to play the guitar. As a young man, I imagined that I founded my own school and initiated new directions in education. That was why I majored in education. Such grand, mythically based fantasies preceded me in my life and ensouled me. They gave me the energy I needed to work toward new life goals and to take on the challenges of everyday living, of my education and profession. Such grandiose imaginings are vital for men.

Today, we are more inclined to allow these masculine grandiosities. We are more willing to develop a culture which has room for male fantasies without men laying claim to better positions economically or more power than women for this reason. Men should not be forced into a psychological corset. We must, rather, allow their grandiosities, their search for the mythic, to better enable them to infuse our civilization with their energies.

The term *masculine grandiosity* makes us think of arbitrariness, arrogance, and the overestimation of one's ability. It conjures up images of men who talk only about themselves and seem to consider themselves the most interesting people in the human race. We think of men who demonstrate the greatest passion for their own egos, of men who bore us with their self-centeredness and lack of self-reflection.

Turning to history, we discover dozens of examples of masculine grandiosity, of men who brought tears and suffering to thousands or, worse, drove thousands to their deaths. Napoleon Bonaparte sent countless French soldiers to the gates of Moscow, where they froze to death for his imperialistic fantasies. It was this same Napoleon, who said of himself, "My name shall live as long as the name of God." Hernando Cortes (1485–1547), leading four hundred soldiers, destroyed the tottering Aztec empire once and for all to the glory of the Spanish King Charles. With his dreams of showers of gold, he delivered the death-blow to an ancient Indian culture. Adolf Hitler signaled catastrophe for Europe and the Jewish people with his racist delusions and ruthless ambitions for Germany to become a great power.

Masculine grandiosity puts us in mind of men who impose their will upon the world, who stake their claims to power, and who persevere in the fixity of their own ideas. Such men believe that the world must adapt to *them*, without their needing to take the environment or their fellow human beings into consideration. Masculine grandiosity is onerous.

Masculine grandiosity seems abnormal and, at best, of interest as a form of psychopathology. It approximates cases of delusions of grandeur or megalomania in which the patient overvalues his abilities, his position, his ideas, and his discoveries beyond measure. Such patients believe themselves the possessors of "trillions," while in fact they live in poverty as miserable figures in public institutions. There are the manic patients who believe they can save the world or that they have discovered Valium. Grandiosity seems to be the overvaluation of the capacities and qualities of a fragile ego, threatened from one minute to the next with depression or its own demise. We can well do without masculine grandiosity!

While my intention is not to minimize or relativize such crimes against humanity, I want to consider grandiosity from another perspective. I want to show how masculine grandiosity, with its thirst for empire, conquest, power, and position, also has a positive side. Grandiosity also characterizes an orientation of the soul concealed within the contributions of Henri Dunant, Albert Schweitzer, Heinrich Pestalozzi, Le Corbusier, John Lennon, Martin Luther King, or politicians like Winston Churchill or Willy Brandt.

Grandiosity motivated all these men. They did not see themselves primarily as single human beings shaped by personal history and relationships. Their activity mirrored a sense of being bound to a collective framework. Because they considered themselves expressions of a greater process, they were prepared to devote themselves to the community and its work. This perspective of human existence brought them a conviction of the rightness of their path and the justice of the causes they espoused. Thanks to this grandiosity, they were able to dispel self-doubt and to overcome the greatest resistance. Their grandiosity manifested itself in dedication to a cause, whether in art, technology, or business, or in an identification with the goals, ideals, or tasks of a movement or a group. We would do well to promote such grandiosity today.

At the beginning of his career, Graf Zeppelin (1838–1917) met with considerable resistance to his project of an airship. Leading experts of the time labeled his ideas, "fantastic," "extravagant," or "crazy." In an open letter, a group of intellectuals including Helmholtz, advocated strongly against any support by the German War Department for Zeppelin's proposals. Graf Zeppelin persisted, however, despite the widespread public rejection. The notion of an airship had taken hold of and ensouled him. He saw his efforts not as the product of his personal creativity, but considered himself a "tool . . . called to create something that the whole world had long desired." As the servant of technological progress, he had no choice but to carry on with the project. Graf Zeppelin's grandiosity consisted of living for an idea, the idea of an airship. He had a vision that made it possible to overcome the limitations of the existing technology.

I do not mean to give the impression that masculine grandiosity is a male quality. That would be an inflated misunderstanding. A man becomes grandiose because of the myth using him as its instrument.

Masculine grandiosity often has as its result an unswerving adherence to an idea or concept. Galileo Galilei (1564–1642) is an interesting example of this phenomenon. Galileo rejected the geocentric perspective and instead believed the sun to be the center of the universe. Based on his astronomical observations, he could not accept the notion of the earth as the midpoint of the solar system. During the Inquisition hearings from December 1615 to June 1616, Pope Urban VII indirectly ordered Galileo to recant his heretical ideas. Galileo allowed himself to be intimidated and obeyed. In the aftermath of the hearings, he spoke only of his "hypotheses."

He was unable, though, to give up his ideas or, to put it differently, his ideas were unable to give up *him*. Although it was not in Galileo's nature to fight heroically for new scientific knowledge, he felt compelled to write down his ideas. In his 1632 *Dialogue Concerning Both Great World Systems*, he argued anew for the Copernican theory. The book evoked hearty enthusiasm and boundless indignation. Galileo was again ordered to appear before the Inquisition. The conflict irritated the astronomer and he requested not to have to travel to Rome. He mentioned his rheumatic condition, the difficulties of the journey, and his age. Rome insisted on his appearing. Finally, in 1633, he took an oath to give up his ideas and to spread no more false teachings.

Galileo is one example of masculine grandiosity. By nature, he was neither a hero nor a champion of new understanding. He felt so committed to astronomy, though, that he could not do otherwise than to think and teach what his science had revealed to him. In the field of astronomy, his soul participated in an *encompassing greatness*, while his personality remained anxious and adaptive.

Masculine grandiosity manifests itself through a man's involvement with a specialty field or a particular collective. The individual male does not experience his activity or perspective as grandiose, but as objectively valid. For Galileo, it was obvious that the sun was the center of the universe, just as for Graf Zeppelin it was clear that an airship could be built. The facts dictated the reality. The man in question thinks and works against the backdrop of a more encompassing reference system than the purely personal, and his certainty derives from that system. His commitment to the specialty field or collective serves as the guarantor for his conviction. In a word, grandiosity is a man's ability to devote himself with élan to an impersonal task in which he believes.

When in 1847, Otto von Bismarck delivered his initial address as a member of the Prussian Diet, the other delegates reacted with boos and catcalls. Bismarck remained composed: "I stayed at the podium, leafed through a newspaper lying there, and, when the noise receded, completed my speech." Grandiosity underlies a man's tendency toward an overvaluation of himself, out of which he lets the facts speak. Thanks to his grandiosity, he can mobilize energies, demonstrate firmness, and strive unswervingly toward a goal. As a specific attribute of the male soul, this attitude can have a fructifying and stimulating effect on the environment.

Let us attempt to illuminate this masculine grandiosity. Where do men derive this power of conviction? What does it mean for their souls? For my part, I believe this male creative ability to be the expression of men's mythological orientation toward life.

Before we address these questions, I would like to clear up a possible misunderstanding. Magnificent works and dedication to the community are, naturally, also possible with a feminine orientation toward life. The motivation to devote oneself to a cause, to fight for it, and to make the necessary sacrifices can have its origin in an individual's psychology as well as in his or her mythological orientation. It is irrelevant to a starving Somalian whether the UNO worker distributes food rations out of personal concern or out of outrage at the economic discrepancy between rich and poor nations. The result is the same even though the background motives differ. If an individual's motivation is psychological, she will see her dedication as a response to a personal challenge or a personal concern.

Pushing her prepared statement aside, Rosaria Shifani cried to the startled mourners, "Troppo sangue, non c'è amore, non c'è amore per niente!" ("Too much blood! There is no love here, there is no love for anything!") She had just lost her husband, Vito Shifani, in the Mafia's bloody attempt on the life of Judge Giovanni Falconi (May 23, 1992). She had been incensed by the loss of her husband, who had served the Mafia-hunter judge as a bodyguard. She became determined to fight the Mafia, personally. Through interviews, speeches, articles, and a book, she tried to convince the people of Sicily that it was vital to take the Mafia on head to head. Her struggle resulted from her personal involvement and concern.

Rosaria Shifani's example is typical. In contrast to many men, women's involvement in an issue stems from their *psychological motivation.* It is more the aspect of personal engagement motivating women and less a concept or myth. This personal engagement serves women as the basis for the ability to empathize with an individual's fate or situation.

When I talk about men and woman and emphasize the differences between them, I am referring to the soul's orientation and not to biological categories. Just as men have feminine aspects of their souls, so do women have masculine qualities in theirs. Feminine and masculine are archetypal predispositions in each and all of us that go beyond biological gender. It would be one-sided to reduce a woman to biological gender alone or to grant her only one archetypal gender. Women, too, possess the potential of archetypal masculinity. As a rule, though, an individual's primary soul direction corresponds with biological gender. Most men also feel masculine in their souls and have a pronounced mythical orientation, even though a part of their personality carries a feminine/psychological orientation.

Now let us examine the soul background of masculine grandiosity.

## THE NEED FOR UNIVERSALITY

Samuel Johnson once said, ". . . a man must take care not to generalize things." Masculine grandiosity finds expression in different forms. It shows itself primarily in the need to have an effect in a collective or a common cause that goes beyond personal interest.

Otto Stich, the Swiss Minister of Finance, was asked by a woman journalist why he was prepared to make the immense sacrifices in terms of family, personal life, and even health, that his office required. Was it worth it, the journalist wanted to know, to work sixty hours a week, to have almost no time for oneself, to be continually criticized publicly, only finally to realize how much a Minister of Finance's hands are tied by circumstances? "My efforts are intended for society," the Minister answered somewhat self-consciously, "to help shape our democracy." The answer was too general for the journalist, was not personal enough, and so she continued probing. She found his answer too lacking in reflection, too much a male platitude, and probably suspected other, unconscious motives like ambition or the desire for glory and power.

From the perspective of masculine grandiosity, the answer is typical, however. The motivating factor is not the personal, but the general and universal. A cause or an idea is the central focus for the grandiose man. His activity is justified by having redeeming social value: he does not recognize personal motives. Such men devote themselves to the organization, nation, economy, military, family, or concept, thereby subtracting the personal factor. What energizes them originates neither in their personal biography nor in self-interest, but derives from a larger context. Energy fills them from the outside, from their specialty field or from the system, so that they are able to pull themselves together and devote themselves to something. For them a universal, encompassing cause or theme is the elixir of life.

The Swiss–American Nobel laureate, Edmont Fischer, explained his 1953 decision not to return to Switzerland as due to "the higher level of biochemical research" in the United States. The determining factor was not his personal preference nor an appreciation for the American lifestyle. Biochemistry had decided for him. Fischer justified his decision with arguments that probably would not have weighed so heavily for a woman in a similar situation. For a woman, relatives, friends, the climate, and aspects of daily life would have been more important.

A man's need to give himself over to a universal or collective task also finds expression in inconspicuous activities. An apartment superintendent pays especial attention to the number of keys distributed. Otherwise, there would be no way to oversee who entered the building and the risk of theft or vandalism would increase. A restaurant owner feels that the quality of the food he serves determines the overall mood in his establishment. These two men live out their need for a collective context in their respective professions. They consider the duties and chores connected with their jobs to be *universally* important. In so doing, they are identifying with tasks that present themselves as existential challenges within a *temenos* framework. Whether the tasks are spectacular or will attract the attention of the outer world is not important.

Whether the personal or the universal is of primary importance depends on an individual. A teacher may struggle hour after hour with his class. He tries to understand his pupils, holds individual conferences with them, and brings fresh material to class to awaken their enthusiasm. His efforts may be due to devotion to *his* class or to *youth in general* and the *teaching profession*. He possibly has no great interest for the individual pupils, even forgetting their names. Instead his desire is to acquaint the coming generation with education as a discipline. The notion of doing something for youth in general may inspire him, while attention to individual children remains secondary. His belief in the next generation, his intent to introduce them to the secrets of biology or the beauty of literature motivates him and not the personal relationships he establishes with the pupils themselves.

Often this soul orientation takes on bizarre qualities. A train engineer gets upset at late-arriving passengers, because as unpredictable factors, they disrupt the railroad schedule. A bank teller finds the individual customers tiresome and annoying. Like the teacher I mentioned earlier, these men's interest belongs to the system, not to the individual human beings participating in it. They see themselves as part of a greater organization, one that is well organized and fully synchronized. The universal quality of an issue or concern determines their involvement and not the needs of individuals.


## MEMBERS OF A MOVEMENT

Another way masculine grandiosity expresses itself is in *inner participation in a collective movement.* Like the adolescents who elevate themselves to membership in real or imaginary gangs, adult males place their activity within a greater social context. Thinking back on the first weeks after his escape to Norway, Willy Brandt remembers ". . . it must have been sometime shortly after my arrival in Norway: I hiked along a fjord and memorized the speech that I would deliver on my return to Lübeck." At the time, Germany was securely in the hands of the National Socialists. Brandt was in exile and any hope for his return was minimal. In his imagination, however, he already saw himself addressing Germany's Social Democratic Party. His grandiosity lies in the conviction that he will belong to a future movement, a social trend, representing values and goals and a particular attitude toward life.

Many men imagine themselves as part of a movement, feel themselves part of a collective. Their thoughts and fantasies involve them in society and social trends. Although their personal views are unimportant in themselves, their thoughts, opinions, and positions have to flow into the contemporary political debate. They locate their activities within a social context as an expression of that movement. This way of perceiving themselves changes their self-image, since the movement or group with which they feel affiliated influences their identity. They see themselves as entrepreneurs, students, progressive educators, socialists, liberals, yuppies, environmentalists, house husbands, or white-collar workers.

The tendency to define oneself by means of a group or movement becomes evident during elections. Men listen to the slogans of their political party, while women are more likely to vote on the basis of personal choice, not party lines.

We should not confuse belonging to a movement, though, with adaptation. Although a man participates mentally in a movement, different possibilities are open to him as to how and where he will locate himself within the movement. Should he identify completely with a movement, he will become typical—a typical bank teller, teacher, social worker, or pilot. If he were an American bank employee, he would wear Boston shoes and a school tie. Were he a social worker, he would have a beard and dress in sweater and sandals. He would judge his environment from the perspective of his particular group.

Men can also participate in a group by differentiating themselves from the group and by emphasizing their distance. A man refuses to be a Yuppie, has had enough of the critical attitude of the sixties and of the consumer economy, and turns, therefore, to ecological farming. His convictions stem from an oppositional position. Indirectly he participates in various collective trends that serve him as orientation points for the direction of his own soul. Such men hold to the opposite of what they see as collective movements: they withdraw and consider themselves outsiders, critical thinkers, or reformers. Their thoughts and actions set a counterpoint to the perspectives of the middle-class, alternative lifestyles, or the career builders.

A successful Jewish business man expressed his suspicion of monolithic blocks by saying, "When everybody shares the same opinion, something is wrong." He developed his own standpoint through an ongoing dialogue with this kind of unshakable, collective conviction, always attempting to decide differently than the masses would. Collective society with its trends and movements was very much a reality for him, an important counterposition that continually challenged him. This man's grandiosity shone through his oppositional posture.

"It would truly be the greatest blessing to be imprisoned in the interest and for the well-being of one's own country and religion . . ." was Mahatma Gandhi's (1869–1948) comment thinking back on his prison term in 1908. The Colonial Government in India had sentenced Gandhi, because of his call for passive resistance to British policies. "The true path of greatest happiness consists of going to prison and bearing the suffering and deprivations there for the sake of one's nation and one's faith," Gandhi continued. Clearly, Gandhi's time in prison brought him an inner strength and conviction.

John Lennon (1939–1980) had a similar experience, although in a very different area. Discussing the beginnings of the Beatles career, he commented, "We were always anti-jazz. I think it is shit-music. . . . Rock 'n' roll was real, everything else was phony—and what is real gets through to you, whether you want it to or not. You recognize something in it that is true, as in all true art." His whole life John Lennon reacted strongly to collective trends and, for this reason, often felt like a "chameleon." Although he rebelled against established movements, at the same time he seemed to have a developed sensitivity for the onset of new movements. He had a strong connection to both the coming and the current themes of his time. "Wherever the wind was blowing, it blew the Beatles in that direction. We were not the flags on the ship, but the whole ship was in motion. Maybe we were simply the highest up and calling, 'Land ho' . . . , but actually, we were in the same boat."

Lennon's comments are an example of the struggle between the ego and the Self, to use the terminology of Jungian psychology. The ego has to come to terms with a suprapersonal entity it experiences through collective movements. The Self anticipates which movements most closely correspond with the needs of our souls and gives us indications of which ones to affiliate with and which ones to avoid. The tension between the ego and the Self is necessary to prevent our becoming marionettes or the victims of a movement. Further, this tension has to be ritualized, since the individual alone does not have enough strength to critically come to terms with collective movements.

Because of their grandiosity, men participate in the current themes of their larger environment. They join with the collective soul situation of their time through newspaper articles, reports on television, or conversations with friends and acquaintances. The existing social or political challenges arouse them and awaken their emotions. When men describe their personal history, they often use images from collective movements as a way of marking turning points. They structure their personal past with the help of trends and problems of the era in question. "During my time in high school, I was fully under the influence of the Hippie movement: I dressed like a flower child and took part in every demonstration. Later I had a quieter phase and the literary scene became important for me. At thirty, though, I had the feeling that something had to happen . . ." ". . . At the time the Korean War broke out, I had . . ." Collective themes and movements provide men a way of expressing their souls.

Women are more likely to shape their past according to relationships. "At that time, I was still married to Herbert . . ." or ". . . that was when I shared the apartment with Carmen." The personal comprises the foreground for women. Instead of collective events, new relationships and personal changes mark the important turning points. Women cite core events from the psychological realm. Cheryl Bernard and Edith Schlaffer reached the following conclusion after countless interviews with men and women: "While women experienced the crises in their lives as especially revealing and key phases, men more readily tended to play down crises as exceptions or to simply ignore them."

Naturally, women are also subject to the influences of social currents, but the *temenos* is not the same. Unlike men, women are more likely to express themselves on psychological themes or from a psychological perspective. The universal, the collective trends or movements, remain abstractions for them and do not become a reality of their souls. Women look for psychological areas in which to participate. Since women view the private and personal as the source of the soul's renewal, events from relationships take on directional potential in shaping their lives. Their soul orientation results from personal involvement and the immediacy of connection.

> In my job as a private tutor, I had to realize, that a permissive, anti-authoritarian attitude by itself was not successful. During one lesson, a boy became insolent and obstinate toward me. He refused to take part in the lesson. I offered him the choice of either cooperating or of sweeping the floor. When he replied by sticking his tongue out at me, I threw sand on the floor and ordered him to sweep it up. I felt silly, but it was the only way I could get anywhere with him. I believe there are times when we have to be authoritarian.

This teacher decided for herself not to use anti-authoritarian or punishment-free methods in teaching children. Her *personal experience* ushered in her change of attitude and not a theoretical perspective from an educational journal. For women, relationships appear to be the channel through which new impulses touch and move the soul. Information only takes on importance for them when a personal connection exists.

New thoughts and ideas often reach men not by way of the personal realm, but through movements. A man hears or reads about a new direction in education and, therefore, wants to try out the approach in his teaching. Knowledge he gains from relationships does not often carry the same weight as does objective information or material printed in newspapers or books, announced on television, or shared by colleagues at work. An older, elementary school teacher reports, "I am completely convinced by Frederic Vester's ideas about learning. After reading his books, I wrote to him, received further material, and have totally changed my teaching." What made the difference for him was not a personal experience or an encounter with a friend, but the feeling of taking part in a new, learning theory movement.

This focus on a concept, on the universal, or on the idea of belonging to a movement gives men their sense of grandiosity. The masculine exerts pressure on men to devote themselves to a task that will connect them with something greater. Men, therefore, look for a system in which to participate or a challenge that will give their existence meaning beyond their individual lives. The masculine draws men away from the individual, psychological world they knew as children to a task or a theme corresponding to that part of their souls.

## THE HIDDEN POWER OF MYTHS

Men's grandiosity is an attempt to engage the myths of our civilization. Behind the fascination for concepts, the universal themes, and the social movements hide contemporary myths, powerful, transcendent realities of the soul. Mythic images carry every profession and every collective movement. They comprise the basic tenets or axioms determining the fundamentals for human action and direction of thought. Myth expresses itself in specific conceptions about man and Nature. Just as physics requires formulas to recognize material processes otherwise difficult to grasp, every field of activity needs a myth with which to construct a corresponding reality.

While Galileo Galilei found his myth in astronomy, Willy Brandt in the Social Democratic Party, and John Lennon in his perception of the musical trends of the time, most men follow the trail of their myth in less spectacular ways. Usually, they serve the myth legitimizing their respective profession. In order to invest themselves, however, they require the grandiose expansiveness and the feeling of participation in a supra-individual system. The myth grips them and allows them to see the world in a corresponding light. A physician develops an eye for diseases, diagnoses, and treatment possibilities by participating in the myth of medicine. He believes in healing and in the potential for therapy to influence the state of health. Interestingly, the newest medications are often the most effective: new medication again ensouls both patient and physician with the myth of medicine. The myth steers their perceptions and produces their conviction of being able to master the current problem from the corresponding perspective.

Men's choice of conversation topics reflects their mythological participation: they prefer general topics rather than personal issues. Sports, technology, politics, or current events are common subjects. From a psychological perspective, men play it safe by keeping to harmless topics. From a mythological perspective, the suprapersonal focus reveals the masculine orientation of myth. Myths use these subjects as a speaking tube. General themes confer energy to the men and make possible assent, but also critical distance. Thanks to this characteristic, it is easier for men to deliver speeches or to debate issues, removing themselves personally in both instances. This quality in men irritates women.

The identification with the mythological shows itself in men's patterns of conversation as well. While women generally hesitate to cut off their partner in conversation so as not to affront them, many men do not even notice when they interrupt someone else. They also tend to talk more than women. "It is so quiet in the country, I only hear my own voice," wrote the nineteen-year-old Bertold Brecht. On a given theme, men are often in agreement. Borne up by a myth, they see themselves as the great spokesmen for an issue, without registering the absence of personal factors and of the realm of psychology.

## INITIATION RITUALS IN MYTHS

Ethnology gives us a description of men's mythical orientation. In many societies and tribes, the boys are initiated through especial rituals taken from the myths of the corresponding group. The process is often painful. For the Samburu—a black tribe of cow herders living in the northern part of Kenya—boys between the ages of fourteen and twenty-six have to go through the so-called, *moran* time, to be accepted by the tribe as men. This testing phase begins with circumcision. During the torturous procedure, the boys may not show the least sign of pain. One sigh and they will be despised as cowards the rest of their lives.

Prior to the *moran* ceremony, initiates may still visit their mother's house. Afterwards this is forbidden. They must swear to never eat meat that a woman has looked upon or to drink milk. The initiates live in a secluded encampment in the bush where they are taught the craft of raising cattle and the methods for acquiring them. They learn to live economically so that they are later capable of starting their own household. If an initiate comes from a poor family, he has to steal cows. As a cattle thief, he exposes himself to additional dangers and can be imprisoned, beaten, or even killed. By exposing himself to such dangers, though, he becomes more attractive to the young women of the tribe. Through the *moran* ceremony, a boy acquires self-awareness and the capacity for productivity and fruitfulness. He becomes a man.

The *moran* ceremony releases boys from their "narcissistic passivity" and their orientation to the feminine. The initiates separate themselves from the personal and private and identify with the more universal values of the tribe. They have to prove themselves in the face of the existential challenges that the tribe as a whole must master. From this moment on, they are initiated into the myths of the tribe that henceforth will form the basis for their identity. "For the Samburu . . . the term manhood . . . implies the concept of the tribe, itself, a concept that is bound to dedication to common goals," notes the anthropologist Gilmore.

Such initiation rites express a man's search for mythical participation. A man does not substantiate his position with arguments from his personal and private life, rather he defines himself in the light of the myths supporting his culture. He learns to submit to what Robert Moore calls, "masculine tradition and the myths of the community." He experiences his own activity as part of a *supraordinate process*. Participating in myths conveys the feeling of greatness as I have described it earlier.

Masculine grandiosity drives away personal self-doubt and a focus on one's own personality and provides a feeling of self-certainty. A man sees himself unconsciously as part of a myth, and his grandiosity draws from the mythic power. Participating in a myth gives a man his task and his role in life.

## THE USEFULNESS OF GRANDIOSITY FOR CIVILIZATION

> *"Socrates remained Socrates, an ability possessed by the fewest of men. First they are children, then they become men, and when they have become men they become politicians, generals, poets, heroes or something else, just not themselves."*
> — Friedrich Dürrenmatt

Men's grandiosity is an important force contributing to mastering civilization's existential challenges. Thanks to their grandiosity, men leave the personal behind and devote themselves to a cause or a collective movement that goes beyond their front yard. Grandiosity that results from men's mythological orientation contributes to their ability to adapt to an organization.

Grandiosity also helps them to sort out the fundamental issues in a personal situation. Men trace the workings of a system, a collective movement, or even a myth from individual experiences. If a boy steals a chocolate bar from a convenience market, men recognize the act as an indicator for the decrease in social morality or the negative effect urban life has on children. Less frequently would they explain the theft based on causes from the individual child's psychology. They strive for a more inclusive understanding. It is not the conductor who was rude, but how badly the railroad system treats its passengers. Naturally, this perspective imparts a feeling of greatness to men and expands their personal realm.

Men's longing to participate in the mythological makes recognition by the universal, by society, important. "I want to create something. I want to be immortalized . . . I want to leave something for posterity." Or, "I believe that success and public recognition is one of the most fundamental motivations . . ." Or, the title of a high school boy's essay, "How Can I Leave My Mark in the World?"

## MEN'S GOALS

The result of a mythological soul orientation is that the goals men envision for their lives usually do not derive from their personal lives and biographies. Men's goals are grounded rather in the myths to which they were introduced as children. They devote themselves to environmental protection, the rights of workers, a particular area of research, politics, a corporation, or to the idea of human rights or social welfare—even though they may not directly or personally have anything to do with the theme or cause. This grandiose desire to be involved in social or political issues helps men to overcome their egoism. It is no longer a question of one's personal happiness, but of the common goal. The masculine spirit relates to the world differently from the feminine spirit. The former seeks the grandiose, expansive gesture, strives for an encompassing concept, or fevers after an ideal.

In 1483, Christopher Columbus (1451–1506) introduced himself to the Portuguese King John II as the future "Grand Admiral of the Ocean Sea" before he had even assembled a fleet. He was completely convinced that he would discover great wealth, islands, and a continent abounding with gold and silver. The idea of reaching India from the west had inspired him to such an extent that he henceforth called himself, Christobal Colon, and turned to the Spanish Court when the Portuguese king would not support his project. He offered his services, instead, to Ferdinand of Aragon and Isabella of Castille.

While personal motives naturally played a part for Columbus, he seems to have been ensouled by the myth of discovery, a myth that brought him energy, conviction, and a readiness for action. He was gripped and enchanted by the myth that exploration and discovery constellated in the culture of his time.

## WORK AS LIFE'S ELIXIR

*"A man who has no office that he can visit—it makes no difference who he is— is on an unbelievably thorny path."*
— Bernard Shaw

Today there are no more continents to discover. Masculine grandiosity has to find other means of expression. One avenue is work and its importance for the soul. "Work is of the greatest value for me. It is the one area of life in which I feel most secure . . . . Work is more important to me than my girl friend. If I were no longer successful at work, I would feel like I did not exist." "If I had to decide today between my private life, say, my wife, and my profession, I would choose my profession, since that is the only thing that originally and causally has to do with me."

Men live out their Columbus fantasies in their careers. They see professional goals as undiscovered continents, climbing the career ladder gives them the feeling of exploring new worlds. For this reason, fulfilling the expectations of superiors or their company is of primary importance for many men. Often "profession defines masculinity" and is a life's elixir. Generally, there is also a direct correlation between a man's feeling of self-worth and his professional activity. Failures, stress, or unemployment trigger major subjective crises.

In what ways is the situation different for professional women? The difference between the masculine and the feminine orientation shows up the most at work. Even when both perform the same tasks, hold the same positions, and share the same training, women still work from psychological motivation, while men look for connection to a myth. The team, the colleagues, the atmosphere, and the distribution of the work load is of greatest importance for women. Men tend to negate these personal factors. Their motivation is grandiose and derives from the suprapersonal system served by their individual efforts.

As school psychologists, they do not consider themselves as working for a particular school district or as the advisor for a given team of teachers, but as representatives of school psychology in general. Men often do not take disagreements personally, but as an indication of dissonance within the system at large. One man concluded, "Teachers clearly have difficulty accepting the advice of psychologists. We are a threat to their positions." A woman in the same situation would have been furious with the teachers or have felt personally affronted.

Since men feel like actors within the greater system, they can overlook personal animosities. "I can't stand him, personally, but we forget our differences at work." It is easier for men to set personal feelings aside when a problem has to be approached jointly and when all concerned subordinate themselves to the same system. From a feminine perspective, the individuals in a working situation are just as important if not more so than the job itself.

## CAREER BUILDING: DISTURBED MALE BEHAVIOR

Our culture does not recognize the soul significance of work for men. The legitimate demand that all professional fields be open to women has caused us to forget that the same activities do not carry the same meaning. Often men's career building is considered abnormal. In popular thinking, men just destroy themselves, when work is the central focus of their lives. They are prisoners of unsuccessful socialization and caught in masculine role clichés. Career thinking makes them unable to allow intimate relationships and to become conscious of their own feelings. They alienate themselves and become subjective cripples.

Our culture scarcely understands the motivation of a career man and looks at him with the greatest skepticism. Why does his work mean so much to him? What good does it do him to slave away for his profession? Is he not actually crazy to be in his office already by seven o'clock in the morning? Usually the career man is portrayed as an infamous and greedy egoist, lusting after power and personal gain with no consideration for those around him. We assume that successful men are brutal by nature and sexually motivated. If a man strives for a specific position, for influence, reputation, or an interesting job, he is suspect. What is wrong with him? Would he not do better to spend time at home with his wife and children rather than spending four evenings a week on the road?

The "new man" involves himself in the housework, assumes an equal share of the responsibility for his children, and is unwilling to have his company assign him to an unfamiliar part of the world. For him, the family and his relationship with his wife are more important than his career. A politician or CEO who storms out of the house at six in the morning and only goes to bed exhausted late at night is a pathological case. How can anyone work so hard for prestige, honor, and recognition from his profession or society? How much better it would be for a man to be content with himself, to have time for his wife or significant other, to devote himself to his personal friends? Where is there any meaning in building a career?

It is noteworthy how many men make use of these same arguments themselves. Hardly a one of them will openly admit to his professional passion. On television talk shows, men try to one-up each other with proof that they, too, are "new men," that their personal life carries greater value than their profession, and that they would naturally be prepared to give it all up for a simple cottage in the country. In a word, they play down their profession. Such comments, though, contradict men's actual behavior and ignore the fact that, without professional challenges, they would not be able to live.

## PSYCHOLOGY'S LACK OF UNDERSTANDING

From a psychological perspective, the value men place on work and career building is incomprehensible. According to relational psychology's reigning understanding, the human soul reveals itself in the private sphere. Psychologists, therefore, study the personality, examine the biography, probe the character, and analyze the personal surroundings to find plausible explanations for human behavior. Professional ambitions and goals depend on the personality. Psychologists seek to understand the ambition of an individual engaged in the outer world as a facet of his or her psychology. They assume the existence of shadow motives—the thirst for power, narcissism, or delusions of grandeur—in the man who attempts to realize himself through his work. A man spends so much time at the office to prove himself to his father or to compensate for an inferiority complex. In psychologists' view, a man overvalues himself, suffers from one-sided socialization, or avoids personal problems if he is convinced that his professional activity has an effect on society or is of importance for his community.

The energies men expend for their profession, for their careers, or the sacrifices they make to the theme or cause to which they feel obligated, do not spring solely from the personal realm. Such efforts cannot be explained only on the basis of biography. Psychological categories do not sufficiently explain men's striving for accomplishment. Why should anyone desire to run a company or to travel from city to city as the director of a not-for-profit organization or to spend one's energies to make the metric system the basis for measurement? Thanks to psychological research, it is possible for us to identify the shadow motives that do play a role in the dark of a man's psyche. But psychologists underestimate the significance of the myths expressing themselves in professional dedication. Psychologists fail to recognize the attractive power myths have on men. Myths infuse men with power in the depths of their souls.

Naturally, since men are also psychological beings and women, likewise, have a masculine, mythical side, the psychological motives might *also* be accurate. A politician or a rock star does satisfy his narcissism in a crowd's applause. A department head does live out a personal thirst for power when he invites employees in his section to an obligatory staff meeting. That does not mean that narcissism or a thirst for power are the *only* motives for the corresponding activity. If we only recognize psychological motives, our understanding is too myopic, and we fail to respect the mythological part of the soul. Of course a man satisfies psychological needs in his profession. Yet, these motives frequently do not suffice to justify the effort and drudgery a career involves. A man requires the touch of myth to mobilize sufficient energy and the necessary dedication required to work for a professional, political, or interest-related goal. Only myth confers the feeling of grandiosity that makes it possible to take on a life challenge.

Grandiose, mythic striving, however, is not tolerated. In the 1992 American presidential election, we noticed how the candidates constantly appeared with their wives. Barbara or Hillary stood next to George Bush or Bill Clinton as a guarantee of "family values." The candidates paraded the relationship with their wives and emphasized repeatedly that their spouse and children held first priority. Therefore, after his election, Clinton first thanked his wife, daughter, and mother. Bush promised to devote himself more to his grandchildren.

The candidates' behavior reflects a general attitude, not just an American one. Since masculine grandiosity by itself is suspect, it has to be integrated with feminine psychology. A man's ambitions are only acceptable with a woman at his side, guaranteeing the psychological emphasis. The show-casing of the presidential candidates' wives served the purpose of disguising the masculine, mythological with psychology. From a psychological perspective, it is incomprehensible why anyone would want to assume the superhuman challenges that accompany the American presidency. No rational, intelligent individual would want an office that draws enormously on one's energies and which few leave with laurels. Since no one understands the masculine desire to serve the myth supporting the American nation, a candidate has to fall back on family psychology to be successful. Outwardly he presents his domesticated side, while otherwise carefully hiding his masculine passions.

## CAREER AS A PATH OF INDIVIDUATION

Men's career building and the importance they give to work are not always pathological or the sign of a loss of soul. This assessment stems from the feminine, psychological perspective that values the personal more highly than the universal. In the feminine view, work primarily serves personal development. This view would consider the psychological *temenoi* only relevant for shaping individual life. It has no sense for the role played by the myths that surround us and in which we grow up.

If we regard career building from the mythological standpoint, we get a completely different picture. For men, a career is not just a vehicle for self-development, a source of personal satisfaction, or avoidance of "real" needs, but *a path of individuation*. By that I mean that men follow their existential purpose through their professions. For them a profession is a possibility of coming to terms with themselves and the forces in the depths of their souls. Soul development takes place through a profession. Through their respective work-related activities, men participate in the myths characterizing their cultures.

The notion of "career" is the attempt to find a connection to the myths underlying a given profession. A mechanical engineer makes an offering to the myth of technology; a teacher pays homage to the myth of enlightenment; or, a policeman serves the myth of civil order. Career building rests in the longing for the myth celebrated by the corresponding profession.

In many an apparently hollow and egotistical careerist hides a temple servant devoting himself at the shrine of his profession. What at first glance looks like acquisitiveness or a power trip, turns out to be a concealed ritual of dedication. To the man in question, success signifies that the myth finds him worthy and that he has been accepted to the inner circle of temple servants. We can understand the importance work has for men as an expression of the longing for mythical participation. A man senses the myth's numinous power in his profession and is subjectively fulfilled.

"My evaluation states that you have performed outstanding work. I am very pleased with you," the Chief of Staff informed me. The position in the psychiatric clinic where I worked a number of years ago as a psychologist was difficult. Other staff members tormented me and intrigued against me. As a psychologist, I felt attacked. The Chief of Staff's comments triggered unsuspected feelings in me. I felt my eyes watering. I could not understand why his praise was so important for me: my other professional and personal activities provided me with enough confirmation. Only with time did it become clear to me that these comments made me feel affirmed in my occupation: I felt respected as a psychologist. For me, the Chief of Staff was a symbol of the myth underlying psychology and psychiatry.

The myth for each occupation defines professional success. While many professions measure success in terms of material wealth, others consider more important things like personal reputation, standing with clients and colleagues, perseverance in the face of temptations, or the feeling of living up to the professional myth.

A forty-year-old mechanical engineer resigns a well-paying job in the research department of a textile machine manufacturer. His superiors cannot understand his decision. What about his retirement benefits? Does he not have a family to look after? Is he looking for a position with a higher salary? The engineer emphasizes how satisfied he is with his income, how much he values the short commute, and how well he gets along with his colleagues. He has no other choice, however, than to resign.

He says he feels some kind of inner pressure. By that he means that a spirit of innovation without which he cannot live is absent in his position. Everything is so regulated, that he does not need to lift a finger. His interest lies elsewhere. He wants to develop new technical systems. He dreams of simplifying the production of textiles or the components for large textile machines. He wants to explore technical solutions for the complicated production processes. In short, his company no longer serves the myth motivating him.

The mythical narrative animating him reminds us of Hephaistos. For the Greeks, this god was lord of fire and the god of the smith's art. He furnished the palaces of the gods with art objects and made presents to his wives, Charis or Aglaia, of marvelous jewelry. Characteristic of this god was that he tried to change the world through *techné*, through art. By forming and shaping material, he created products that opened new possibilities of life for humans and gods alike. For Hephaestos, salvation took place through his craft.

This mechanical engineer's dedication belongs to the myth carried by the archetype of Hephaestos. He would have given up himself, denied himself, had he not remained true to his myth. In all probability, he would have felt beside himself and have been intolerable for those around him had he chosen the easier path and stayed in his old job. He was able, however, to find the courage and to receive the necessary support from his family to follow his profession, his calling. The strength for his difficult transition he drew not from the personal realm, but from the feeling of connection to something greater—the myth of *techné*. His grandiose notion made it possible for him to quit his job and seek out a more fitting channel for the energies moving through him.

## THE MARVELOUS QUEST FOR A FATA MORGANA

The desire to realize oneself in the light of myth parallels the quest for a fata morgana in the wilderness. Driven by the belief that they are making an important contribution to society or to their profession, men sacrifice hour upon hour, often risking their personal well-being. Superficially, they want to develop a new computer program or solve a particular problem at work to diagnose a patient's disorder, or bring a legal case to trial. Yet, their dedication belongs to the myth that supports their activity and grips them. Only in this way does work convey the feeling of doing something essential. Only from the perspective of myth does personal investment acquire meaning. Filled with the hope of climbing the career ladder to a certain level or of completing a specific project charged with mythical substance, men invest themselves in their professional disciplines.

Of course, they are following an illusion. It belongs to the nature of myth to remain ungraspable and transcendent. Men live from the fascinating power of myths and are drawn by the corresponding *temenoi*, even though the myth remains out of their reach. Their longing drives them, even though the ultimate satisfaction remains unattainable. A man strives for inclusion at Arthur's Round Table, even when he knows those knights will never find the Holy Grail.

Winston Churchill (1874–1965), the British Prime Minister, was an untiring, skeptical politician. Driven by his vision of a free Europe, he succeeded in giving the peoples subjugated by the National Socialists new hope in the decisive months of 1940. Churchill's performance was superhuman. His energy

disappeared, however, when he felt himself shut out of the decision-making process. This feeling overcame him during his brief
imprisonment in the Boer War and after his defeat at the polls in
1945. Unable to participate in meeting the challenges of the
moment, he succumbed to a dull passivity. He felt cut off, unable
to participate in the "great events."

In other words, he missed the opportunity of serving a myth
through his actions. His whole life, Churchill was in his element
when struggling with the collective forces of his era. Following his
withdrawal from politics, he fought with bouts of depression, sat
silently for hours before the fire, and could find no meaning in
life. Without the possibility of engaging the great myths of his
time, his superhuman energy left him. He was a Mana Personality
only when he was in the light of a myth and as long as the myth
could shine through him. Churchill did what he did not for himself, but as the myth's servant or participant. His role was that of
an instrument, not a mythological hero.

## THE HOUSE-HUSBAND AND HIS HIDDEN MYTH

Of course, not all men devote themselves to a myth. Many decide
against a career and make their families, their personal well-
being, and relationships with others the center of their lives. Work
serves the purpose of earning a living. The great themes of our
time, the expressions of prevailing myths, interest them only mar-
ginally. They want neither to submit to the compulsiveness of a
profession nor to involve themselves politically nor to transform
society. Such men reject the combative, impersonal engagement
with the challenges of our time and opt for a private life.
Apparently, they have no need for participation in the myths, no
longing for grandiosity.

"I decided against the stress of the business world," commented one thirty-five-year-old social worker. "There is no point
in just chasing after money, in having no time for your kids, and
in venting all of your frustrations from work at home."

Appearances can be deceptive, though. Perhaps, there really
are men who are living out their feminine, psychological side.
Often what we see is but the apparent focus on psychology. The
demonstrative dedication to the private realm may conceal a
protest gesture. Many house-husbands turn out to be heroic

objectors. They, too, feel the fascination flowing from the current myths, but live out their mythical side differently. They consciously decide on another path, while sensing the power of myth in themselves. These men stage their myths as house-husbands or by sharing the housework with their partners. "Men have come a long way since they first began to think about the concept of equality . . . I was a house-husband and I was proud of it. It was an experience that taught me the facts of life, because it was the total reverse of my own upbringing. It is the wave of the future, and I am glad to be along in the first ranks." This was from John Lennon.

The outsider, house-husband, or objector frequently fights with himself and only superficially distances himself from the collective themes. His secret fascination for myths pervades his protest attitude. "In this patriarchal society, men have to do something so we can achieve a democratic society in which women have equal rights." A man like this lives out the crucial myth of equal rights. He shapes the world of his private life mythically. He expresses his grandiosity through an oppositional position—he devotes his life to the private realm—but nonetheless follows a collective model.

He views his role as house-husband from the mythical givens of his society: patriarchy, ecology, equality, alternative lifestyle, and so forth. He may even turn with ardor to "organic gardening," to writing articles about being a house-husband, organizing a neighborhood group to campaign for protected residential streets, or defending theories about proper nutrition. He expands his domestic existence into the mythical dimension when he adds contemporary and collective themes. Masculine thinking pervades the shaping of his familial life. Men seldom can orient themselves through psychology alone.

The difficulty of this path lies in the limited number of external ceremonies through which the myth can be represented. A living myth requires collective rituals and insignia as a manifestation of its content. In business, the rituals are the office, corporate buildings, technical apparatus, staff meetings, Franklin planners, discussions, hierarchies, positions, and functions. They express the reigning myth. A house-husband can only turn to himself; he has only the private realm for support. For many, this is asking too much. They miss the insignia of grandiosity provided by jobs in an institution or a system. They feel helpless without *the power of a celebrated myth* that also includes participation in group rituals.

Because men want to bring in the mythical element, the profession of house-husband inevitably takes on different accents than that of housewife. Women are often capable of drawing strength from themselves, because they can live out of psychology. Most men, at least ideally, need a mythical context to individuate. A social worker turned house-husband organized a weekly musical group on his block, set up a workshop to build his own furniture, and in addition bought a variety of animals to look after. Indirectly, he reconnected with myths by creating existential challenges to master that otherwise were lacking in his new profession.

## THE COUNTER-MYTH

It is important for men to live up to their grandiosity. Grandiosity, though, becomes dangerous, when it is not relativized by a counter position. Masculine grandiosity can only be tolerated by society in a mythical arena. Without a counter-myth, without opposing positions in other words, inflation threatens. After returning from his campaign in India, Alexander the Great ordered his soldiers to henceforth consider him a god. This decree was too much for the Macedonians, despite the fact that claims to deity status meant less to people than they do now. Alexander had gone too far.

In 1945, Winston Churchill was completely convinced that he would win the election. He had organized the dinner party to celebrate his victory before the votes were counted. British voters, however, did not forgive him his self-certainty and his rhetorical insults: comparing the Labor Party with the Gestapo and characterizing Laski as the "second Führer" (after Adolf Hitler). He lost the election.

What happened with both men is something that is possible with the mythological orientation. They became inflated, succumbing to the myth they were subject to instead of serving the myth. They saw themselves as myth, presumed divine authority, and lost their perspective for the *mythical struggle*, the dialogue between different myths. Every myth implies its counter-myth, an alternate position on the same level that calls into question the inherent grandiosity of the first myth. When someone celebrates only one myth, he or she can fall victim to arbitrariness, spiritual desolation, or, in the worst cases, the use of violence. In pathological cases, as I mentioned earlier, men consider themselves identical with the myth that grips them. The mythical grandiosity seizes them, personally: they *are* the myth instead of serving it. Personalizing a myth betrays the mythical dimension. When men personalize a myth, they feel supreme and superior in their positions, possessors of the truth, and fail to realize that only one truth speaks through them.

A collective example of this mythical one-sidedness is certain tendencies within the Roman Catholic Church. Many Church representatives consider the teachings and dogmas carried by the Christian myth as possibilities—with God's help—for finding new strength and taking on the questions of earthly existence. Others place themselves on the same level as the dogmas. They do not serve the Church's teachings, but they *are* those teachings. They no longer recognize the myth as an external, grandiose reality to which human beings can turn, but consider it the absolute truth. They no longer recognize Christianity as a wonderful myth through which God makes himself known to us, but as the one and only truth—a truth that must be lived out with no awareness of other realities. The Jungian analyst, Wolfgang Giegerich, says, "Myths do not lay claim to *the* truth, to be *the* final word about the world . . . Myths always tell only one particular story."

## THE MYTHICAL SENSORIUM: THE NEED FOR OPPOSITIONAL IMAGES

Being gripped by a myth gives us the conviction of being in possession of *a* truth. In an intellectual debate, we are completely capable of acknowledging other positions without believing our own to be wrong. As I mentioned in chapter 3, participation in myths necessitates a dialogue, an open debate or struggle in which the ego takes its position over against the myth. When we live in myth, however, we feel as if we represent objective truths. Against these truths, subjective, psychological insights or other mythical standpoints do not have a chance. An English teacher vehemently supports the importance of formal English and observes a general degeneration of language usage in the younger generation. A specific, mythical attitude shapes his perspective as surely as a different mythical attitude shapes that of his colleague, who argues for the use of vernacular idioms as the only way to reach the younger generation. Myths guide both teachers.

It is practically impossible, though, to recognize the mythical bases for one's own convictions. Only some historical distance provides us with the necessary skepticism. What we today consider truth and irrevocable reality, will perhaps only evoke bemused head-shaking in a hundred years. The grandiose myths to which we now devote ourselves will later be superseded by other, superior myths.

Many earlier ideas and suggestions for dealing with existential and societal challenges seem absurd to us today. The mythical realm is constantly changing. In the seventeenth century, for example, a member of the British House of Commons, Andrew Fletcher of Saltouns, suggested that the government might reduce the number of the unemployed by creating a hereditary class of servants. Parliament seriously discussed this proposal. Fletcher and many of his contemporaries believed in hierarchies and class distinctions determined by birth. Their collective, mythical models emphasized the differences among human beings. Equality was not one of the themes or myths of seventeenth century England!

Our ideas, thoughts, and suggestions depend on the myths by which we orient ourselves. To be conscious of our own position, we have to remain aware of these mythical influences. It is also important for us to remember that incomprehensible, alien ideas are probably grounded in a myth different from our own. A different mythical foundation generally causes us to reject the thought or idea in question.

Just as Churchill had to take his opponents seriously, those identifying with the masculine orientation also need to pay attention to the *other side*. Grandiose men require a sensorium, a sensory apparatus, for the myths of their time as well as knowledge of the past. Confronting other myths, current and historical, provides the tension necessary to avoid seeing themselves as bearers of *the* truth. Grandiose men usually experience other mythical positions as oppositional images. Environmental activists consider representatives of the UAW to be opponents. Or, a small businessman thinks of the president of the Chase Manhattan Bank as a mindless, unimaginative and self-serving materialist.

 We need oppositional images to experience the tension of opposites and the energies characterizing the interplay of myths among themselves. Grandiose men should acknowledge their oppositional images, should attend to them, and study them.

When we come to terms with them consciously, these images protect us from our own arrogance. To distance ourselves formally from or rabidly combat a counter position is fatal, for we lose the opportunity for evaluating our own model.

As men, we must fight for our myths and devote ourselves to them. At the same time, we must listen to our opponents and take their myths into consideration in the awareness that there are also *other* myths. Such a dialogue provides the basis for honing, relativizing, or rejecting our positions. When, however, we are unshakable in our perspective and give no hearing to the demons possessing our opponents—in our perception—our own myth loses its power. We become boring and mentally stale like the fanatical botanist who never questions his view of nature or the  dilettante for whom everything is cosmically meaningful.

Masculine grandiosity is a vital motif calling men to devote themselves to society, their country, or their fellow human beings. The feeling of grandiosity rests in the participation in one of the myths our collective formulates as an answer to an existential challenge. As men we strive for this relationship with myth as a way of coming in contact with a part of our souls that only reveals itself to us through an objective, outer world task.

As a teenager, I was a member of numerous rock 'n' roll groups. We practiced our guitar riffs, drum routines, and vocal harmonies in dingy cellars. The music greats of the time were our inspiration: the Beatles, the Rolling Stones, the Kinks, the Who, and the Animals. I, myself, heartily rejected Stones's fans and imitated the Beatles, the Kinks, and the Animals. A Stones' fan looked different to me and was someone I could not tolerate in my band.

These musical groups were the bearers of the different myths current at the time. The conflicts we engaged in as Stones', Beatles', or Kinks' fans mirrored the tension of our culture's relevant myths. By rejecting the Rolling Stones, I became more conscious of my own myth. I did not see myself as an upright member of the middle class playing the bad boy—so my perception of the Stones—but as the carrier of a new message. For me, the Beatles incorporated genuine creativity, not something aimed at meeting the expectations of the public, but daring to listen to its own voice.

Naturally, the vast majority of men do not experience their relationship to their profession or other interests as mythical. They focus on the task to be performed or the duties included in a specific job or function. "Object compulsion" determines that the committee for departmental policy meet at six in the evening and, consequently, a man has to miss his son's birthday party. The notion that this "object" also results from one's soul's orientation and produces a particular perspective, is beyond the scope of most men in my acquaintance. They do not reflect on their mythical orientation. It is the nature of myths to draw us into their wake and to cause us to register the world only through that mythical pattern.

Personally, I am convinced that it is time for us as men to become conscious of our myths. We need new cognitive instruments of reflection to recognize the forces working in our souls. It is no longer acceptable for us to either hide our masculinity in hushed tones or to live out our grandiosity in unreflected one-sidedness. We need a new guiding image allowing for grandiosity and dedication to collective goals without the risk of succumbing to superiority or of barring the way to women's emancipation.

We need myths that both convey certainty and mobilize our strength to master existential challenges. Only myths ready us to confront society's challenges and make sacrifices. Through myths we come into life and are prepared to become politically active. They provide us with a foundation for action and the capacity to chose to meet existential challenges. Myth is the basis for the masculine part of our souls. We must respect this mythical, grandiose quality of men if we want to truly live into the future with its problems and challenges.

# 5

# The Shadow of
# Grandiosity

♂

# Masculine
# Mythopathologies

The gambler who loses his last cent with unflinching demeanor, the egomaniac for whom career and public standing come before his family and children, or, finally, any man who asserts his will with violence—all of these are forms of masculine grandiosity's shadow. In this chapter, I speak to that shadow side. We will look at the dark side of men's mythical orientation—in sexuality, in public life, and in the private realm. In part, these soul disturbances rest upon a lack of relationship to myth. Actually, men who otherwise receive little recognition in their lives attempt to find their masculine side through violence, posturing, egocentricity, or addictions like gambling.

In other words, I turn to the mythopathologies of men in this chapter. I analyze the shadow of masculine grandiosity as I describe it in the preceding chapter. I explore the significance of morbid, exaggerated, and abnormal forms of grandiosity from which both men and their environment suffer. Together, we will study aberrations of the male soul and male perversions to avoid the dangers that men have to expect. Some of these soul disturbances we recognize in women, since the dividing line between the pathology of men and women is fluid.

The pathologies I describe here, however, are disturbances from which men are more likely to suffer: compulsive gambling, the insatiable desire for recognition and prestige, boastfulness, the need for originality, violence, delusions of grandeur, and grandiose arbitrariness. This list is not complete. It is not my intention to make a definitive presentation of masculine mythopathologies, but to provide insight into possible forms of unhealthy mythical orientations. Many of these disturbances are the other side of positive male characteristics. Notions of greatness are the motor for creative male accomplishments and for the courage to incur risks. Men—and our culture—need such notions to venture the new, to keep the economy from stagnating, and to discover new technologies. At the same time, in exaggerated forms they can degenerate, for example, into manic overvaluation or compulsive behaviors.

Most of the soul's disturbances described in this chapter manifest themselves in conflicts with public life. The distinction between public and private life is important for me, since these two realms of life correspond largely with the spheres of influence of mythology and psychology, respectively. While the private realm remains the reserve of intimacy, of personal life, and of the laws of psychology, myths reign in the public realm. The male soul strives for realization in public life, while the female soul elevates personal life into its primary focus.

Even though, as I have already mentioned, both realms of life are important for men as well as for women, men tend to define themselves more readily in the light of the myths from the public sphere, while women base their identity in their private life. Women who work often see themselves as mothers pursuing a career, while men experience themselves as politicians, businessmen, or professionals who have families. The thesis of this chapter is that specifically male pathologies manifest themselves in the public sphere.

Researchers like Ariès, Duby, and Sennett have shown how every society develops concepts of what belongs to the public and what to the private realms. Where the dividing line occurs between the two changes continuously. What once was private will shift to the list of public discussion topics and public themes become private. The *Zeitgeist,* the spirit of the time, and the social structure determine what the public discuses, deals with, and determines.

At one time religion was a public theme and one did not hesitate to discuss one's faith with others. Today, the relationship to God has become private to such an extent that psychiatric or psychological evaluations often do not include the question of religious affiliation. Sexuality, on the other hand, has become a public topic, wrenched from the private realm. For centuries, discussion of women's capacity for orgasm was taboo. When Empress Maria Theresa of Austria complained to her personal physician about her flagging libidinal interest, the latter conveyed his advice, written and in Latin, in a top secret message. "*Praeterea censeo vulvam Vestrae Sacratissimae Majestatis ante coitum esse titillandam.*" ("In addition, I believe that your most Holy Majesty's vulva should be titillated before coitus"). Today we speak openly, in newspapers and on television, about women's sexual experience, rather than relegating the subject exclusively to the personal, private sphere.

The mythopathologies I describe here concern aberrations in men's public persona, disorders of the mythical component of their personalities. The pathologies that reveal themselves in the public arena can break through despite a perfectly normal private persona. A charming, attentive bank teller, who for years has been an exemplary and wholly satisfactory employee, removes 10 gold bars from the safe one day and disappears to South America. The father of a family sits in front of the television with his two sons watching the program, "America's Most Wanted." Police and FBI are searching for a sex murderer, who raped a woman at a freeway rest area and subsequently strangled her to death. All three men are horrified at the crime. Next morning the police expose the father as the assailant and place him under arrest.

We all know of other examples from the Second World War. Hitler is supposed to have been extremely loving in caring for his dogs. The report of Heinrich Himmler, head of the SS under Adolf Hitler and responsible for the murder of countless thousands of Jews, is also shocking and perverse. With sober objectivity he describes how he planned their deaths, observed piles of corpses, and succeeded in spite of everything—"aside from exceptions of personal weakness"—to retain his composure. He was unaware of the pathology of his public persona. He split off his bestiality and lived it in the public realm while simultaneously identifying with a lofty personal ethic. As long as the private persona was intact, there were no grounds for alarm or self-doubt. Like many men, Himmler remained unconscious of his ugly, diseased public face, his dedication to a perverted and delusional myth.

The discrepancy many men demonstrate between their public and their private behavior is frightening, leading to an intensive search for plausible explanations. We cannot comprehend this split from a psychological perspective. Psychologists comb through individual life histories, laboriously constructing psychological connections to find a reason for the atrocities. Supposedly, a Jewish male friend's rejection of his sexual advances triggered Hitler's hate for the Jews, and Napoleon developed fantasies of grandeur because of his small, physical stature. The idea that a man can be respectable and charming or, at the least, inconspicuous in private, while behaving like a monster in the public or mythical realm remains intolerable. It unsettles our existing ways of judging people and taxes our knowledge of human beings. Until now, we have sought explanations almost exclusively in men's psychology. Since we have declared psychology the basis of personality, we investigate the private life for motives. This perspective eclipses the mythical side of men's personalities with its basis in public life and in those myths current in society.

In this chapter I take a different approach: I do not examine the background of male pathology from the private, personal realm, but from the public, mythical one. I do not explain the disorders and aberrations of the soul on the basis of personal relationships and life history, but in conjunction with the mythical orientation of the male soul.

Due to the concept that there are diseases of the soul specific to the mythical aspect of men's personality and deriving from men's mythology, the explanations and suggestions for improvement will turn out differently. I do not search for disturbed relationships with father or mother, for early childhood trauma, or for Oedipal conflicts, but for disturbances in men's mythical orientation. To return to psychology for understanding would be inappropriate and would result in the psychologizing of a mythical phenomenon. We would then understand the mythical out of our subjective reality and lose its objective aspect.

## COMPULSIVE GAMBLING

I begin with compulsive gambling, because it is an addiction that is not easy to account for and one that primarily affects men. Also, it clearly arises from the dynamic of men's mythical being.

A conversation:

> "You are an academician, have a good job and are known for your pointed legal expertise. I do not understand why you still want to lose thousands of dollars in casinos!"

> "Because the ball is round!"

Men who are compulsive gamblers feel an overpowering need to walk the aisles of casinos or to seek out one of countless gambling establishments and to chance "it." They think about winning yet know full well that, in the final analysis, the house or the slot machine collects. They love the thrill; they are fascinated by the rolling ball that determines whether they will double their hundred dollars, win five times that, or simply lose. Gambling becomes an obsession when a player can no longer tolerate the tension, expectation, and hope he experiences with each bet. By gambling, the men concerned have the feeling of giving themselves over to a greater power. Their fate lies in the hands of Dame Fortune, who brutally and arbitrarily decides whether they will leave having been favored or ruined.

For gamblers it is not a question of the pleasure they experience when they bet a given amount in the faint hope of winning. It is a question of *existential surrender*. The compulsive gambler has no choice but to abandon his money for which he often worked hard to the arbitrariness of the ball or the cards. This gambler cannot stop when he arrives at the edge of ruin. He has to play until he has wagered the last penny and has perhaps even pawned his property.

"It has to be 27," ran through the mind of the thirty-two-year-old bookkeeper as he sat working at his desk. As soon as the work day ended, he jumped into his car and raced from Zurich to Constance. At the casino he bet two thousand German marks—even though he was deep in debt. He promptly lost his money.

For some time this man had lived apart from his wife and his children. His gambling had driven him to ruin. His wages had been garnished and, although he was a successful bookkeeper and the financial conscience of a number of firms, he lived in a meager room in an outlying suburb of Zurich.

We might ask why this man would risk his existence in this way? How is it possible for an intelligent, rational individual to give himself over to this kind of nonsense and gradually destroy himself? Seen superficially, the hope of winning is the primary goal of compulsive gambling. The gambler dreams of showers of gold, of becoming rich "overnight." The fact, however, that most gamblers do not stop until they have lost everything should give us pause. The compulsive gambler keeps playing and does not leave the tables when he pockets considerable winnings. He keeps at it until his winnings are gone. Is it really the chance of winning he hopes for and that he asserts is his main motive?

We need to take the results and the context of this behavioral pattern into consideration. The gambler we are talking about operates in a public sphere. The atmosphere is impersonal: the croupier acts distanced and bored. Compulsive gambling occurs in the outer world, not in the private realm, and almost exclusively in anonymous groups. This is where the gambler achieves financial ruin, where he seeks out the destruction of his personal existence. This is where he feels the yearning to go to the limit and beyond. The gambler's real goal is just such a *personal catastrophe*. He is not trying to win, but to stage his personal downfall. He seeks out a contained, public arena where what he fears and at the same time yearns for can take place: existential catastrophe. A gambler's goal is giving up himself. To understand this motif, we have to take a brief detour.

We are all beset by fears and anxieties throughout our lives. To be afraid of accidents, personal mistakes, or natural catastrophes belongs among the fundamental qualities of human existence. On one hand, we fear for our own health and our death and, on the other, we worry about those closest to us, our partners and children. Existential horror accompanies us always. Before human beings could illuminate their environment with gas or electric lights, this "abysmalness of existence" confronted them every night. "Night overcomes human beings with fear and terror," notes Wolfgang Giegerich. Mountains and thunderstorms were a further source of fears.

At the same time, we want to live free of fear, to keep the "world of terror" from our door. We hear of terrifying events in the media and see the pictures on television, but we only experience fear and terror directly when it touches us personally. In other words, we have constructed a fenced-in environment so we do not have to notice existential horror. We do not want to be personally reminded of fear and terror. We are not ritually bound to the abysmalness of existence the way people were, for example, in seventeenth century Europe. The man of the house would gather family members around him to revive the night fears in chorales and recitatives. "Since the night's danger and horrors / awaken fears and worries of ours . . ." "Oh, look, here lies this wretched soul / by fear of night surrounded."

We assign our existential horror to life's periphery. In our perception an economic catastrophe, an automobile accident, or a collective epidemic might effect our personal downfall. Calamity befalls us from the outer world. Today we identify the mythical terror belonging to archaic human beings with external events. We conceptualize the abysmalness of human existence: the plane could crash, the food might be irradiated, or such and such an acquaintance might be HIV-positive. Horror is a possibility in the outer world and not a reality of the inner realm, of our personal being. We try to hold out in our pacified, private sphere and to avoid participating in this mythical horror.

The situation is especially unbearable for an individual with a mythical orientation. He senses the terror; he knows about the potential catastrophes. It becomes increasingly difficult to devote himself to his activities within such a well-contained space without experiencing the horror directly. Naturally, he tries to avoid the existential horror through his profession, his family life, and his leisure activities. He concentrates on the tasks at hand, attempting to live according to his ideals. Yet, the existential terror intrudes again and again as a dimension of life demanding respect. He does not want to think of all that could happen, but the certainty that "it" could actually happen to him gnaws at his mind anyway. The terrifying thing could seize him as well and wrench him into the abyss.

To understand the gambler we have to visualize this existential situation for ourselves. Compulsive gambling is an attempt to encounter the existential horror. A gambler places himself in extreme situations—like those in dangerous sports such as freeclimbing, sky diving, bungee jumping, or motorcycle racing—to reach the limitations of his own being. He seeks to look in the eyes of that horror he knows exists and constantly fears. For the compulsive gambler, it is not a question of winning, but rather of the quest for personal catastrophe and the staging of his own downfall. The financial loss and the consequences arising from it produce emotional shocks in him from which he can directly experience the existential horror. He encounters the mythical terror—and is still alive!

We need, therefore, to understand compulsive gambling as a condition stemming from a blocked mythical relationship to life. By gambling, a man seeks the horrifying, alarming, and divine spark to free him from the routine of the everyday and to allow him to experience existential horror. The gambler surrenders to the powers of fate ruling the gaming tables. In losing, he again experiences the overwhelming forces he senses in the outer world, forces capable of plunging him into the abyss. A wager offers the possibility of confronting these uncanny, superhuman powers determining our being.

Through the terror he experiences in losing, the gambler expects to establish a mythical relationship to the world. Gambling allows him to participate in the myth of fortune as it favors or ignores him. Paradoxically, therefore, he perceives personal catastrophe as deliverance: the inexplicable and horrifying "it" occurs in the comprehensible realm of the game. What in secret he has always feared has happened, leaving him still standing on his own two feet. Losing a bet frees the gambler from the terrifying uncertainty of when and where the terrifying event will strike.

## THE ADDICTION TO ATTENTION, HONOR, AND GLORY

The next addiction we will address is the exaggerated striving for public recognition. Attention, honor, and glory become the central focus forcing other interests into the background. A man with this addiction directs his efforts toward what the outer world notices, values, and honors and expects the general public to respect him. The *theatrum mundi*, the theater of the world, has chosen him for a leading role. He defines himself on the basis of the attention that comes his way from the outer realm and sees such recognition as affirmation of his outward-directed, risk-taking masculinity. He has left the private sphere behind and moves on the stage of the common weal, braving the dangers of the outer world. He is not one to sit fearfully at home, hesitating and fixating on himself, but dares to step out into the great, wide world. The confirmation or admiration of others provides the common denominator for his activity.

We find evidence of the place and importance of honor for men as early as the ancient Greeks. Achilles is willing to exchange a long, uneventful life for a short and glorious one, and Agamemnon is prepared to give up a few months of his life for an honorable death on the field of battle. The obsessive search for glory and honor became a part of the Greek ideal of masculinity and found expression in *The Odyssey*. The hero of the epic, Odysseus, engages in countless dangers with monstrosities of the world and overcomes them through his physical strength, cunning, and sly tricks. He finally returns home covered with glory to his waiting wife, Penelope.

Wanting and working for public recognition is normal and healthy. When public attention is important to them, women as well as men mobilize energy and are ready to act and sacrifice for society. Those involved in this way take their orientation not from the private realm, but view their activities in a larger context. When a man feels the eyes of society resting on him, he will carefully gauge the effect of what he does and says. The image of standing before an audience in an imaginary auditorium spurs a man on and increases his level of performance. We speak of an addiction to honor and glory, however, when public recognition supplies the *exclusive motivation*. This man focuses his attention solely on the public's reaction and, without the feeling that others notice him, he collapses. He needs to hear the applause and admiring murmurs of an audience, to shine in an impersonal arena. He grows restive if a week passes without questions from reporters or gets angry if a colleague is interviewed on television. His focus is not an object, a project, or a theme, but always his own glory. Leaves on the trees should whisper his doings, even though his activities are merely a means of acquiring the outer world's attention. In the meanwhile, his private persona atrophies.

One researcher describes the director of a firm who was highly esteemed for his many contributions to society. The man served as chairman of the city council, board member of various organizations, director of the church choir, chairman of a charitable fund-raising drive, and, additionally, was active in politics. The public showered him with honors. One day he left on a short vacation and hanged himself. He lived on the public's reflected glory while woefully neglecting his psychological side, his private persona. Left to himself he was overcome with feelings of meaninglessness. We can find similar examples in politics. Pierre Bérégovoy, the one-time Socialist Premier of France, put a bullet in his head when the public denied him its recognition.

There are different paths for acquiring recognition in the public sphere. Next to a media presence, titles and awards convey a feeling of one's own greatness. Most men consider a professorial title, an honorary doctorate, a political office, or an award of any kind proof of public recognition. Naturally, it is even better to have a street carry one's name, to have a statue remind coming generations of one's personal physiognomy, or to have a written or artistic work known to one's grandchildren's generation. Such things make the longed-for place in history a certainty.

The ambition of the former leader of the Central African Republic, Bokaska, took on downright grotesque forms. As president of this poor country in the African interior, he built an immense palace and surrounded himself with an extensive staff of servants. Felix Houphouet-Boigny, President of The Ivory Coast, had the ambition of building a cathedral exceeding St. Peter's Basilica in Rome in size.

We all know of situations that occur because of a wounded sense of honor. Dueling, a widespread practice in the last century, was a means of rectifying an affront to one's sense of honor. Alexander Hamilton, the first American Secretary of the Treasury, lost his life in one such encounter. The following is a contemporary story.

A certain Albanian caught his wife in bed with another man. He immediately shot his rival who was attempting to jump out the window. From prison, the affronted husband informed his father-in-law. With a loaded pistol, the latter traveled to Switzerland, waited at a church christening for his daughter's family, and calmly shot at his three- and six-year-old grandchildren and his daughter. While his daughter survived the father's vengeance only grazed by his bullet, one grandchild was seriously wounded, and the other died from a head wound. The grandfather allowed himself to be taken into police custody without resistance. He had accomplished his purpose: he had saved the family's honor.

During the reign of Kaiser Wilhelm II the notion of an authoritarian state dominated the German empire. Duty and obedience were considered a citizen's primary obligation. Nothing had greater significance than to be recognized and honored by the state. Cabinet ministers, therefore, appeared in the German parliament wearing sabers at their sides and high school teachers wore their officer's uniforms on national holidays. What mattered was recognition by someone in a public position; anything from private life was secondary. Wilhelm II served as a towering father figure and his countrymen considered an audience with him the highest form of success. He, himself, enticed his subjects with titles, medals, and uniforms.

Wilhelm II appears to have been obsessed with a mania for uniforms. Photographs of him seldom if ever show him in civilian dress. He appears constantly in uniforms of different regiments: the Life Guard Hussars, the Guard du Corps, or the First Infantry Guard Regiment. He was not satisfied, though, with just German uniforms or Austrian uniforms, but wore English and Russian uniforms as well. As Kaiser, he held the position of honorary commander in several non-German units. He seems not to have grasped the symbolic significance of these titles and spoke of inspecting "his" regiments in England or Russia. The English could only protect themselves against his painful importunity by stationing the Kaiser's regiment in India.

The obsession with recognition during this period also expressed itself in the sixty-two levels of the Prussian court hierarchy. Accordingly, university rectors belonged on level forty-seven, members of parliament on level fifty-eight, and so forth.

Today the need for honor and recognition does not reveal itself so apparently. Failing the rank and station associated with an aristocracy—today found only in Great Britain and the Scandinavian countries—we use *material goods* to signify our importance in the public sphere. Since we cannot hope for a title such as Lord, Sir, or at the very least, O.B.E. (Order of the British Empire), we have to appease our need for recognition in other ways: the discrete Volvo, a not-to-be-overlooked Mercedes 300 SEL, or a cellular telephone betray public significance. The simple house in Aspen, the Caribbean cruise, or the custom-built mountain bike serve notice to our fellow human beings whom they have before them. We look for recognition through material symbols that point to our standing in the public realm. We thereby differentiate ourselves from the masses and expect them to notice our uniqueness. While men are more likely to find recognition in titles, positions, and material symbols, the desire for honor among women often manifests itself in their choices of friends and colleagues.

A man's public persona may stand in *striking contradiction* to his private persona: the role that he plays in public diverges markedly from his psychology. Privately the same individual may cut a sorry figure or present contradictory values. The Englishman John Wilkes (1727–1797) is an impressive example of this disparity.

The son of a well-to-do wool manufacturer, Wilkes was known as a *bon vivant*. He drank in excess, loved to eat, and was continually entangled in love affairs. Nevertheless, he became one of the

most significant political figures of his time and was considered by
the working and lower classes of London as an "incarnation of
lofty ethical principles." Wilkes introduced ethical and moral standards into politics. Although his personal lifestyle contradicted his
public persona, he defined himself by his public role and importance. He followed the myth of his time that required one to be
ethical and decent. Certainly, personal authenticity was unknown
to him as a criterion.

   We can trace ambition back to longing as a way of locating it
within the mythical canon. An ambitious man takes his direction
from the existing mythical images dominating the public sphere
and works toward achieving the position due to him within that
context. By achieving importance in and from the collective, he
hopes to burst the bonds of his private being, to escape the psychology of his personal life. Thus, ambition stems from his desire
to escape the drudgery of personal being and fate as well as the
banality of everyday existence. By securing a place in history, an
important position, or public recognition, he reduces the necessity of confronting questions of personal relationship and of
reflecting on his private biographical issues. With confidence he
can be boring, disgusting, or a cripple in relationships since he
has long since legitimized himself on the basis of his public image.

   An ambitious man concentrates his efforts exclusively on
those themes and projects that yield benefit for him in the public
eye, in his job, and in his profession. What he says, knows, and
reveals of himself reflects the mythical expectations that his imaginary audience places on him. Often he lives out or personifies a
myth, like an actor playing his role in the collective realm. Like
John Wilkes, he splits off his private persona. He needs no private
life to play a myth!


## THE ADDICTION TO ORIGINALITY

A further and frequent male pathology is compulsive originality.
Someone suffering from compulsive originality distinguishes himself from others by his unconventionality. A unique idea or an
unusual performance defines the profile of his collective personality. Perhaps, he dramatizes his uniqueness out of fear of the
banal aspects of existence or because he fears the psychological
side of his life. "I'm not like everybody else," he thinks and

attempts to attract notice by sailing the Atlantic solo, climbing a 14,000-foot peak in record time, or displaying himself as an art object. Originality serves as the medium by which he attracts attention, maintains his difference, or becomes a public figure. These men attempt to catch the public eye by interpreting their roles other than the way dictated by the corresponding myth. They reject the mythical givens and identify themselves through their differentness.

Their compulsive originality may create new ideas or motivate them to extraordinary performances, yet they often think primarily about possible media exposure or at least the reaction of their acquaintances. They feel a thorn in their side, because they would not want to be a common bank teller, a typical teacher, an everyday journalist, or just another consultant. They strive for originality for originality's sake, for so they acquire a place among the gods.

A successful Swiss bank director with a reputation for being an unconventional thinker was invited to appear on a radio talk show to discuss a topic of his choosing. The show's format was to have public figures address any theme for two minutes. Instead of talking, however, the bank director remained silent for the two-minute period. His listeners could only hear the dripping of a water faucet in the background. He intended his action to be a way of calling attention to a world flooded with noise pollution. It is very likely, however, that originality was his true goal. For him to have simply discussed some issue would not have been original!

Originality compulsion is a variation of the male addiction to honor and glory. While in the First World War young men hoped for glory from their display of bravery in battle, today the extraordinary or especially irreverent activity or idea promises a place in the sun. The unusual carries mythical value, and the mythical overcomes the vulgarity of everyday existence. By identifying with originality, a man takes on an identifiable role in the *theatrum mundi* and acquires a vehicle for representing his personalized myth.

## VIOLENCE

I now turn to the problem of male acts of violence, a pathology that receives much attention and from which all of us suffer as individuals, as groups, or as a society. Violence is a permanent challenge we have to face constantly. Given the right excuse, men allow themselves to be seduced into violence again and again. They throw themselves into the melee, go looking for a fight, and want, literally, to see blood. A criminologist notes that, "Many young men long for violence, experience it as enjoyable, and . . . take pleasure in it." Criminal statistics make this very clear. While women commit offenses like theft or fraud relatively often, men make up the vast majority of offenders for acts of violence. The prison inmates in Switzerland and Germany are overwhelmingly of the male gender. What is it about violence that so fascinates men?

For myself, I can feel my conflicting relationship to violence. Consciously, I reject violence as a means of resolving conflicts. I consider it primitive and uncivilized when we go at each other with bare fists, seek to solve disagreements with physical force, or strive for a goal with no consideration for other people. I despise these methods of resolving differences.

At the same time, I feel another side in myself, a terrible strength slumbering in me that can be awakened by specific situations. At such times I am filled with rage. There is the careless driver who passes me while I am stopped for someone at a pedestrian crossing. There is the colleague at work who intrigues against me. There are the gang members who spray paint on my house and try to intimidate me with threats. Images flood my mind of how I could set the situation right with a few well-placed right hooks or how I might blow up undesirable neighbors with a bomb. The images have a freeing effect on me, absorbing the emotions that rise in me. Am I really as peaceable as I like to believe?

Our acts of violence wear different faces. We can be brutal toward women. We are capable of hitting and tormenting them and attempting to make them submissive with our physical superiority. Of course, it is always the other one who is at fault. The fact remains that thousands of women suffer from the results of rape or brutality on the part of their husbands or partners. They feel inferior in the face of a man's physical strength.

The moment of violence also surfaces in conflicts between men and within male systems. Under certain circumstances, violence constellates rapidly in groups of men as the riots at soccer games or at demonstrations have shown. "Power to the people," comes the cry, and city hall or the administration building are pelted with paint bombs.

The German public was shocked by the wave of violence that exploded against foreigners in Cottbus, Dresden, Halle, Görlitz, and other East German cities. Right-wing radical youths joined in groups, called out, "Heil Hitler," and set fire to homes for those seeking political asylum. "Often there are no more than ten or fifteen activists who punctually assemble large numbers of action-oriented and brutal collaborators for assaults on 'foreigners,' leftists, and anything 'non-German,' " observed one commentator. The adolescents of the former East Germany feel that they are German and better than Turks or Greeks.

We men have a tendency to violence. History reminds us that violent conflicts have occurred in Europe many times over the last two hundred years. In addition to the First and Second World Wars, Europe also suffered through the Russian Revolution, the Civil War in Spain (1936–1939), the uprisings in East Germany (1953), in Hungary (1956), and in Czechoslovakia (1968), the "troubles" in Northern Ireland, and now the brutal war in Bosnia-Herzegovina. It would seem that warlike, brutal conflict is the norm, not peace. Since political systems are, for all practical purposes, controlled exclusively by men, we are justified in regarding violence as inherently male. Men act violently in given situations and feel compelled to resort to violence or to react with violence.

What is the meaning of this male brutality? It is not my intent to study here the economic or political causes that can lead to violence, but to examine the question of the meaning violence has in the soul of men. Men seek out violence, reject it, avoid it, demonize it, or delegate it. As a theme, violence will not let them go and, as I discuss in the third chapter, attracts them already as children. It seems too simplistic to me to trace this tendency to elevated testosterone levels or to explain it through gender behavior, imitation and modeling, parental conflicts, the economic situation, or phallic-Oedipal behavior.

We have to consider the meaning of violence as an *act of soul* and question to what extent violence and being a man belong together. We have to try to examine *violence, per se*, not only as an activity of someone else, but as our own soul's potential. As men, we carry violence in us. We need to trace this soul quality to understand violence without legitimizing it. We have to try to understand violence in its shimmering, archetypal fullness even if we come to conclusions that we, personally, do not find appealing. We have to look the hateful face of violence full in the eye, for only through

unbiased consideration can we ever hope to grasp it in its significance for the male personality. Trite demands that "men just have
to change," or appeals such as, "violence should not exist," help little when we are not familiar with the soul background for men's
violent tendencies.

I will explore violence in conjunction with men's mythological orientation. That, I believe, is the only possibility of diverting
violence's destructive effects.

When we consider the place of violence in fairy tales and myths,
we notice that *violence* often goes hand and hand with *creativity*. In
the Lettland fairy tale, "How the Woodcutter Tricked the Devil and
Won the King's Daughter," the hero only wins the princess after having changed himself into a lion and fought with the devil. In the fairy
tale, "Kagsagsuk, the Poor Orphan Boy," the orphan can only free
himself from the figures that were mean to him by smashing their
heads or crushing them to death. Violence brings something new
into the world, initiates a transformation, or destroys something old,
cumbersome, or outmoded.

In different myths, demons free the people through acts of
violence. The Germanic thunder god, Thor, defended gods and
men with his hammer, Mjöllnir, against the threatening powers of
Utgard, the giants, and the Midgard serpent. Hercules strangles
the Nemean lion with his bare hands and, with the help of his
sword, poisonous arrows, and fire, he succeeds in killing the multi-
headed monster, Hydra. Violence occurs over and over in
Christian mythology as well. On one hand, the prophets are violent and, on the other, the God of the Old Testament and even
Jesus display violence. Moses angrily destroys the golden calf,
David slays Goliath with a sling-shot, and Jesus drives the merchants out of the temple. We ought not to forget that Christianity
begins with a murder: the crucifixion of Jesus. In the Old
Testament, God reduces Sodom and Gomorrah to rubble and
ashes, commands Abraham to murder his son, and, in the New
Testament, goes so far as to sacrifice His own Son. In all these
examples, violence serves as the tool to alter the world. Violence
furthers new development and establishes a new attitude or a different level of consciousness.

We also can observe the relationship between violence and
creativity in the history of our political systems. Our democracies
did not come into being on the basis of evolutionary processes,
but thanks to the willingness of men (and women) to resort to

violence. Louis XVI did not abdicate his throne of his own free will, nor did the Nazis lay down their weapons in the face of convincing verbal arguments from the Allies. Violence often stands on the threshold of a new social order or orientation.

The world took the movement of 1968 seriously when students in France called for a general strike and pictures of street battles between young people and police flickered in living rooms around the globe. Without these excesses this movement never would have reached the public consciousness. Those bloody street battles created the 1968 movement, at least in part.

In retrospect, all this may seem well and good to us. Yet, when I remember that during these acts of creation, people lost their lives, then my old rejection of violence surfaces once again. Did Louis XVI not have a right to life? Were there not other ways of punishing the inhabitants of Sodom and Gomorrah? We have to reject violence, because it damages the integrity and the will of our fellow human beings, individually or as a group. Violence stands in contradiction to the ethical principle requiring us to respect the life, will, and lifestyle of other human beings. I have difficulty comprehending the creative aspect of violence when homes for political refugees are burned, IRA bombs tear children to pieces, women are raped in the open street, or villages in Bosnia-Herzegovina are "sanitized." I gaze in the ugly, disgusting face of male violence and feel pain. Am I a coward, then?

Violence always takes place in a field of tension, where opposites are manifested: Germans against foreigners, Serbs against Muslims, Catholics against Protestants, blacks against Chicanos, Socialists against Capitalists, Dallas Cowboy fans against Denver Bronco fans, men against women, criminals against police, and so forth and so forth. The prerequisite for violence is that the world be divided into dichotomies, into clear polarities. I am here, you are there. A separation is made and an opposition results. From the perspective of the one pole, the other side appears as a demon or an otherwise antagonistic other.

Violence arises from this tension of opposites. Two individuals or two groups stand opposite one another, each registering the other as enemy. At least one side feels itself existentially threatened and challenged. The individual or group attempts to assert its own position. The individual attacks what is foreign, criminal, different, evil, disgusting, or also fascinating to validate his position, eliminating everything that does not correspond to that position. Violence, therefore, leads out of the tension of opposites and frees me from my inner division.

We have established that myths are characterized by their *polar structure*. They contain an oppositional tension, a disjunction dividing our environment. When we participate in a myth, we perceive the world in contradictions. I devote myself to education and thereby oppose ignorance. I expend energy for social well-being and strive to eliminate social injustice. When I participate in a myth, I am confronted by two poles that encompass existential challenges: life or death, security or danger, order or chaos, society or individual. The oppositional tension brings differentiation to the theme in question. When we deal with existential challenges, mythical polarity grips us, and it is up to us to find our way out of the dilemma.

Violence means that we have opted in favor of one pole. Through violent action, we free ourselves from ambivalence and decide in favor of one side or the other of the myth. We destroy or eliminate the opposite pole and thereby place ourselves deliberately in opposition to another expression of the myth.

In terms of our lives, this means that we take a position in favor of equality or the liberalizing of the economy or the protection of refugee shelters without considering the counter position. Naturally, we are aware of human differences or of how liberalizing the economy can lead to the exploitation of the workers. Yet, we want to make a decision and to effect something. Violence occurs when we choose to follow only one mythical pole and intentionally ignore or destroy the other one. Violence follows from the feeling of having to find a solution, to finally effect some change. It is no longer a question of pro and con, but only of con.

We men tend to violence, since the tension of opposites is an essential characteristic of our souls. We perceive ourselves and our environment by means of opposites. The oppositional tension is stimulating to us, and we can tolerate it for extended periods. We sense discrepancies and try to position ourselves in relation to them. Confronted by opposites, a woman would be more likely to react ambivalently, perceive them less clearly, register the feeling that both positions have validity, or decide on her attitude at the outset. As a man, I willingly surrender myself to the tension.

A verbal duel, a struggle, and impossibly contradictory positions provoke me. I seek out the oppositional tensions for the sake of finding some solution. Developing a new fighter/bomber makes no sense; the Dallas Cowboys will win the Superbowl; labor/management arbitration is pointless; sending marines to Grenada is morally untenable; golf is for snobs; we have to integrate foreigners more effectively. We men live from and in oppositional tensions. They stimulate us and animate us to renewed activity.

We can observe this in the self-images men conceive of themselves. As a therapist, I have noticed how men's self-image also includes a clearly negative side. In addition to the positive qualities, men also see the egoistic, power-hungry, or narcissistic sides of themselves. Men who go into therapy frequently develop a polar image of themselves so that their good side struggles constantly with an "inner son-of-a-bitch."

When we resort to violence we are trying to free ourselves from one of the fundamental dilemmas of our soul's orientation. We are trying to rid ourselves of the tension and the emotions generated by the opposites. In doing so, we believe we have complied with the task the myth has set for us: the criminal is imprisoned, the bridge is built, the leak is plugged, the country is pacified, or the employee is terminated. Different themes present themselves within the oppositional framework depending on our profession or activity. Through an act of violence we attempt to escape an existential dilemma. We either destroy or incorporate the other, the alien pole, so that the new and better pole of the myth might prevail.

Am I deluding myself in believing I am not violent? Perhaps I have been fortunate enough not to have been provoked to such an extent. Perhaps it has not been my lot to defend one of the underlying myths of our civilization. Under different circumstances, in another era, or as part of another social class, I, too, would have been violent. I, too, would have felt called upon to oppose evil or to resolve the tension of opposites.

One such tension of opposites played a not immaterial role in the outbreak of World War II. A sharp dichotomy marked the public realm in Germany following World War I. The German people felt an existential challenge. The unacceptable national role ascribed to Germany by the Allies, on one hand, and the need for a positive national identity on the other were the cause of the tension. The Allies portrayed Germany as the perpetrator of World War I, forced enormous sums in reparations from her, and decimated the country geographically. At the same time, the

Germans, still nursing their dream of national greatness and a corresponding place in history, could only watch while England and France sunned themselves in their colonial empire. The Germans were torn back and forth between their desire for greatness and accepting their actual, mediocre national role in Europe.

In this situation, National Socialism presented itself as the solution. It offered the vision of greatness and simultaneously provided reasons for the German disgrace and insufficiency in the war. The magnificent Aryans, characterized by discipline, strength, and communal identity, would rise again. The counterpole of this myth, egoism and materialism, the National Socialists projected onto the Jews by declaring them the enemies of German culture. The Jews became the split off opposite to the Nazis' grandiose German myth. The abominable act of eradicating the Jews was supposed to relieve the tension of the opposites.

The extermination of the Jews was declared a heroic act in the perverse assumption that it would assist the Aryan population in taking its rightful place. "Yet, only paradise justifies hell. Therefore the stakes could be nothing less than salvation, than the redemption of the human race. For that reason the Germans took upon themselves—as a mission—the saving crime," says one writer.

The Jews stood for the opposite of what the Germans wanted. The Germans were striving for racial community, while the Jews held out for a parasitic and egotistical existence. This counterpole had to be exterminated for Germany to redeem itself and to attain a more exalted purity and genuine ideals. A German historian observes that, "The Jew was the one and identifiable figure on which the Germans could focus all the anxiety and aggression of their damaged self awareness. With the extermination of the Jews, the modern-day original sin was, symbolically, eradicated, the burden of isolation wiped out, and all disaster of contemporary history transformed back into a suprahuman salvation secured in superiority."

The Germans committed the outrage as the "saving crime" to make possible their redemption. For such a goal, they were willing to take on this monstrosity. The destruction of the Jews did not appear to them as evil, but seen in the light of the common goal, as an "unconscious yearning for a new life." They resorted to violence in the hope of transformation.

The similar, age-old yearning also manifests itself in the horrifying ethnic "cleansing" carried out by the Serbs in Bosnia-

Herzegovina. To them the Croats and especially the Muslims represent the counterpole of their national myth. For the goal of Greater Serbia, the Serbs have been capable of the most disgusting and disgraceful of actions. The myth of national identity demands this "sacrifice" of them and brands the "other," the foreigner, a threatening presence. Instead of confronting the counterpole position in a ritual struggle, the Serbs think in terms of "solutions," of extermination.

Unfortunately, we can observe similar tendencies in certain youth groups in Germany. Behind their attacks on Vietnamese and Turks hides the attempt to come to terms with the uncertainty that the German national identity brings with it. These youth groups, too, act out of a tension of opposites. They are reacting against the collective image celebrated by the politicians and in the media. They hear a double standard in reassurances of German peacefulness and of generosity and openness toward foreigners. They are suspicious when politicians send out the message that the rest of the world has nothing to fear from Germany. They sense the unbelievable forces concealed in Germany's shadow.

The national ideal serving Germans as their orientation reveals itself to be a defensive, magical spell. Where do we see the feelings of superiority, the rejection of all that is foreign, and the claims to uniqueness existing for centuries in German culture? German youth's acts of violence are the despairing attempt to bring the full breadth of the national myth to life so it can be fought out directly.

In their own eyes, the youth groups' violence is grandiose. Through their actions they have hit a sensitive nerve in the German people. Their terrible feats have released emotions, fear, dismay, and serious discussions. To provoke a reaction to what they say and do, they chose the insignia of the National Socialists for themselves. They have made the need for greatness—something very natural in a country of Germany's size—into a theme, and have taken up the Third Reich as their metaphor. Effect is important for them. The notion of past greatness mobilizes energy for all Germans and awakens the sleeping dragons.

The problematic aspect in all of these examples is their one-sidedness. Every myth has two sides, a light one and a dark one. Violence arises when we live out only one side of a myth. If we are starry-eyed enough to live out only the positive pole, the neglected one will force itself violently upon us. We have to acknowledge both mythical poles as possibilities. As Swiss, American, or English, we are not simply tolerant, appreciative of foreigners, and fascinated by what is strange and different, but have at the same time powerful feelings of rejection for the unknown and alien. When we identify with the culture in which we grew up, if we participate in the myth of our homeland, we feel superior to those from other nations. During their early contacts the indigenous Australians considered the whites inferior, because the poor beings had no knowledge of Aboriginal dream time.

We may not leave the expression of these split-off feelings to right-wing, radical youth groups. We have to consciously acknowledge them in ourselves just as the pre-war Germans should have acknowledged their simple-mindedness and egoism instead of projecting it onto the Jews. Only in this way can we hope that acts of violence will not be carried out concretely, but will be understood as challenges within a mythical arena.

From different historical examples we have learned the impossibility of splitting off the counter pole of a myth. The beginning of the French Revolution took place in 1789 with the storming of the Bastille. In 1793 King Louis XVI was beheaded and Robespierre's Reign of Terror followed. The revolution eradicated everything aristocratic in the name of *liberté, égalité, fraternité*. The revolutionaries, however, forgot that those who are not equal, the aristocracy, for instance, are part of the myth of equality. No sooner had the French nobility been executed or driven out of the country than a counter current promptly set in and reached its peak in Napoleon's crowning himself as emperor. All this despite the democratic sentiments of the revolution's credo.

A similar development accompanied the Communist takeover in Russia. After the "glorious" October Revolution of 1917 and the brutal shooting of the Czar's family, the revolutionaries did not establish the rule of the proletariat, but a new dictatorship. Stalin, Khrushchev, and Brezhnev ruled just as brutally and dictatorially as Nicholas I, only under different principles. Since the aristocracy, the counterpole had been physically eliminated and was no longer present in the public realm, the creative, revolutionary act degenerated, becoming the opposite of what the revolutionaries had originally intended. The split-off pole revenged itself and took over control.

What is the upshot of my argument? A friend told me of a strange experience. He shared an apartment with a black man from Panama. For six months everything went well. In time, though, the many guests the Panamanian invited for supper and their criticism of our society began to get on his nerves. To be sure, he usually agreed with the accusations: we are racists, oppress minorities, and exploit the Third World. Yet, suddenly, after one lengthy discussion accompanied by global criticism of the West, my friend lost his temper and cried out, "If you go on carping about our culture and using the color of your skin as an excuse for your own problems, I'll give you a plane ticket back to Africa. Simple!" Profoundly shocked at his emotional outburst, he tried later to apologize to his roommate. He wished he could have bitten his tongue off to avoid his thoughtless comments.

Strangely enough, from that day on his relationship with his roommate was more relaxed. They mutually liked and respected one another. Their relationship had been dominated by the myth that there are no racial differences and that xenophobia is unknown among civilized human beings. My friend had not acknowledged his racist attitude, his feelings of superiority, and his xenophobia to himself—and those feelings became split off.

As men we have to guard against denying our negative ideas and feelings. Violence results when we fail to acknowledge our brutal fantasies, destructive ideas, and impossible desires. We need to accept these inner currents as the opposite pole to the light side of our myth. We do not become noble by pretending to be noble. We must never eliminate or split off the counterpole, but have to respect it as the other side of our conscious attitude. As men we need places where we curse, swear, and can express ideas that are inconsistent with our considered, conscious attitude. In public life there should be room for such inappropriate thoughts and tolerance for our fellow human beings who dare to express such notions. If we can acknowledge our inadmissible images and ideas, there may be hope that they will lend us energy and motivate us truly to work for transformation.

"I would love to grab you by the hair, give you a shove, and rub your face in the mud," my biology teacher growled shortly before my high-school graduation. I was shocked. How could he dare to talk that way to a pupil? His face, however, betrayed a smile. He had admitted to a fantasy that had sprung to his mind when I failed to show much interest for his subject. The image carried energy, conveyed a message, and because he delivered it playfully, motivated me to take biology more seriously.

I am suspicious of men who pretend not to be violent, who
behave peaceably, and claim they are open, tolerant, and friendly.
I am suspicious of men who pretend never to enjoy scenes of violence or never to have grandiose fantasies. They frighten me. I
wonder when and where their repressed demons will make themselves known?

## RAPE

Sexual violations also belong to the shadow of the male soul. The
most frequent form of sexual outrage is not the compulsive perpetrator, who climbs into a woman's apartment at night, ties her to
the bed, and violates her sexually. Neither is it the reclusive, unob-
trusive man who violates twenty-three women on the street by forcing them with a drawn pistol to satisfy him manually or orally. The
most common form of sexual violation are the hundreds of
molestations that occur in semi-private life. These offenses share
the common element with pathological ones of occurring outside
the circle of the perpetrator's personal acquaintances.

In addition, I will here direct my attention to the innumer-
able violations that take place in the personal realm. The friend
who unexpectedly forces his attention on a woman who has
invited him in for a cup of coffee. The colleague who makes a
pass on the way to the car in an underground parking garage.
Like violence, sexual violation or molestation offends against the
integrity and worth of other human beings. Both are ethically
and morally reprehensible. This circumstance does not release
us, however, from the task of tracing the significance of sexual
violation for the male soul. Although only a small fraction of men
violate women, we must ask about the meaning to the soul of
rape. To answer this question, we will first examine the place of
sexuality in and for men.

According to the perspective of our culture, sexuality should
remain in the private sphere. Sexuality is a wonderful vehicle for
mutual communication between men and women. It allows us to
devote ourselves to our fantasies and to experience physical sen-
suality, thus enriching our intimate relationships. By means of sexuality, we express our relationship to another human being, show
our love and esteem, and allow him or her to share our sensual
ferocity. Sexuality belongs, according to common consensus, in

the private realm. Demonstrations of love in the public realm are subject to various taboos. By relegating sexuality to the private realm we simultaneously subordinate it to psychology. In public, sexuality glimmers through eroticized behavior, but our culture only allows this expression to a limited degree. We consider a public display of pronounced erotic energy a professional invitation for the dispensing of sexual favors. Our culture has effectively banned sexuality from the public realm.

The situation was not always so. As some researchers describe it, "pilgrimages to the kingdom of desires" belonged to the image of a "public man" of the eighteenth century. Men lived sexuality as an *impersonal act*, whether in bordellos, with prostitutes, or with other women. Relationship was not the primary emphasis, but sexuality for its own sake. The French considered, *l'heure bleue,* the hour immediately following work and prior to returning to wife and children, the time for impersonal sexuality, the hour of lovers. People did not have to live sexuality exclusively in the private sphere, but could experience it as a quality of the impersonal realm as well.

Men perceive sexuality as impersonal more than do women. The male soul is drawn to sexuality in the public realm. I mean that for men sexuality does not have to be bound to relationship or be an experience they share with a select woman. Rather it is a force that manifests itself in the outer world. Men turn their heads when an attractive girl walks by and react immediately if a waitress is wearing a low-cut blouse. Their reaction seems to be relatively undifferentiated—to the irritation of many women. It is not a question of appreciating a beautiful physique or a pretty face, the way many women do with men. Men's head turning happens almost as a reflex. Men are capable of neglecting a beautiful wife, because they are fantasizing about an unknown woman on the subway. This aspect of male sexuality is often hurtful to women. They gaze at the exhausted Romeo, who once again has nodded off in front of the television, and ask themselves whatever became of the fiery suitor and lover from way back when. They do not want to be reduced to the roles of wife and mother, but would also like to experience themselves as seductress or woman of the night.

One night, during my military service, I sat with others from my company in a bar. I mentioned in passing I was going to be the co-director of a camp for eighteen women between the ages of twenty and twenty-five. It was like throwing a match into a box of sparklers. The men painted scenarios of how all these women of the

night would fall all over me. Several threw envious glances in my
direction. What annoyed me, however, were not just the men's
insinuations, but the fact of how familiar I was with similar fantasies.

Problematic for men is their experience of sexuality as an
outer world fascination. The thought of an impersonal sexual
encounter with an unknown woman carries a powerful attraction
for them. Such attraction stems from the longing to experience
sexuality in a masculine way without awkward psychologizing.
Men are looking for an encounter with the anima, itself, and not
one with Michelle Carpenter from Peoria, Illinois.

With the exception of dance halls and discos, our culture has
largely de-sexualized the public realm. Roles men take on in public do not define the sexual aspect of their being. We consider flirt-
ing to be a prelude, an invitation to relationship, while impersonal
eroticism is either not an issue or has been relegated to prostitution. Not only do we not cultivate impersonal sexuality, we scorn it
and have withdrawn it as an experiential possibility from the realm
occupied by myths. Men as well as women, therefore, encounter
sexuality not through mythological figures, through the archetypes, but through psychology. We have psychologized sexuality.
Only relationship permits sexuality. Otherwise it is punished. For
this reason, we cannot live out sexuality by way of mythical models
as was possible, for instance, with temple prostitutes in Greece.
Sexuality has become a purely personal affair. Consequently, we
only encounter sexuality's distorted forms in the public realm.
Aside from naked women at newsstands—which are now discretely
covered—and the tiresome sex films on television, sexuality has no
place in the outer world.

I consider sexual violations to be pathological attempts to
experience sexuality in the public or semi-public sphere. From
the perspective of the masculine soul, perpetrators are trying to
return the absent feminine to this realm. They want to encounter
the feared, fascinating, and arousing feminine directly without
having to become involved psychologically with a woman. They
are seeking sexuality, per se, as an impersonal act. Violations in
the public or semi-public realm are the abnormal attempt to
engage sexuality mythically. Men need to live the archetype of sexuality without the troublesome complications arising from personal relationships. They need to encounter Woman as the
powerful counterpole to the masculine orientation. Through
rape, a man can also separate himself from the feminine and

reconnect with his masculine orientation without having to come to terms with psychology.

He had molested five women. One mother with an infant he waylaid in a pedestrian underpass. With erect penis he advanced on the woman pushing a stroller in front of her. With a confused expression on his face he looked at her and pushed his penis against her skirt. The irate woman was able to defend herself. Now this seventeen-year-old, would-be rapist sits before me, a skinny little boy, who hardly dares to speak and turns red if I try to talk to him about girls. No, he does not know any girls his own age. His attempts at rape were impersonal actions: he was looking for the Feminine. Since our culture offers no ritualized forms for impersonal sexuality, this young man turned to rape for an initiation into the uncanny world of sexuality. As my conversations with him showed, women for him were not individuals, but half-real, even mythical figures.

Feelings of fear and anxiety always accompany confrontations with our mythical depths, since the powerful forces of myths endanger our ego position. When we are gripped by the power of a myth, we sense a shudder, a shock, or an unusual fascination. As Mircea Eliade notes, "The God of mystics and theologians is terrifying and sweet in one." The encounter with the myth conveys depth to our experience.

This fear and fascination also surfaces in cases of molestation. By contrast to other mythically motivated activities, men do not take on the feelings of fear, themselves, but project them onto the woman. Although men register fear in other situations, on the job, in wartime, and during duels, for example, in cases of rape, the victim is the one seized with panic. The victim lives out the fear, thereby granting the act archetypal qualities and locating the mythical terror. From a mythological perspective, the victim participates unwillingly in a degenerated ritual invoking a myth. The perpetrator seeks union with the Feminine, itself, with a mythical figure. Therefore, in instances of sexual molestation, the man errs by not taking on the terror and the fear the way fighter pilots, mountain climbers, or adventurers do. Instead, he cowardly delegates these feelings to his victim.

Actually, women should return the fear to the men. Were women not to react with fear and shock when they were molested, it is imaginable that the demons would fall back on the perpetrator and cause him panic. Modern forms of self-defense emphasize this phenomenon. By defending themselves, women show their unwillingness to assume the terror and to carry it by themselves. Instead, they send it back to the perpetrator who then, paradoxically, is more likely to find what he was seeking. In the Dionysian mysteries, the maenads gave themselves over to ecstasy and, wildly excited, traveled through the villages teaching men to fear. In the same way, men prone to sexual molestation must learn to fear. Be that as it may, as long as our culture possesses no public, ritualized forms of eroticism, the problem of impersonal, mythical sexuality will continue to exist.

## DELUSIONS OF GRANDEUR

> *"I am the greatest."*
> —Mohammed Ali

Men with delusions of grandeur are suffering from exaggerated grandiosity. Their notions of greatness seize them, and they ascribe superior, personal influence to themselves. They may believe they are brilliant inventors, new Messiahs, or the personification of a new movement. They have lost their contact with reality, overvalue themselves, and can no longer assess their influence realistically. Delusions of grandeur are forms of grandiosity exaggerated to the extent that those in question identify with a myth instead of allowing themselves to be directed and ensouled by it. One psychologist has described delusions of grandeur as a condition of the "public persona." Such a man confers cosmic significance on his actions, considers himself to be an all-father figure, a new prophet, or at least an extremely important figure in public life. In chapter 4 I describe how grandiosity could inspire a man to greater performances out of a sense of being so close to the myth. Here I am speaking of grandiosity's pathological dimension.

Psychiatrists have described delusions of grandeur as a mental disturbance, a psychosis in which the individual identifies with a figure from politics, business, culture, or history. He believes himself to be the President of the United States, a famous movie star, Napoleon, or Einstein. Women suffering from psychotic delusions of this kind confer noble or aristocratic lineage on themselves. Men, on the other hand, see themselves as significant figures from public life.

Mark David Chapman believed he was John Lennon. At work he wore the name tag, "John Lennon," over his own and married a Japanese woman four years his senior. (Yoko Ono was six years older than Lennon). When he quit his last job, he signed Lennon's signature. Lennon was the figure from public life with whom Chapman identified. Since, in his mind, he was the true John Lennon, he had to kill the "false" John Lennon.

Delusions of grandeur manifest themselves in *persistent feelings of superiority*. A man with these delusions feels he is better than others and believes he possesses unique characteristics or capabilities. The psychological literature describes the case of a sixteen-year-old who suffered a psychotic break during a trip to Paris. In therapy, it became apparent that he perceived himself as someone unusual. Because he had received the best grade in his class on one assignment, he felt he was "top of his class." A subsequent trip to Paris gave him the feeling of being a "world traveler." The class assignment and the trip to Paris triggered feelings of superiority, and his public persona became intensely narcissistic. Additionally, his sense of his own uniqueness made him believe he would find a place among his peers and overcome his personal isolation.

In these cases, the identification as well as the self-overvaluation point to an exaggeration of the public persona. At the same time, the integrity of the personality can be maintained completely even with extreme delusions of grandeur and feelings of superiority. The individual assigns himself a prominent role and believes he is extremely important with important tasks to perform. This sense of his own greatness frequently stands in blatant contrast to the importance those around him perceive.

A man I knew lectured at one of the psychology institutes in Zurich. At his own insistence, he had been invited to come to Zurich from another country and speak on the topic of his recently published book. The lecture had been announced well in advance. When I asked how his talk had been received, he proudly informed me the audience had given him a five-minute standing ovation. I was naturally impressed, little suspecting that his audience had consisted of only three people.

At the same time, a man's overvaluation of his public persona can have a very positive effect on morale at work. A middle-aged man who worked for a city sanitation department was happy to let me know how he and his supervisor had decided to order different brooms. The brooms from Taiwan they had been using, although inexpensive, wore out very quickly. He had, therefore, recommended that the management purchase more expensive Swiss brooms that would last longer and be more economical in the long run. The department's management had enthusiastically accepted his proposal. According to his account, the management had decided to distribute Swiss brooms to all of the city's employees thanks solely to this man's intervention. He obviously considered himself one of the most important men in his department. I, myself, was a little skeptical, since he held a rather subordinate position with the city. As a street sweeper, he was seldom if ever asked for his opinion and could only perform his job under the direction of his immediate superior. He had never met his boss face to face. Nevertheless, his overvaluation of his position involved him in his work and made it interesting for him.

A characteristic of a man's overvaluation of his public persona is the absence of any counter positions that might relativize his position. In extreme cases, the public persona expands and grows until it suddenly bursts and collapses on itself. Men with such notions of greatness know no boundaries. They expand farther and farther, wanting to see themselves in an ever brighter limelight. Intentionally imitating Charlemagne, Napoleon I had himself crowned hereditary emperor in Paris on December 2, 1812. President Sese-Seko Mobutu of Zaire commanded his officials to hang his portrait over every crucifix. Nicolaie Ceausescu built a gigantic governmental palace in Bucharest out of megalomaniacal blindness. These men attributed divine importance to themselves, believing that they were predestined to assume a public or national responsibility. They had received the "call" and, for better or worse, had to devote themselves to this overvalued undertaking. Clearly, they had overstepped the boundary between a healthy identification with a supraordinate myth and self-delusion.

Someone suffering from delusions of grandeur and the overvaluation of his public persona is identifying with a mythical figure. In this inflation, he becomes the carrier of the myth instead of remaining the myth's humble servant. The temptation to overvalue ourselves is great when we hold office and recognition or have become public figures. It is easy to accept the mythical projections of the public personally. We then live the myth.

Men with delusions of grandeur or who overvalue their public persona are capable of developing unbelievable strength and energy. Their energy comes from living one side of the archetype manifesting itself in the myth. This personal identification with the myth, however, can also lead to existential loneliness. Gods are alone. Because they lack the counterpole, they live in a desolation of soul. They, therefore, unconsciously seek a catastrophe to bring them down from the heaven of the gods. An inflated overvaluation of their role is inevitably followed by a collapse, since the soul cannot bear to live out a myth. The character of Nixon, in Oliver Stone's film of the same name, is a good example of this phenomenon.

## SELF-GLORIFICATION

We find a similar overvaluation of one's own person in a condition related to delusions of grandeur, namely, self-glorification or egomania. In this pathology, the individual does not identify with a cause, a social responsibility, a position, or a mission. Instead, he "loves himself best" and is convinced that he is the most interesting of human beings. An egomaniac waits for an appropriate position in a corporation, in academia, or in business to confirm his sense of his own greatness. His primary focus is his own personality, and he declares himself to be a worthy object of general interest. His ambition is directed toward promoting himself, for he, himself, is the goal and the vehicle of his notions of greatness. His fantasized public persona is filled with narcissism. Egomaniacs tend to cultivate their lifestyle unduly and are convinced that they deserve more than other people. In their minds, their ideas are highly interesting, their hobbies most unusual, and their plans and projects uniquely original.

Although unintentionally, mothers frequently propel their children toward egomania. They express fascination at how their son develops ideas and begins projects. A six-year-old boy draws up plans for a hydroelectric dam. An eight-year-old recognizes the flags of all the sea-going nations. The nine-year-old son has already published a newspaper as part of his schoolwork. Since they cannot personally relate to this level of interest for things outside the private realm, mothers genuinely believe their sons have extraordinary abilities. Because she reacts psychologically, a mother only reflects the personal aspects to her son. She interprets his budding mythological interest psychologically: "you are an extraordinary human being," is the message she sends. She mistakes his mythical orientation for his personality.

Egomaniacs may conceal their pathology beneath an apparently hypercritical attitude toward life in general. They sit, self-satisfied, in a bar or at home, holding court for colleagues from work, acquaintances, or their family. They complain about "corrupt politicians," the miserable state of the country, and the world at large. Their hypercritical verbosity or monologues serve as justification to themselves and others for not engaging the public realm. Of course, he would do a better job of it, yet why should he have anything to do with "these idiots?" The egomaniac belongs to no political party, because no party suits him. For him, just participating in a demonstration or signing an initiative seems to be intensive political activity. Egomaniacs convey to their environment the message that they can (and will) do it all better as long as a throne is held in constant readiness for them. Their self-centeredness, with its noticeable disinterest for others' activities, often betrays them. As a projective defense, they suspect material power-driven motives behind the efforts of their fellow human beings. Cynicism not uncommonly colors their judgment of other people. The egomaniac stages himself, directs his own greatness within *his private circle*, and fears the confrontation with the public realm.

Such men may be too ambitious to chance the move into the public realm. They dramatize themselves without the wider public taking any notice of them. They hesitate to plunge into the turmoil, but expect honor and recognition from those around them. Should they finally obtain an outer-world position, they become even more expansive and feel legitimized in presenting even the most tenuous of ideas under the guise of that position. Perhaps they unconsciously fear that their notions of themselves might be criticized by the public.

The egomaniac has never risked entering public life and displays disrespect for the outer world's myths by living his own life as a myth. Others may consider him extremely musical, yet he refuses to learn to play an instrument. Perhaps he is rumored to speak three or four languages, but does not speak them for fear of disgracing himself through incorrect pronunciation. He may be said to be extremely sensitive and cannot, therefore, have anything to do with other people. In cases of delusions of grandeur, a man identifies with the myth. Egomaniacs autistically dramatize their perception of myth in private.

An acquaintance, who demonstrated tendencies to egomania, attracted attention by furnishing the apartment he shared with his fiancée entirely according to his own needs. There was no space for guests in the living room, because he used it for his hobby of building model airplanes. Visitors had to be content with two chairs and a small sofa and were rewarded by being allowed to marvel at the completed and semi-completed works of their host. Another room served as his office and the common bedroom was littered with his books and sports equipment. On the walls hung pictures of the man, himself, and in conversation, during which he completely ignored any common themes, architecture, his own field of expertise, soon dominated. Guests quickly realized that they had entered a small, private kingdom.

The egomaniac identifies himself with a myth as well. Unlike the man with grandiose delusions, though, he does not live out the myth in the public realm, but in private. The egomaniac uses the private sphere to stage his notions of greatness, although he often hides them behind a psychological facade. Seen superficially, he gives the impression that he has made private life and his personal relationships the primary focus of his life. In reality, he only uses them to play out his grandiosity. A compromised mythologist conceals himself in his psychological attitude. Psychology is not really his focus, but a means of misusing his personal mythology. Behind apparent shyness and public reticence is a self-anointed king.

He is the great thinker who has never been challenged, the great actor who never played a role, or the quintessential citizen who has never assumed public responsibility. The egomaniac's attitude cannot be religious. Rather than believing in the transcendent power of mythical models, he has canonized himself as a mythical figure. Music does not evoke emotions or stir up human reactions, but merely provides a possibility for him to show what a brilliant musician he is. He attempts to compromise the myths by avoiding the oppositional tension characterizing mythical arenas. Instead of exposing himself to the difficulties, the shadow aspects, and the polarities of mythical tensions, he withdraws into his inner world and distances himself from the mythical struggle with his grandiose notions.

Depression is the greatest danger for egomaniacs. Their catastrophe comes from inside and begins when the carefully constructed system collapses or the internal self-congratulations fail.

## PSYCHOLOGICAL CRIPPLES

I will just mention the man who is completely mythologically oriented as the last male pathology. These are men who totally
neglect their psychology. Such men have no capacity for relationship and neither reflect on their personal life situation nor accept
their personal biography as a factor in their thoughts and actions.
These are extreme rationalists, who view the world around them
only from a mythological perspective. Because of their one-sided
orientation, they have difficulty recognizing the individual human
being in the policeman, the bank clerk, the teacher, or the salesman. They reduce other individuals to public or collective roles.
His profession, alone, is important for the psychological cripple.
Only his career receives any attention even when his wife sits
home suffering from depression and his children know their
father from watching him on television.

The psychological cripple is incapable of registering his own
feelings and is often characterized by his level of insensitivity in
relationships. I will not address this form of pathology further
here since a number of other books and articles on male psychology have already addressed this topic.

## SUMMARY

Compulsive gambling, an exaggerated need for honor and recognition, violence, delusions of grandeur, and self-glorification are
among the most remarkable male pathologies. We could also add
other pathologies such as workaholism, alcoholism, or various,
specific neuroses to this list. As I mentioned, however, the goal of
this chapter is not to elaborate a definitive pathology for men, but
rather to point out how male pathology might appear from the
mythological perspective. My hope in presenting this brief
mythopathology is that the reader might sharpen his awareness
for the possible relationships between a soul disturbance in a man
and his mythology.

I have described two categories of male pathologies here.
The first concerns disturbances in which men are not engaged in
the interplay of archetypal forces. Men suffering from pathologies
in the second category succumb to a myth, because of a weak ego
and a limited capacity for self-reflection. The egomaniac, who in

my experience we find quite frequently today, fails to see the existential challenge that myths create.

Men with these conditions seek the *tremendum*, the horror, the dread, the fascination, or the euphoria of myths. They want to feel the mythical spark of divinity, although it is too much for them. Due to their soul's disorientation, they withdraw from the public realm (self-glorification, egomania), stage their own direct, self-destructive confrontation with the myth (compulsive gambling, addiction to fame and glory), or identify with a myth (delusions of grandeur). All of these pathologies compensate for the feeling of being excluded by the divine power of myth. Perhaps these men—the compulsive gambler and the addict to recognition as well as men suffering from delusions of grandeur, violent outbursts, or self-glorification—hope for the divine, enlivening spark, for contact with the suprahuman power of myth to give them purpose and meaning for their existence. Lacking a *temenos* to connect them with the corresponding myth, they live out mythical aberrations. Finding it impossible to define their roles in the light of a myth, these men avoid any confrontation in the public realm.

The myths shaped in the public realm draw men to them. Men need to register and confront the forces "out there," whether at work, in politics, in sports, or in culture. In this regard, our culture needs to strengthen men so that they are prepared to face the struggle in the outer world. The public realm, however, will devastate anyone who withdraws into the private realm, builds his identity exclusively on his private persona, and follows only his private interests. The "great necessities of life" (Freud) demand a mythical answer and a grandiose resolution.

If our culture forgets or fails to support the connection men have to the public realm, that realm will suffer. Additionally, if we do not recognize men's mythical role, they will flee into pathology or concentrate primarily upon psychology. They will no longer allow themselves to be ensouled by the myths, but will assume a feminine definition of existence. No society can survive unless at least some of its members are willing to take up the struggle with the myths.

# 6

## The Tension between Archaic Savagery and Overcivilization

♂

## Mythotherapy for Men

Men's relationship to psychotherapy is ambivalent. On one hand there is a small number of differentiated men who are willing to work on themselves, to reflect on their personal feelings, and to take personal aspects seriously when they suffer from soul's problems. Opposing them are the vast majority of men who categorically refuse therapy. For them to turn to a therapist would be a sign of weakness or proof of extensive mental disturbance. Work, profession, hobbies, or politics are important for them, not time spent in psycho-babble. Feminism demands of these men to think differently, to be prepared to look at themselves. Are they really resistive to therapy?

I am convinced that the problem lies not with men, but with the existing therapeutic perspective. If therapy focuses on the personal, on everyday relationships, private life, and individual biography, it fails to address the male soul. Mythical existence and the public persona are excluded. Psychotherapy for men requires consideration of other aspects. Therapy must again bring men face to face with existential challenges, address their public persona, and direct attention toward the breadth of their mythical environment. In this process the therapist cannot simply take the position of the empathetic companion, but must also play a devil's advocate role to constellate the mythical tension.

The orientation of soul differentiates the sexes. Women experience themselves as psychological beings, while men attempt to realize themselves through mythical patterns. With this in mind, we might ask what therapy for men might look like? In the first chapter, I describe how most men instinctively avoid therapy. They sense that therapy's emphasis upon the private, personal, and relational is one-sided and foreign to their being. They sense that the masculine requires a different form of therapy. The conventional therapeutic approach of working through the personal biography does not provide the help many men are looking for. A part of the man's soul balks at digging through childhood experiences, discussing the relationship with parents, seeking out solutions, and reflecting on the relationship to the therapist. The confidential, personal atmosphere of the consulting room does not touch the core of the male soul.

A well-known psychotherapist sent a publisher a manuscript for a book. He offered the small publishing house exclusive rights to this book. He effusively assured the publisher that he had chosen this company because he felt it would do the best job and had the most impressive list of other publications. The publisher and his editor studied the manuscript and discussed the possibility of publishing it. The contents were interesting, for the author had written from his experience. In a convincing way, he asserted that only someone who was "genuine" could be effective as a therapist. Psychotherapists, he went on, should practice according to their beliefs and feelings and not manipulate their clients. While the publisher considered whether to publish the book, he discovered by chance that another company had listed the work in its catalog. Apparently, the author had not felt it necessary to inform the first publisher about his multiple submissions and the impending publication by the second publisher. Does this seem like the action of someone who is "genuine?"

This anecdote points up a further problem of psychological therapy. Although psychology may reflect on, analyze, and, perhaps, even heal the private persona, the public persona remains untouched. In the private realm, an individual may be conscious and well-adapted, while in public his demons may be completely unrecognized, let alone directed or controlled. While a man, therefore, may present himself in private as genuine and self-reflective, a completely different and unconscious side comes out in his public life. Publicly he is capable of betrayal, power-seeking, insensitivity, and even violence, not to mention a rebellious attitude, perseverance, capriciousness, and originality. Traditional therapies do not speak to this public, mythical area of a man's life.

We need another kind of therapeutic approach, another setting, a different language to address men's mythical side and to
enable them to recognize issues of masculine orientation. We
have to broaden therapy to include the mythical dimension. Only
in this way can men come to terms with the suffering, the shadow
aspects, the difficulties, and the fears they encounter in their
engagement with myths.

## MYTHOGRAPHY

> While I was still a child, we did not have the economic prosperity of today.
> It was during the depression and sacrifice was necessary. At fourteen, I got
> my own chest-of-drawers as was the custom in middle-class families of the
> time. At sixteen, I was allowed to wear long pants for the first time and to
> go out in the evening. The political climate was not good, though. The
> Germans had just occupied Paris.

Listening to this man, we notice how he connects his personal
experiences with events of the time. His first chest-of-drawers
reminds him of the economic situation, and he connects the
beginning of his social life to phases of the war. Although he is
telling about his childhood, parallel themes of the outer world
interrupt him. Politics, the economy, thoughts about his social
class, and the general state of affairs invade his personal narrative.
Could he be avoiding the subject at hand?

This childhood narrative points to a disposition in men that
therapy must take into consideration. When men reflect on their
personal lives, they tend to include their background myths. If
they try to focus on their personal history, to recall significant personal events and situations, collective themes push forward as
well. Behind these themes lie concealed the myths that influenced
them. They recall the national economy, particular technical
developments, political events, the different social structures, or
the mood of the nation at large. Therapy must attend to this mythical context that influences men so powerfully.

Masculine therapy must, therefore, begin with *mythography*.
Therapists need to identify the mythical environment in which men
grew up and that characterized the region of their childhood. A
therapy for men does not focus initially on a personal anamnesis,
but attempts to get an overview of the myths in which the client lives.
What, for example, was the mythic environment of his birthplace?

Recognizing these myths is frequently difficult. We are either not conscious of them or we have split them off or psychologized them. If I think back to my own childhood, isolated memories come to my mind: driving in the car through a flooded street or an incident in elementary school. How could I start a mythography with this material? If we hope to recognize and reconstruct the mythology of our childhood, we need a gradual and systematic approach. We can recognize the myths when we view our family and region of origin from an outside perspective. Instead of restricting ourselves to family history as the gateway to our soul's history, we need to extend our gaze to include the breadth of our environment. What characteristics were attributed to the inhabitants of the town or city in which I grew up? What effect did these qualities and the general environment have on me?

Rudolf Steiner (1861–1925), who reports of his childhood that it was "things, not the personal, which challenged" him, writes:

> When I was a year-and-a-half old, my father was transferred to Modling near Vienna. There my parents remained for half a year. Then my father was placed in charge of the little station, Pottschach, on the southern line in lower Austria, close to the border. There I spent the time from my second to my eighth year. A beautiful landscape surrounded my childhood. The panorama extended to the mountains that separate lower Austria from Steiermark: the Schneeberg, Wechsel, Raxalp, Semmering. With its barren rock near the peak, the Schneeberg caught the rays of the sun, and what they heralded, reflecting from the mountain toward the little train station, was the first greeting on lovely summer mornings. . . .
>
> At the little train station, however, all interest focused on the railroad. In those days, trains only passed through the region at considerable intervals. When they did arrive, there was usually a crowd of people, who had time, gathered from the village. . . .
>
> I feel that it was significant for my life to have experienced my childhood in such an environment. My interest was drawn strongly to the mechanical aspects of this existence. And I know how this interest again and again would darken that portion of my childish soul going out toward graceful and, simultaneously, generous Nature into whose distance the trains, submitting to mechanical laws, would each time disappear.

Steiner's childhood memories bear traces of a mythography, in which the interaction between Spirit and Nature, between the technological and the earthly, comes through. These external realities occupied Steiner throughout his life.

Frequently, attributed qualities can further mythographic analysis. There are behavioral patterns and peculiarities that supposedly characterize groups of people or regions. The inhabitants of Fallanden, a village near Zurich, are said to indulge in extensive celebrations and orgiastic bouts of drinking. Students of the Free Gymnasium in Zurich were accused of elitist, intellectual narrow-mindedness and snobbery, while the Guggenbühl family, who came from the right bank of Lake Zurich, were known for their strong hands. Mythic images are often concealed behind such simplistic characterizations. Strong hands point to a Protestant myth that marks my family of origin: work gives life meaning. The accusation of snobbery betrays the social hierarchy constellated around every school. Such apparently superficial attributes provide keys to the myths in which we all subtly participate.

Even clichés can provide mythographic clues. Students majoring in psychology are accused of being, "not entirely normal," and of studying psychology because of their own psychological difficulties. A psychologist would indignantly reject such accusations, recognizing them as defenses or an avoidance of one's own difficulties. From the mythical perspective, though, this accusation includes some truth. Naturally, psychology students are no crazier than other students, but they weigh abnormality differently. They do not exclude unusual, pathological, bizarre, or strange behavior, but see it as a source for change. According to this myth, dark becomes light, fecal matter becomes gold. The accusations or the clichés suggest the very myth that grips many students of psychology.

Mythographic therapy would also direct its attention to the myths developed by a client's social grouping. To legitimize socio-cultural positioning or to make such positioning tolerable, social classes create axiomatic explanations. These explanations define an individual's identity as a member of the class in question as well as how he or she is expected to behave. Members of the upper middle class in Zurich do not consider it appropriate to invest a lot of money in an automobile or to show outward signs of wealth. A member of the English upper class does not take an interest in soccer, technology, or knowledge gained from books. Instead he cultivates his wit and sense of humor.

If someone grows up in the lower class, he probably experiences the effects of the myth that intellectual work is a form of loafing. He may also share an attitude I have observed especially among those from lower class neighborhoods: take advantage whenever possible of those who are better off. When the English rock musician Peter Townsend of The Who appears in faded jeans and a grimy pullover for an interview, he reveals the myth with which he identifies. He is telling us he is "from the street." Even as a multimillionaire, he takes his orientation from the myth of his working-class origins.

Especially in countries with strongly hierarchical class systems, myths have an enormous influence over the behavior and perceptions of the various classes. Class myths determine what an individual thinks, believes, and perceives, even how he plays, talks, and fights. While in one social grouping it is possible to scream at each other without further consequences, in another displeasure is expressed through hints or intimation. The first group orients according to the myth of "being genuine" or "expressing one's real emotions," so its members can live together harmoniously without becoming neurotic. The other group places greatest emphasis upon disciplining one's affects.

A mythography does not concentrate on the personal, but analyzes the message to the soul from an individual's larger environment. The perspective is of breadth, not depth. Mythography does not start with personal relationships, but begins with things, with the outer world, to become acquainted with the *temenoi* that shape and fascinate the client. It filters out the collective and mythical forces that have influenced him. "In Quarter Four where I grew up in the city of Zurich, a special atmosphere reigned," remembers a well-known Swiss writer. "We boys joined together in gangs, wandered the streets, and pelted the rich people with snow balls and clods of mud as they were on their way to shop on the Bahnhofstrasse." This writer orients himself by the myth of a working-class child, who knows the stench of the streets.

Frequently these myths come to light through details in our memory. One analyst I know described how the emphasis on the vertical impressed him in the city in which he grew up. In his memory the city was filled with churches towering impertinently into the sky. He, himself, believes that this characteristic of his hometown colored his personality. He, too, sought for the vertical all his life and to rise above his roots.

A mythographic anamnesis also includes the consideration of the history from the client's family, hometown, and nation. By history, though, I do not mean the written history, but the stories that are told, the orally transmitted history. I mean those things that people in families, in a region, or in a country talk about and want to know about their past. Myths gather their material from the lives of our forebears and the everyday events of the past, selecting the incidents to tell their stories. Like the example of the man from the Swiss interior in the first chapter, historical events sink into the depths of the unconscious. From there they provide mythical material that is referred to depending on the circumstance. That man's rejection of the European Community had its roots in a myth belonging to the region and represented in the remembered historical events. Many men carry traces in their imaginations of the myths from their hometown area or their family of origin.

The late British Labor Party leader, John Smith, is known for his calm temperament and self-assurance. According to the family history, the Smiths are descended from the sole survivors of the Scottish fishing village, Ardrishaig, on the North Sea. All the other inhabitants of the village lost their lives to a typhus epidemic. The story developed into a myth among the descendants and shaped their attitude toward life. They do not easily lose their composure. It is, perhaps, this family myth to which John Smith owes the temperament that allows him to sleep peacefully in the back seat of a car racing through London with flashing lights and wailing siren.

The national myths in which we naturally also participate are often difficult to recognize. When we are surrounded by our native culture, reflecting on it tends to become emotion-laden and banal. We do not discuss the myths of our own country, but our prejudices and clichés about other nations: the Swiss are restrained and egotistical; Germans are unduly thorough and lack a sense of humor; Americans are loud and eat hamburgers. Although we defend ourselves against these clichés, such prejudices can also provide the means for discovering national myths. Behind every national attribute, exaggerated or not, may lie a myth.

National myths may also be concealed behind the affects we express toward foreigners. Especially among European men and young men in particular, their expressions of hate toward citizens of one-time Yugoslavia are frightening. They label them drug dealers, traitors, and thieves, who can only think of violence. These accusers see red when they are even introduced to someone with an eastern European name. No matter how coarse, simplistic, or xenophobic the reproaches, they still point to mythic content. Who are you as a German, an American, a Dutchman? What characterizes you? Therapy needs to make room for xeno-phobic comments so that therapist and client may recognize the latter's national myth.

It is always easier to recognize our own national myths from a distance. Since they rest upon the axiomatic principles a nation develops to master its specific challenges, national myths require some perspective if we are to identify them. Only by living in a for-eign country does an Englishman notice the side of himself that longs for the lifestyle of the landed aristocracy, while someone who is Swiss realizes the importance for his country of personal autonomy. An American, in the same situation, recognizes the propensity his countrymen have for grandiose solutions.

A mythographic anamnesis is a journey of exploration to the myths that touched the client in childhood, adolescence, or adult-hood. The landscape of the soul in which an individual lives emerges in mythography.

## MYTHICAL CORE EVENTS

A successful, forty-five-year-old lawyer reminiscing about his past says,

> I was there when the Globus riot broke out. It was a hot summer. We stood all lined up on one side with the police on the other side. I felt a rage in myself toward this society, toward the war in Vietnam, and the perennial yes-men. We were united. It was clear to me that I could never just fit into this society without voicing criticism. It had to be changed.

The myth of the 1960s had gripped him and continues to influ-ence his behavior today. It serves as his inner orientation.

Therapy for men must uncover this kind of *mythical core event*. I mean those upsetting, frightening, fascinating, or brutal experi-ences that make us feel as if we were cast into the world. I mean experiences that burst the private cocoon of our existence and thrust us into the confrontation with life's impersonal forces. I mean experiences in the realm of a *temenos* that touch us to the quick. We sense an existential challenge and an extraordinary power makes existence appear in a different light. Myths break through in such core experiences, enabling us to recognize myth-ical qualities and the possibility of the soul's regeneration. Core events often take the form of professional difficulties or life's catastrophes. I, myself, remember such an event that had profound meaning for me as a young guitarist.

It was a concert tour. I sat on the stage in a tuxedo before the large audience. After performing two pieces brilliantly, I came to one by the Mexican composer Ponce. I had played "Scherzino Mexicano" on numerous occasions in concert and felt like I could play it standing on my head. The first notes came readily to hand and the music flowed. Suddenly, my fingers sought vainly for the next chord and lost themselves helplessly on the frets. The rest of the piece had disappeared once and for all from my head and my hands. Icy stillness thundered in the hall. Never had an audience been so close and so real.

Curiously, I experienced that moment when every eye in the hall was fixed on me and not the slightest sound could be heard, not as traumatic, but as *divine.* To be sure, it was personally unpleasant, but seen from another perspective, it was "up-setting." It tore me from the limitations of my being, allowing me to feel the overpowering expectations of the audience. I was completely present, had experienced an interruption, and had been freed of my own professional and personal expectations. In that moment, I sensed the limitations the profession of a classical guitarist had brought me.

My failure was a rebellious act through which I forcibly interrupted a socially established pattern and, at the same time, tried to revivify myself. The man in me resisted the perfectly staged musical presentation and refused to become a servant to the composition. From my perspective, my collective act tamed the music so that it lost its demonic and chaotic power. Naturally, I enjoyed the sound of the music, yet no one's soul was touched by it and I, myself, became an onlooker. What at first glance appeared to be a defeat for me, was in reality a mythical core experience.

In a masculine therapy, it is important to reflect on those occasions when the client was caught and lifted above the personal realm. In contrast to personal events or traumas such as a difficult relationship, a ruined marriage, a terrible childhood, or a life-threatening illness, mythical core events take place in an interaction with the outer world, with the myths that find their expression in professions, institutions, or politics.

Mythical core events are often connected with violence, although not necessarily with concrete violence. Violence may express itself as a conscious, aggressive act of will staving off overly civilizing influences: a provoked suspension from school, active opposition to one's boss, or a crusade for a particular political idea. Men seek out this kind of experience to come in contact with the myths and to sense meaning in life.

There are those who seek the mythical connection through concrete acts of violence. The Scottish writer, Alexander Stuart, gives an example in his novel *Tribes:*

> "Let's put the frighteners on them!" the Neck growls, feeling different suddenly, feeling ugly in a powerful way—ugly and beautiful at once in the knowledge of what is to come. And his solid, muscle-ringed throat constricts, as his skull notches back and he calls out to the youths in a voice misinformed with centuries of hate and perfectly pitched to bring dread to their rimorous souls:
>
> *"Oiii!"*
>
> They know. The youths know they're out of luck. They look hopeless for a minute, as the Neck and his mates close in. Even to the Neck they look helpless: young men, younger than him, wearing high-street-smart casual clothes and the fear of God or Allah or whatever it is they believe in on their foreign faces above their foreign moustaches.
>
> So he advances, Trevor and Simon beside him, and the youths stand ready to retaliate, but their hatred is responsive, it doesn't have the clean clear line of stupidity and disgust which fuels the Neck's. And when they run there's nowhere to go, because some shape of things has decreed this beating—this isn't just between the Neck and his mates and the boys, this is something wider, something encouraged by certain newspapers and politicians, by ingrained attitudes that those who settle here, wherever "here" is, must live the way the locals do, the way the Romans tell them to.
>
> And this beating isn't just a beating it's murder. Not that anyone dies, but it's murderously vicious because it has to be: to make a point, to let them know. And because it's fun. . . .
>
> And when he is winded and panting and slick with not only rain but the blood of his prey; when he has given better than he's got, dished out the dirt, taught the coolies a new trick; when his heart is pounding and his lungs are hurting and his head is in some higher sphere of happiness— higher even than the fantasies entertained of crab-legged dollies waiting behind the doors of dawn deliveries before the Post Office untightly gave him the push; when he has chased the last terrified youth to the farthest against boot, jaw against glass; when he has seen the tears in the young man's eyes, and the shattered tooth spat from his lip, and the broken bone protruding through the gash in his tracksuit trousers; when he has punched and locked and stomped the hatred out of him and has no energy or will to do more, he sees the final grope of consciousness in the boy's being and holds back, letting him breathe a moment.
>
> And then he kicks and kicks and kicks and kicks again, murmuring "You cunt! You cunt! You cunt! You filthy cunt!" in time with his blows as

he drives himself beyond pleasure, beyond duty—as if some outside force has taken hold of him and let him watch and experience everything, feel the pain, taste the vomit in the boy's throat, share the welcome rush of darkness enveloping the senses, dulling the suffering, bringing peace.

In war, men often experience the kind of core experiences like the one Stuart describes for Neck. It is unusually touching to hear veterans of World War II who fought in the trenches, were wounded, taken captive, and had horrifying experiences describe their wartime service as the most wonderful time in their lives. As perverse as this may sound, the war for them was a chance to play a part in an impersonal conflict and to participate in mythical forces.

## BOASTING AND SPONTANEOUS SPEECHES FOR IMAGINARY AUDIENCES

Boasting and spontaneous speeches are further important elements of masculine therapy. By boasting I mean the exaggerated presentation of our own performance and abilities. Spontaneous speeches are extended monologues on a theme of interest to the speaker. Boasting takes place in the narrating of *stories* and *dramatic events*, in the telling of vacation experiences, anecdotes, or events at work. I mean stories we usually tell our circle of friends, in a bar, colleagues at work, our partners, or our assembled families. They are stories men insist on telling others whether they are asked or not.

> It was absolutely calm. We sat on the deck of the ship, enjoyed the mood of the evening and our dinner of fish. Suddenly, a voice resounded on Channel 18, a frequency reserved for emergency communications. Highest alarm phase! A hurricane was approaching. In the distance we actually caught sight of a band of black clouds. Thanks only to our immense physical efforts and the competence of our captain were we able to sail out of the danger zone.

With these stories listeners may marvel, be frightened, rejoice with the narrator, or nod here and there. When men boast this way, they often show astonishing self-confidence. Even when they are normally awkward, clumsy, or shy in personal interactions, boasting or spontaneous speeches bring about a change in them. New energies awaken in a man when his tongue loosens. Then those around him get to hear about a canceled vacation, sporting activities, the story in a novel, experiences in military service, the demands of a job, or political opinions. Many use their professions as the focus of their bragging: the company they work for is wonderful or their efforts were extraordinary.

Boasting and speeches are another way of attempting to establish contact with the impersonal realm. When men give way to such stories, they are not looking for dialogue or an exchange with others. These communications are one-sided, their subject matter determined by the speaker's achievements or areas of interest. The listeners' psychology may not interrupt these magnificent narrations.

In therapy, on the other hand, a client tailors his words to the therapist, presenting his story to correspond with the therapist's conscious or unconscious expectations. The psychology of the therapeutic relationship determines the exchange: two human beings encountering each other in their individuality. In masculine therapy, the therapist must not be the focus of attention for boasting and spontaneous speeches. The focus must be on an *imaginary audience,* a circle of friends, forebears, the nation, those at home, or a group of colleagues. When the client begins these presentations, his gaze should not be directed at the therapist, but at the mythical figures he is actually addressing.

Following this approach, it will be possible for a man to revivify his mythical participation. When he boasts and delivers speeches, he is feeling his way toward the great connections in the world and toward his original, existential challenges. He is letting his grandiosity shine through, revealing his dream to just once do or experience something determining and overwhelming. We could see boasting and speech making as a form of self-intoxication. We could see it as a way to avoid the banality of the everyday by connecting primarily with the impersonal challenges of existence. From my perspective, however, speeches and boasting are a man's attempt to revitalize his own mythical canon, to again take possession of mythical substance. Men desire to rediscover their fundamental myths and to experience their mythical relationship with the world. Therapy should serve to breathe life into this mythical substratum of the individual personality.

What a man conveys when he talks this way should not be understood personally, but needs to be interpreted mythologically. When he complains about an "all-nighter," shows his over-filled appointment book, fumes over completely unreliable colleagues, or reports how, with great effort, he was able to meet a deadline, he is narrating a hero myth. He is tired, worn-out, and has a night-sea-journey behind him. The unreliable colleagues or suppliers are the enemy, whom he must fight, outmaneuver, and overcome to reach his goal. We are hearing a heroic epic!

When clients lack the capacity for measured boasting, I try, as a therapist to awaken it. This can be difficult. Many men are plagued by self-doubt and consider their role at work, in the family, or in society to be insignificant.

A forty-year-old man suffered from anxiety attacks at work. Whenever his boss looked over his shoulder, he started trembling. He worried about ending up on the street. He felt inferior to his colleagues, who had taken the traditional educational path, while he had worked his way up by taking classes at night. In therapy he described his professional development haltingly and self-consciously as though he ought to excuse himself because of it. Any tendency to boasting was completely absent. His task in therapy was to learn to see his career differently. Instead of being a failing, his unusual development was a grandiose performance. As an uneducated immigrant in a foreign environment, he had managed to acquire a well-paying job. Reflecting on his Mediterranean origins and the myths of his childhood finally enabled him to be boastful about his profession.

## THE THERAPIST AS DEVIL'S ADVOCATE

In the next phase of therapy, the therapist takes on the role of a devil's advocate. This begins as soon as the client, based on the mythography of boasting, complaining, and spontaneous speeches, has established contact with his most important myths. Now comes the actual dialogue with his personal myth. The speeches and boasting soon resemble self-adulation or hypochondriacal laments, if the therapist does not take up the struggle with the pertinent myth presented through the client.

A myth can grip a client one-sidedly, allowing no room for other perspectives. This one-sided identification with the bright side of the myth leads to inflation. The client then trumpets his philosophy out into the world, believing he has found the Truth and the solution to the world's problems. He does not notice what he has split off. He considers his myth the objective truth and his experience a legitimization of his one-sided attitude. He does not register criticism, since the distinction between subject and object collapse in a myth lived one-sidedly. He considers the meaning system, by which he orients himself, to be the sole reality.

Myths, however, are characterized by a *tension of opposites.* In myth, two forces compete or fight against each other. Each myth, therefore, has two sides. The myth of progress opposes tradition, the appreciation for what has stood the test of time. The belief in technology stands over against the potentials of nature, and health competes with the significance of disease. Myths serve us as axiomatic explanations through which we come to terms with the challenges of human existence. Nevertheless, we must guard against one-sidedness when we permit ourselves to be gripped by a myth. Since myths are always polar, there is always an "underworld," a negative counterpole, that challenges and angers us, makes us uncertain and rejecting. When we are gripped by a myth we are likely to lose the vision of this underworld. We become blinded and see only one side of the myth. Technology solves all problems; wholeness frees me from inner discord; increased personal contact will end interpersonal tensions.

Jung says that, whenever we concentrate on one side of a myth, the other pole will tend to split off; the opposite becomes constellated in the unconscious. The demons come together in the underworld and plan their next appearance. To the myth of technology, then, belong the chaotic forces of nature; to the myth of the hero, the cowardly momma's boy; and to the myth of the understanding teacher, the power hungry know-it-all.

It is the therapist's task to express the counterpole by lending it his voice. In feminine-oriented therapy, the therapist attempts to understand the client from the inside out, to study her biography, and to explore her complexes. In mythologically oriented therapy, the therapist plays the role of a representative of the underworld. Although he lets himself be led by the myths that surface in the consultation room, he always tries to identify the counterpole. He keeps his attention focused on the shadow of the client's reigning attitude.

A forty-year-old director of a small industrial concern informed me how supporting his workers was his highest priority. He practiced "management by going around" and wanted to be informed about all the worries and concerns of those working for the company. Instead of allowing his employees to come to him, he visited them unannounced while they were working and asked them personal questions. I listened to his description, thinking how wonderful it sounded until I became a bit uneasy. I imagined what it would be like to have my boss constantly interrupting me and to have him take the liberty of asking me personal questions. I would probably find it irritating and would worry about placing myself at his mercy. When I described my reaction to my client, he became angry. "That is not at all true for my employees," he answered and was insulted that I would even express such thoughts. The following week, though, he came back to my comments and admitted that he probably did need to be mindful of evoking similar reactions among his employees.

From the perspective of the client, the therapist poses tiresome questions and is a pessimist, a nitpicker, or also a naive optimist. From the mythological perspective, the therapist takes on the role of a devil's advocate, who prevents the spread of self-satisfaction and dreariness in the client's soul. The therapist listens with a critical ear to the client's speeches, bragging, and complaining, but keeps his gaze directed toward the other side. The client cannot expect subservient applause like that at a meeting of the Chinese Communist Party, but a discomfiting, opposing voice like the minority party in the British Parliament. The therapist takes on the role of a heretic, of the "loyal opposition."

In masculine therapy, the therapist must prevent one-sidedness. He does so not that his client eventually finds his way to a more balanced position, but because the confrontation with the opposites, with the demons of the underworld, helps the client keep the myths alive in an ongoing way. The therapist confronts the client so the latter continues to sense the existential challenges and to allow himself to be ensouled by the corresponding myths.

Through the therapist's heretical attitude the therapy evolves into a ritual struggle. The therapist questions the validity of the client's basic beliefs, and grapples with his client. Of course, it is important that both parties openly acknowledge this ritual struggle. The client knows what to expect and understands the therapist's critical attitude as a part of the therapeutic approach. He knows the criticism is not personal, destructive, or absolute, but a part of the therapeutic dialogue. The client's trust in the therapist is, naturally, an essential precondition. The client knows that both

he and the therapist will deal with the criticism within the framework of therapy and that it is not a sign of ill will.

The point of this confrontive technique is to bring new life
to the fundamental principles of mythology. The client comes
back to the myths without one-sidedly identifying with them. By
doing so, he is freed from his indifference, suffering, or depression. He also reconnects with the basis of his soul without falling
victim to some doctrine of salvation. His belief in life gets awakened when the therapist introduces the demons of the underworld. The therapist's dissent awakens new energies in his soul;
the tension constellates the myths. The original, existential challenges become palpable in the therapeutic encounter. Therapy
activates the masculine, myth-building spirit. Through his heretical and contradictory attitude, the therapist revivifies the client's
sense of paradox and relativizes an all-too-grandiose, one-sided
identification with a myth. Because of the ritual struggle, the
client is irritated, shocked, stimulated, or angered. He, thereby,
mobilizes new energy to bring himself renewed into the world
and his work.

## EXISTENTIAL CHALLENGES

The goal of a man's boasting, his spontaneous speeches, and his
confrontation with the contents of the underworld is to lead him
toward his existential challenges. What does the world want from
him? What tasks are his to fulfill? Usually men experience these
existential challenges in their profession. They see tasks that they
cannot avoid: the reorganization of the company, a presentation
on the new animal protection law, or the organizational meeting
of the Association Against Freeway Proliferation have top priority.
Such tasks give men the feeling of being necessary.

Men can, however, also perceive tasks in the personal, private
realm as existential and mythical. "The world must be peopled,"
declares Benedict in Shakespeare's, *Much Ado About Nothing* (II, 2),
as he decides to woo Beatrice.

A man's soul longs to place itself in the service of an existential task. By doing so, it sees the possibility of participating in a
greater whole or of dedicating itself to a cause. Personal well-
being or power needs do not always comprise the main goal of
men's activities. Frequently that goal is a collective task. Men,

therefore, experience these tasks, these challenges, not only as personally enriching or as opportunities for self-realization, but as service. "The work in the orphanage is important to me, because that is the only way I can do something to meet the need of millions of children in the world." The rationale derives from the cause, *from the object,* and not from one's own person.

It belongs to men's personality to define themselves by way of an existential task. This emphasis is foreign to the feminine, psychological perspective. The psychological perspective gives priority to the person and the personal, while career, intensive hobbies, or a passion is only a means to an end. On this point the different perspectives clash and this is the reason why, in addition to psychological therapy, we also need the masculine, mythological approach. Through mythography, the speechifying, and the ritual struggle, a man will find his way to that task demanded by his orientation and providing him grounding.

In addition, it is important in mythically oriented therapy for the client not to think in terms of solutions. The goal is a connection with the existential challenges. Naturally, a challenge will make *life more problematic.* The client registers the task and wants to make himself available. He does not think that he already has the solution in the bag. The notion of "solutions" originates in psychology, the goal of which is to reduce tension, settle dispute, and eliminate discrepancy. The belief in problem solving is antithetical to mythically oriented therapy.

## MEN'S GROUPS

"You understand nothing," a distinguished man in a gray sport coat yells at me. I react just as vehemently. Two other men join in, objecting that the discussion is taking place on the wrong level. Applause comes from the right, laughter from the left . . . I am leading a weekend course for divorced fathers. The atmosphere is unlike any I have experienced in women's or mixed groups: coarse, tense, aggressive, but focused, respectful, and concentrated at the same time. I sense how much I like the nature of this group. I feel an energy in myself that is ready to take up the engagement with these men and willing to confront our common themes.

Men's groups can produce this kind of atmosphere provided the leader does not make the men uncertain or psychologize them. Groups can constellate a mixture of measured aggression, mutual respect, dedication to the task, and anarchic savagery. I remember the men's cliques in college, when we threw wild parties, raced through the streets on our motorcycles, played pranks, outfoxed our teachers, and practiced rebelling at every opportunity that presented itself. Unpleasant memories also surface of times when we went too far: when we threw a classmate into the shower against her will or were vulgar or threw beds out the windows or drank excessively or were rowdy in restaurants.

Today I am a bit more civilized and seldom am only among men. In discussion groups, I do argue regularly with men about cultural or political themes that are important to us. Here and there the old savagery emerges with these avowed gentlemen. We yell at each other, attack each other verbally, and tease each other. Astonishingly, we then part peaceably after the greatest of quarrels as though nothing had happened.

By participating in such groups, men can protect themselves from being excessively civilized and experience beneficial savagery. In groups, men also find their way to their myths. The tensions arising in these groups make palpable the existential challenges that are the source of our myths. Group therapy or men's groups help men to experience the mythical part of their personality.

Robert Bly has shown us the importance of men's groups. In his groups, men come together in secluded places, recite Greek myths, and attempt to discover "the wild man" in themselves. As he describes the process in his book, *Iron John,* the point is to experience the original, archaic man. A man needs mythical, masculine images to develop, a vacuum that needs to be filled. For Bly, the fairy tale, "Iron John," serves as an example of the struggle a man has to go through to reestablish his connection to masculinity. Bly has certainly called attention to an important need in men's souls.

I am of the opinion, however, that the archaic savagery of men's groups is not something men find only by drumming in the woods and reciting poetry. Rather, men discover their savagery through the myths alive in our culture today. We need to replenish the myths of the past with the study of current myths and not be satisfied with a romantic retrospective of the Greeks and Romans. Since the faces, the *temenoi,* of myths are continuously changing, the examination of contemporary myths is not easy. While we need "Iron John" as a starting point, we must subsequently turn to the hidden mythical images in our work, family, and public life. Men's groups must also reflect on which myths appear where and the places where myths touch us. The mood, the aggression, in men's groups helps men to understand their own mythography or the myths in which they participate through life at work or at home.

Men's groups need the element of the existential challenge. Only when men live out the feeling of being challenged, of fighting against the horrific, does the possibility exist for their own myth to come alive. This kind of challenge strengthens the ego and gives it the ability to critically engage the myths. Too, when a man consciously confronts the myths of his time, he reduces the danger of succumbing to a myth as occurred in the Third Reich and still occurs in radical ideologies.

There are different possibilities for men to participate in a group experience. Sports are an important area in which men are challenged and have the feeling of belonging to a group. The fact that men prefer group sports indicates the extent to which athletics satisfy their need for association with other men. Although activities such as football, ice hockey, or handball offer men an outlet for channeling aggression and ritualizing the release of tension, they are not associated with any particular images. Sports, in other words, do not have a mythical underpinning. For this reason, men need group experiences in which contemporary myths are staged and can be confronted.

One example are the "gotcha" games. In these staged war games, either indoors or outdoors, two teams attack each other. They wear protective uniforms and are armed with special air rifles that shoot dye markers. The dye shows where participants have been hit. When played outside, the goal is to capture the enemy's flag. When teams play inside, one team has to push a button defended by their opponents and a bell sounds.

A "gotcha" game is reminiscent of the various, terrible civil wars that we hear about and see on television. To see a gotcha player would put us in mind of Sarajevo or Northern Ireland. We would react with indignation or alienation. How could anyone take pleasure in a game so perverse as war?

The mythological perspective sees it differently. "Gotcha" lives from the myth of the jungle fighter, the warrior who, with his comrades, has to shoot his way through enemy-held territory. It is an image that carries considerable attraction for the minds of thousands of men, expressing as it does the longing for freedom from civilization's restraints. Many young men imagine themselves as street fighters in urban jungles. Fortunately, they usually repress this desire, rejecting the use of violence, and admitting the notion only as fantasy. It only requires an ideology, that permits this form of confrontation, however, for the jungle fighters to stream into the streets. It only takes the "justified" occupation of a condemned building, the "legitimate" setting fire to some symbol of repression, or a "necessary" political demonstration. Then the hateful face of actual violence comes to meet us.

So that matters do not go as far as concrete violence, we need athletic activities like "Gotcha" as a way of living out the jungle fighter myth. We need groups in which the current, anxiety-evoking myths come to life and, at the same time, take place within certain boundaries. In the game of "Gotcha," a young man feels the tension, fascination, and fear this myth radiates, but is able to chose a different way of experiencing it. If we want to prevent violence from literally spreading through the streets, it is up to us to promote "Gotcha" and similar games. We must promote games that allow the terrifying aspect and the existential challenge of contemporary myths to come through without turning destructive. The reality is certain should we choose to repress the myth of the jungle fighter: it will come to life in a very real way.

Men's groups live on contemporary myths. In group therapy with men, it is important for these myths to come to life, whether they are myths about money, career, family, the economy, or politics. Together, the members of the group can confront the myths and, as a group, come to terms with them. Therapists should not just lead men's groups in a vacuum, but should facilitate their drawing energy from the myths present in our society. They thereby help men to awaken their warlike potential and to introduce it into society in positive and creative ways.

## THE BORDER BETWEEN PSYCHOLOGY AND MYTHOLOGY

In conclusion, I want to repeat that therapy based on the mythological perspective can not replace psychological therapy. When individuals wrestle with life problems of a personal nature in a relaxed, private, and confidence-inspiring atmosphere, they address another side of the human soul. In this setting, they experience themselves as psychological beings. Mythography, the boasting, the speechifying, and the confrontive technique speaks to a man's mythical side.

Psychological therapy, as we usually think of it, frequently fails to touch this quality in a man's soul. With his therapist, a man discusses his family, his fears, his past, and his relationships. The myths that serve as his orientation in the outside world, however, he leaves at the consulting room door. He views his ideologies, his principles, experiences, and attitude to life as objective facts. He overlooks the mythical soul material hiding in them.

Often there is a striking difference between a man's psychology and the myths he lives by. A fifty-year-old man storms into a therapist's office. He feels miserable and alone. No one listens to him. He feels as if he were living in a capsule in total isolation. He considers his life to be meaningless and wasted. "A shattered man," the therapist thinks to himself. To the therapist's astonishment, he discovers that the man is CEO of one of the leading corporations in Germany, with over 10,000 employees depending on him.

The man begins to become conscious of his psychology; he begins to examine himself. Although such therapeutic work is valuable and can help him progress, the question of whether this therapy will analyze the mythical part of his personality remains completely open. The mythical material, his participation in a collective narrative, has not yet reached the level of consciousness. He differentiates between the personal questions and the themes he discusses in his sessions and those events in which he takes part in the world of his profession. To his mind, the latter are not intended for the therapist's ear. He presents himself the way he is expected to in the therapeutic context. He celebrates regression, reflects on his relationships, and tries to find harmony and solutions to be able finally to return to the tensions and challenges of his battlefield.

Most men in therapy are differentiated and self-aware, ready to undergo this kind of analysis of their lives. Analysis, though, generally pays too little attention to their mythical connections. What expresses itself in the feelings of meaninglessness of the above-mentioned client are not psychological problems, but mythical ones. Perhaps, he has identified his work with the myth of the creator, of the king. He sits on the throne, gives orders, takes action, plans ahead, and attends to the problems of his subjects. He is inspired by a myth!

His complete identification with the myth, however, is difficult. He has sacrificed himself to a myth and has lost the contact to the source of his own being. Mythologically oriented therapy would, perhaps, give him the strength to distance himself from any one specific myth, or at least to reconsider it. Perhaps the expectation, the desire for struggle, and the fear that originally connected him with his current myth will come to life again. Perhaps, he will find his way to a new myth.

# 7

## The Alienation between Men and Women

♂

## The Battle of the Sexes

We have to move collaboration between the sexes to a new level. Instead of starting with the current idea of equality, we need forms of dialogue that allow for gender differences. Women speak a different language and emphasize different themes in their actions and their perceptions. While personal engagement and authenticity play a central role for them, mythical validation is determining for men. These fundamental differences result in men's and women's experiencing the private and public realms in their own separate ways. We must find the means for men and women to come together, to disagree and to cooperate, without one or the other having to deny their gender uniqueness or attempting to make one-sided claims to power.

*— But why?*

In the preceding chapters, I have attempted to demonstrate to what extent men and women differ not only biologically, but in the nature of their souls. Men and women are alien creatures to each other even though what they have in common far outweighs their difference. In this chapter, I explore the question of how best to configure the relationship between the two genders. Is it possible for men and women to agree when they differ in their thinking, perception, and in what they consider to be central to life? What will their life together look like if men's souls thirst for myths and women look primarily to personal relationships? Who will be responsible for the public realm and who for the private one? Do questions like these not threaten a regression to the time when women were tied to home and family while the glorious men constructed their domains in the outer world?

In this chapter I show how a new phase has begun in the relationship between the sexes. Equal rights for women and their emancipation will and shall continue in the public sector without women having to subordinate themselves to male thinking or simply having to adapt. Men and women will develop ritualized forms of dialogue that will create a place in everyday life for their respective differences. In this way it will perhaps be possible for all of us to live our lives based not only on psychology, but also on myths.

Consider the following exchange as an example of the hurdles we have to overcome.

> Wife: "Look at the advertisement in this magazine. I think we should take the children to Hilton Head again this year!"
> Husband: "Go to the same place twice? I can't see the point in that!"
> Wife: "Then plan our next vacation yourself!"

There are various messages in this brief dialogue. The wife is looking for some confirmation of relationship. She secretly hopes to hear how successful the last vacation at Hilton Head was. Her focus is on the idea of a vacation for the whole family and the possibilities for relationship it could bring. Instead of hearing this message, the husband focuses on the content of the wife's statement. He cannot see the sense of going to the same place twice. He objectifies the wife's information and is deaf to her psychological message. His mind goes to the possibility of travel in general: getting to know strange cities, exploring unknown regions, canoeing down the Orinoco, or driving a Hummer through the Sahara.

The man's lack of understanding is not due to any negative intention, but because his soul's fundamental perspective interprets the question in a different way. His thinking is mythical and identifies the wife's comment with a myth that is important to him. Misunderstandings like this happen continuously in communications between men and women and lead to mutual irritation and frustration.

## DIFFERING PERCEPTIONS

Women perceive the world psychologically, their attention directed toward the individual human being. They hear on the level of relationship and they transmit signals expressing their personality. For a woman, verbal communication serves as a means of noticing an individual, discovering her condition, exciting her to anger, intriguing against her, or grasping her as a human being.

During an evening's conversation with a guest about a trip to South Africa, a woman will not only concentrate upon the content of the discussion. Instead, she will wonder why he is perspiring and pulling nervously at his sleeve while describing his experiences. She will be curious about his relationship with his wife and whether he had a romantic liaison during his trip. Thoughts will come to her mind that men would not have. She will perceive her partner in conversation more fully than her husband, who will be carried away by the theme of South Africa. Before they go to sleep that night, he will want to offer her lengthy explanations on his understanding of that country's political situation. He is absorbed by the topic and the guest becomes an abstraction.

Female psychological perception takes in the whole of an individual: his appearance, his behavior, how he dresses, the way he speaks, his posture, and his gestures. Verbal communication is but one aspect of what a woman registers. A woman's psychological orientation causes a woman to define life from the perspective of the private realm, regardless of whether she spends her time as a business woman, a politician, a housewife, or a bus driver. Important for her are her circle of acquaintances and personal encounters with others. Her thinking is occupied by questions of how her partner is doing, what others think of her, what the children are doing, why a friend of hers believes possessions can be harmful, and how she can state her opinion without hurting someone's feelings. Her focus is on matters of relationship.

Things look different inside the heads of men. "Who is going to the Super Bowl?" "Shouldn't the city build another spur for the freeway?" "What jobs do I assign the department's new employee?" "How come this supermarket charges four dollars for a quart of milk?"

Although these examples are oversimplifications, the private and personal carries primary importance for women, regardless of whether they work inside or outside the home. By contrast, men seem quickly to become helpless with the same themes. They have difficulty formulating feelings that might lead to personal interaction, and it is almost impossible for them to discuss the nature of a relationship. In psychological matters, women are men's superiors. For this reason, women are the ones to speak out in marriage or couples' therapy, the ones who want to resolve problems in the relationship.

Men come across as being somewhat awkward and often withdraw into silence. As I have mentioned before, mythology is their primary orientation. Their souls are moved by the myths manifesting themselves in public or collective circumstances or determining family interactions. They, therefore, become active and talkative when the discussion turns to general or objective topics where they can apply their mythological perspective. A man may spend so much time explaining to his wife why a particular politician should resign, how little a fellow employee understands about marketing, or how the municipal transportation system should be organized, that he forgets their wedding anniversary. Such wordy explanations usually bore women, especially if they have no personal connection to the topic or if they are unable to detect some message for relationship. The mythical inspiration men derive from participating in external fields like sports, bird watching, or technology is not always understandable from a woman's perspective. Women experience men as mildly autistic, incapable of relationship, and frequently less interesting than other women. They perceive men's one-sided absorption in a myth—"all he can talk about is work"—as alien and antagonistic to life.

Since women are more strongly oriented toward psychology than are men, they tend to seek a consensus. To be in agreement is important and conveys the feeling of security and acceptance. Women, therefore, work to achieve harmony in the personal realm. Sharing their opinions with others takes on great importance, since women register disagreement as threatening and antagonistic.

Men place their emphasis differently. For them, disagreement and tension are normal. In their view of the world, dissension is but another possibility. They look for the tension contained in every myth with its inherent polarity and follow the movement of the opposites in a theme or discussion. Correspondingly, men will criticize the work of others, tear a movie to shreds, or question the comments of a friend. Unquestioning agreement is difficult for many men since, by so doing, they distance themselves from the mythical and become bored.

Men want to follow the myths, to trace their movement in the public realm. During a social visit or at a meeting they come alive when they can carry on a monologue about their hobbies or interests. At home, the same men are capable of lying on the sofa for hours without saying a word. During meals, men frequently prefer to stare at a newspaper or watch television and avoid conversation with their wives. The media's reflection of everyday myths hold their interest, while their wives' comments about difficulties at work more than likely leave them cold.

Men's and women's differing soul orientations also result in different expectations of their respective environments. Women expect psychological authenticity from those around them. What someone says should also correspond to his or her personality. Women want to know if others truly live according to the attitudes they espouse. They would not accept an educator like Jean Jacques Rousseau, who promoted the cause of children, but sent his own children to an orphanage. His writings did not correspond with his actual life.

Women's expectation of psychological authenticity results in a different understanding of politics and business than that of men. Women do not separate private life from public role and, consequently, the credibility of a politician's public statements depends upon whether the two realms of his or her life correspond to one another. They judge a politician based on how he is as a human being, how he talks, how he relates to women and children, and whether he does his share at home. Women look for consistent behavior and reject any separation of public position and private existence. In this regard, John Wiles, whom I mentioned earlier, would have had no chance in the political arena.

Women consider even details that have nothing to do with fulfilling an office or position important since they reveal the overall personality. Men are less likely to expect this correspondence between public and private. They may tangentially register that so-and-so "has difficulties at home," or is an "impossible human being," but these factors seldom serve as a basis for their judgments.

In fact, men's readiness to separate public role from personal life often takes on grotesque qualities. A famous professor of psychiatry and medical director of a psychiatric clinic was known to have slept with his patients on more than one occassion. Additionally, he had the arrogance to bill the patients' health insurance for these hours. Elected to Parliament, the same man dedicated himself to establishing rigorous ethical guidelines for psychotherapists. Men react less to this kind of contradiction, even if they consider the professor's behavior intolerable. Commenting on him, one of the professor's long-time colleagues said tersely, "Yes, I know. He still has a problem in that regard . . ."

Men's tendency to split off the realm of the personal from the psychological also manifests itself in the selection of intimate partners. Most men are astonishingly unpsychological in this regard. Rather than considering a woman psychologically, they elevate objective aspects to the determining criteria for their decision. Instead of following the lead of a sense or feeling, they are convinced, for instance, that a woman who grew up on a farm would be good for them or that they need a wife with spontaneity. They choose a partner because she is intelligent or beautiful and do not even think about her character or the quality of their relational dynamic.

The selection of an intimate partner brings to light the system of reference men use as their support. They project a particular mythical image onto the woman in question, thereby avoiding the confrontation with their anima. They usually do not select a woman who upsets or irritates them or triggers powerful feelings. Since they would find living with such a woman threatening, they follow the more secure path of myths that are known to them. It is difficult to say whether, because of this, marriages are better or worse. In the West, though, where marriage is supposed to be a psychological relationship, this tendency on men's part often results in an intensive coming to terms with each other after the couple has exchanged vows.

Men neglect psychology and seldom apply it as the basis for their opinions. What someone represents, accomplishes, and communicates is important. To look behind the facade would be indiscreet. Men like to judge each other mutually as role carriers or actors in the universal drama. They question whether someone fits the mythical image he bears in himself. The myth someone represents is of interest, not their private situation and their character. Such an emphasis also explains how men can work for years next to each other without any private knowledge of each other or any personal connection. After the fact or through the office grapevine, they learn that a colleague filed for divorce or that his wife is pregnant.

Men judge their fellow human beings according to the roles they play in the public, mythical realm. They seek out the myth that will best describe someone. They identify the man at the next desk as a typical *Reader's Digest* reader, someone who is hypercritical without having any depth, or as an intellectual reader of *Time* magazine who has difficulty taking a position. The myths serve them as an opinion screen, while they tune out psychology. We could say, therefore, that *mythological correctness* is most important for men. They ask whether the expression and the behavior correspond with the myth that someone supposedly expresses. Does he really act like an author, a psychologist, a musician, or a businessman? They consider *psychological authenticity*, the agreement of private and public behavior, secondary.

## DIFFERING MOTIVATIONS

One result of women's psychological orientation is the importance of personal involvement. Women legitimize their efforts for a cause or theme, changes in business or politics let us say, on the basis of their personal experience. Where they confront a given problem, at home, as part of their wider life, or in conjunction with their acquaintances, determines their engagement. They campaign against a highway bond issue, because, in their own neighborhood, they have experienced the effects of a community cut in half by freeway construction. They dedicate themselves to the cause of better schools, because a nephew or niece has suffered the effects of poorly planned classes. A woman's motivation stems from her personal experience with a problem or situation. "I know what it is like to be sexually assaulted," was the justification one woman gave for demonstrating against the mass rapes in Bosnia.

Personal involvement plays less of a role in men's motivation. They look primarily for objectivity. The impersonal, sober presentation of a problem is most important from their perspective, and personal factors lead to one-sided and less sensible decisions. Involvement is either unimportant or serves as an obstacle in coming to terms with a given issue. Objective judgment, not personal involvement, should be the determining factor for the majority of men. This characteristic results in the accusation men often hurl at women, namely that they are too emotional, cannot be objective, and cannot think logically.

Behind this objectivity, however, usually hides a specific myth. Men talk about objective perspectives, quote facts, and make reference to "reality," even when they are participating in one of the collective myths. Myths, not personal involvement, serve as their point of reference and as grounds for their activity.

It is most interesting to observe this phenomenon in the field of psychological research. By expecting empirical verification of their experiments through replication and the generalization of their findings, psychological researchers represent the opposite of a feminine perspective. The same psychologists also find it incomprehensible that a psychology, based on the uniqueness of relationship and focused on the centrality of individual experience, could have anything to do with human beings. By expecting general verification, replication of experiments, and objectivity, the academic psychologist celebrates the myth of natural science.

When he starts by assuming the identity of psyche and matter, the psychologist eliminates what, in chapter 1, I have called "psychological thinking." By insisting on the replication of psychological events under similar conditions, he negates the uniqueness of *individual experience.* For him there is no place for a psychology that operates with concepts such as personal involvement and psychological authenticity.

On the one hand, this attitude expresses a masculine rejection of the feminine perspective. On the other, it bores us by its fixation on a single myth. When we cannot discuss the assumptions behind a way of thinking and cannot recognize it as *one possibility* within the mythical canon, we invite spiritual desolation. The findings of psychological research will not touch the human soul as long as the discipline remains rooted in a single myth and rejects other myths or rejects the feminine perspective. Research psychologists will neither practice mythology nor pursue meaningful psychological research as long as the myth of natural science is their legitimization. In what I am calling, "psychology," that would be analogous to applying *one* life history to all human beings.

Personal involvement is not men's primary focus. Instead, they pose the question of whether a theme or problem fits within the mythical canon occupying the public realm. It is not a question of whether they have experienced or felt the theme, but where and how society discusses it. Should the discussion invoke one of the great myths of our time—the myths of progress, redemption, equality, the eternal return, natural science, or sacrifice—men will begin to show interest for the topic. Violence, as a theme, interests men when the public takes it on and debates the question as the counterpole to the myth of human beings as peaceful creatures.

Their mythical orientation and, for the most part, the absence of personal involvement results in men's categorizing of new themes and challenges within a mythical context. To approach a theme mythically is to deal with its oppositional quality, to consider its light side as well as its dark side. The question is not whether a demand or claim will be accepted or rejected, but whether the theme will find acceptance in the mythical canon. Often this process evokes head shaking or resistance in women. They either repress the topic and do not talk about it or they react indignantly: "How can you even talk about the atrocities in Yugoslavia without *doing* something about it?"

Unlike psychological discourse, mythological discussion allows for contradiction and opposition. Against the background of mythology, men can accept the opposites within a theme and deal with them. It is not a matter of "pro" or "con," but the weighing of advantages and disadvantages. The existential tension of opposites shines through and lends the discussion its particular stamp.

On the question of legalizing abortion, many women find it irritating how dispassionately men can discuss the different aspects of the issue. Out of personal involvement and because the question affects them directly, it is alienating to women to have it discussed in this distanced manner. From a woman's perspective, one is either for it or against it! Because of men's mythical orientation, however, both sides of the question become constellated.

## OPPOSING SUGGESTIONS FOR RESOLUTION

Differences in men's and women's soul orientation, such as personal involvement versus mythical objectivity, psychological authenticity versus dedication to myth, and consensus versus an appreciation for dissonance, make it almost impossible for the sexes to understand each other. Due to their soul's disposition, men and women are too different to feel genuinely with each other. They will have to learn to apply mental constructs to begin to understand the other's position. Naturally, there are considerable areas of agreement and delightful common experiences. Yet, these should not blind us to the fact that men encounter unknown, alien beings in women and women in men.

The fundamental differences in men and women make it obvious that opposing suggestions toward resolving these differences are in order. From women's side, the suggestion would be to promote conversation, communication, and above all, personal involvement. Women would place importance upon the encounter of one individual with another in the hope that through increased contact, the sexes might draw closer and begin dismantling the opposites. The key word here would be "relationship."

Of course, this approach stems from psychology and, according to the thesis of this book, is one-sided. Conversation is important, but it will not cause the mythical undercurrents to disappear magically from our world. From men's point of view, relationship and mutual contact will only partially solve the problem. Take the following example.

In Israel a woman was murdered by a Palestinian from the Gaza Strip as she drove him to his job in Tel Aviv. The woman had lived among the Arabs in the Gaza Strip for years and supported the Palestinian cause. Her personal involvement and her relationships did not prevent her falling victim to an act of terror. In a land where opposing national myths collide with each other, the resulting tension could not be dissipated by personal relationship.

Unfortunately, relatedness does not prevent tension, violence, and despair. The chasms of human myth gape wide even when individuals know each other personally. We no longer experience the other person as an individual personality, but as the symbol or expression of a myth. We have witnessed this fact during the civil war in the one-time Yugoslavia as Serbs massacred Muslims with whom they attended school. We have seen it happen as well in Nazi Germany when "good" neighbors failed to stand by the threatened Jews next door. Unfortunately, the fact of being related to someone or knowing someone well does not charm away such brutalities.

The belief that we can prevent such crimes with more psychology ignores the mythical side of human beings. Certainly relationships are important. We cannot live without them. Yet conversation and mutual getting-to-know-you are not always appropriate methods for solving problems. Men respond to relationships and allow themselves to be influenced by them, but this approach still does not touch a part of the male soul. In the conflict between men and women as well as in the attempt to solve public and private issues, psychology cannot provide the only resolution.

Men offer another suggestion to alleviate the fundamental difficulties arising from the tension between the sexes. We will not solve the problem, they would say, with more relationship, closeness, and contact, but with objectivity. We need to strive for clear, objective assessment to make decisions based on the object. They would subtract the personal element from the problem to better concentrate on the actual situation. "It is not a question of what I think is better, but whether these measures are right *for our school,*" states one teacher.

In couples' therapy, it is striking the way the men try to introduce organization, structural difficulties, or the social context into the discussion. "Well, if my wife is so unhappy, maybe it would help for her to plan her day better!" A specific myth, however, conceals itself behind this objectivity. If the man cannot reflect on the myth and believes it to be the "truth," he only persists in his unconsciousness. "I think it would be good for us to do our grocery shopping *together!*" "I don't think it is part of *the man's responsibility* to have to clean the house as well. I don't understand why you have to get so upset!" In their confrontations with women, men often fail to hear messages about relationship and concentrate, instead, on the objective aspects. What men believe to be logical, on the other hand, sounds completely devoid of feeling to women's ears.

Men, of course, use dialogue to settle disagreements, but such male exchanges have a different significance. They differ from the ideas women have about the nature of discussion. For men, it is not so much a matter of getting to know each other, sharing areas of involvement, and exploring the other's psychology. Male discussion aims at establishing position, opinions, interests, and hierarchies. Male discussion is more a dialogue within a given system. What position does one's partner in conversation hold in the system? Is my position better or worse? The dedication to objects or to the common myth holds the primary position and not the individual, not the personal. In men's eyes, the object, the topic, or the task is uppermost. Women find this approach disturbing and unrelated.

What men are doing by emphasizing the object, is displaying their mythical orientation. Since they are constantly in search of devotion to whatever myth animates the public realm or their professional field, they need the mythical substance that contact with the "sacred realm" confers on them. In other words, they see themselves and each other as middle managers, as telephone company employees, or as members of the teaching profession. This is, perhaps, one reason men clearly have less understanding for the psychology of a problem. "What I want, personally, is unimportant. What matters are the interests of the company."

Men's and women's differing orientations often mean that in many current political questions, psychological ideas collide with mythological images. Frequently, the two genders cannot understand one another. In many marriages, conversation is limited to the seven minutes a day that, after six years of marriage, an average couple talks to each other. After having probed the strangeness of the other sex so that it is "known," the areas a couple "has in common" disappear. Man and woman stand facing each other in their respective beings and realize that they speak different languages, pursue other interests, and have divergent fantasies. The greatest danger is for them to deny their differentness and project the unconscious conflict onto the other.

As I have mentioned, Analytical Psychology emphasizes the importance of polarities. Whether we are masculine or feminine, we always carry the sexual counterpole in us. The feminine part of a man's soul Jung called the anima, and the corresponding masculine part of a woman's soul he termed the animus. Together the masculine and feminine form a synthesis and fructify each other.

Psychologically, this perception of gender certainly has its validity. The masculine and feminine *can* be mutually fructifying. The notion, however, of "alternating complementarities" by means of which man and woman complement each other, only partially applies to the human soul's dynamic and orientation. According to this model, neither the masculine nor the feminine sets the tone exclusively. Instead, through the constant, fertilizing dialogue, we bring as much masculine as feminine to every situation.

This model, though, does not consider masculine and feminine existential aspects of being, but as complementary parts of a whole. Since masculine and feminine are fundamentally different, they do not totally fit in a Yin/Yang polarity. Men strive for grandiosity within a mythical framework; women seek confirmation, intimacy, and involvement in areas of personal importance. When men try to come to terms with women, they always run the risk of opening a deep chasm. They may find common ground through their intelligence or through physical intimacy. If not, either the man or the woman will lose the essential connection with their soul's orientation.

## OLD GENDER ROLES

Society incorporates the differences between men and women by allotting each gender specific spheres of action and influence. The resulting division of labor attributes definite tasks to men and to women. According to the traditional allocation practiced in many cultures, men are responsible for the outer world, the public realm, while women tend to the private realm. The classical patriarch fills a public role. He fulfills a function in public life whether that be as a lawyer, policeman, salesman, teacher, garbage collector, or con man. He may attempt to extend his role into the private realm and his relationship to his wife. The allotment of the different spheres of action is grounded in the existential differences between the sexes.

The notion that, because of this role allocation, the man holds a more powerful position, rests on a misconception. When an individual defines himself on the basis of the myths shaping the public realm, he appears powerful or weak. Terminology such as, "position," "standing," "acclaim," "honor," or "recognized power," belong to the collective sphere. The collective identifies the function that a given individual fulfills to establish his area of action and influence. The mayor rules over the municipal employees. The medical director manages his clinic. The branch manager is responsible for his department store. Outside of these areas of influence, however, such individuals have no voice.

In the private realm, the spheres of influence overlap and are, therefore, difficult to recognize. A mother influences her children, for instance, even when they exercise power and hold positions in the public realm. Since individuals exercise power in the private realm indirectly, through relationship, its mechanisms are more difficult to perceive and to understand. The titles of the public sphere are usually absent, since we are unable to identify and separate out psychological spheres of influence. In the private world, personal influence goes unrecognized, while activities in the public one derive from a societal mandate or an assigned position.

If a man declares himself to be the head of the household, he is emphasizing his position in the public realm. Yet, even if he sees himself as the "Lord of the Manor," it does not necessarily mean he holds the actual power in the private realm. The term, "head of the household," stems from the masculine perspective that regards the family as the basic unit of society and requires identifiable figures for use by the public realm. In other words, "head of the household" points to a collective myth of family. Whether the "head" actually determines the psychology of the family is another matter. He does participate in the thinking and the ideas projected by society or the nation onto the family, something that may mean very little at home. In reality, assigned public roles are of less importance for relationships within a family. The power structure in the private realm generally avoids the practice of attributing functions.

Even within the public realm, though, there were for a long time areas relegated to men and those relegated to women. Restaurants and bars were reserved for men. Women maintained their social contacts in cultural or charitable organizations and within their circle of acquaintances. Otherwise, they were exiled to the home. The professional world as well had gender-specific areas. The career path for men was, at the same time, admission to a male domain. In their professional world, men celebrated their grandiosities and surrounded themselves with the necessary attributes. The professional world offered a man the opportunity to free himself from the claws of psychology. In their imagination, these men participated in the world of myth and believed they were helping to solve the great tasks of our civilization. Here, a man's suit, his office, or his automobile betrayed his actual standing in the public realm.

We are also familiar with the practice of allocating spheres of action to men and to women from the field of ethnology. Most cultures separate areas of work and everyday life according to gender. Women are responsible for collecting wood and tending the fire; men direct their attention to hunting and the construction of houses.

## THE CONTEMPORARY ROLE MIXTURE

It is to the credit of the women's movement that our culture knows fewer specific areas restricted to only one sex. In general, our society has taken on the task of abolishing these various areas. There shall be no more domains reserved exclusively for men, nor shall there be any activity from which any individual is excluded on the basis of gender. In other words, the traditional division of labor has been abolished. Women now work toward their own self-realization in professions and do not allow themselves to be pinned to a role.

Our ideal is a society in which everything is open and accessible to everyone. We will not discriminate on the basis of gender, and gender shall not prevent an individual from developing his or her interests or profession. This newfound equality naturally applies as well to politics, the classic male domain. Women should become politically active and take on leading positions locally and nationally. Business, too, should be open to women and no position or type of work should be limited to only one sex. We are promoting greater homogeneity in the military as well as in corporate upper management. We have decided to overcome a divided society and to work for one devoid of gender limitations and a confining division of labor. Men and women should have the same rights.

This step in the direction of a gender-neutral society is both necessary and daring. Only the dissolution of gender-related conventions, regulations, and role expectations will enable women as well as men to find a life task that corresponds to their abilities and inclinations. It is no longer acceptable for women to be forbidden from performing any activity.

## THE OPPOSITES REMAIN

At the same time, we must realize that eliminating sexual discrimination does not solve the problem of men and women. Despite the opening of male domains to women, of the acceptance of women in the public realm and men in the private one, the opposites are very much with us. Even when men turn their energies to child-rearing and tending the sick and women become politicians, soldiers, or professors, the oppositional differences of gender continue to crash into each other. Only the mode of expression is different. Even when men and women turn to the same jobs, even when they move in the same areas of life, they still remain dissimilar beings in opposition to each other.

The fundamental dilemma has not changed just because women have taken their places as pilots, crane operators, politicians, engineers, or bankers. The essential differences between men and women do not just dissolve into thin air simply because both engage in the same activities. They will also not disappear magically from our world through social measures like quotas or equal opportunity employment. If anything, the reverse will be the case. Through the increasing numbers of women entering male-dominated professions, feminine perceptions will, more and more, come to confront masculine understandings.

Now the conflict between masculine and feminine takes place in both the public and private realms: no longer do different territories and spheres of influence define the differences. Instead they manifest themselves in all areas of our lives. Masculine and feminine thinking competes in politics, education, family, and business. With the gender apartheid revoked, men today have to come to terms with feminine thinking directly and women must learn about the masculine. Through this circumstance, perhaps, the battle between the sexes will intensify, and we will have to discover new forms for the struggle between men and women. Since two fundamental perspectives confront each other, it will not be possible always to have understanding between the sexes, nor for them to follow a common path.

The differing soul orientations become that much more pronounced the more issues concern important existential challenges. The polite distance collapses and the rhetoric of equality disappears when a man feels that circumstances threaten the foundation of the nation or when a woman registers a man's behavior to be heartless. Perhaps men will feel threatened should psychological authenticity and personal involvement become determining political criteria. Their open-mindedness may disappear when women couch complex issues in the metaphors of personal life. They will miss the sense of the great necessities of life, the enthusiasm for grandiose solutions, and the courage to be one-sided. Women, on the other hand, will criticize objective compulsiveness and impersonal analyses. Since masculine thinking contradicts feminine thinking, conflict is unavoidable. Until that sublime moment when a combination of both positions becomes possible, we will have to tread a long and difficult path.

Women are noticing, however, that some areas of public life are foreign to them. No matter how much they would like to participate and to fill positions in the outer world, they have an uneasy feeling that the public style of thinking and working does not fit for them. For them it is alien territory. Why do meetings always proceed strictly according to an agenda? While equal rights are talked about in public, the realm, itself, remains uncomfortable for many women. "I cannot support a topic in my department that does not interest me. Why do I have to make a decision when I find both positions convincing?"

Often they succumb to feelings of boredom and alienation. The differing soul orientations come to the fore with concrete questions and with the execution of tasks and duties within a profession. The esteem men grant women verbally reveals itself as empty rhetoric if, during discussions, women are continually interrupted and their arguments are ignored.

Psychology has difficulty making itself heard in the mythically oriented public realm. If a woman representative in Congress bases her arguments on personal involvement or refers to situations from her private life, men will at best humor her with their attention. They will hardly be convinced by her approach: "too personal, too emotional." The "experts" found it extremely curious when Mrs. Thatcher tried to make the problems of Great Britain's national economy understandable by using terminology from her household budget. "How can one compare so complex a structure as the entire nation with private housekeeping," they complained. They would have preferred complicated analyses studded with quotes from authorities in the field of economics. Arguments from private life do not readily lend themselves to integration within a myth. Is this market economics, socialism, or interventionism to demand that the country should only purchase what an individual needs "at home?"

Further, men interpret as weakness the feminine tendency to show understanding for both sides: there is no room in the outer world for ambivalence. In the public realm, we should celebrate mythical patterns, not give expression to our personal processes. From men's perspective, we need to split off the personal to make way for the corresponding myth. We talk about the significance of "mobility" or of "sexuality," not about driving a Chevrolet or our own sex life. It is easier for men to focus on a topic or theme, to censor the personal, and to quiet any inner skepticism.

Men believe that, in the public realm, not only is their way of dealing with issues the correct way, but that it is the only way possible. Objective arguments with cited facts to support them are what count. In the outer world, those who receive respect are men or women holding identifiable positions within the existing ideological structures. Men perceive such figures as representatives of their valid myths, those through which they experience public life. Because of women's psychological orientation, it is more difficult for them to make their influence felt in this mythological environment. Psychology has a difficult time of it in a milieu in which mythical discourse dominates. Any discussion addresses "objectives," while "personal reasons" usually announce the withdrawal from the public world.

Women's psychological orientation makes it more difficult for them to deal with criticism in the outside world. When their work or their opinion is called into question, they perceive these attacks through a psychological screen. They experience criticism, in other words, as if it were directed at them, personally. They become angry and hurt. Lacking the relationship with the mythical perspective, women register criticism not as mythical, but as personal. Women do not experience themselves as representatives of myths, but have the feeling of being personally engaged with the world.

Women's comments and activities in the public realm frequently trigger anger in men. Although feminine thinking is also fascinating and stimulating due to its personal coloring, the personal aspect does not belong in public discussions. Because they do not hold to the defined framework of the mythical canon, women's opinions irritate men. "We are discussing marketing strategies that have proven successful and not your brother-in-law's experience of watering his lawn!" Men quickly find personally influenced opinions irrelevant, even though this approach to a discussion can be superior in intellectual clarity and precision to the verbal approach men use.

In personal discussions, men miss the tension that results from the mythical aspect. Unconsciously, they want disagreements to flare up. It is not possible to criticize or to take positions, defend them, and to attack another's position when the other person draws her arguments and metaphors from the personal realm. It is also not possible when the other person takes criticism personally. Feminine thinking irritates men, because it does not lead to the great solutions and answers of existence and because it leaves no room for impersonal critique. There is no room for men's preference for decisions and for one-sidedness in discussions dominated by the personal and the importance of harmony. Men end up feeling stuck in ambivalence.

For these reasons, careers in the public realm are easier for men. They are not as bound by their private lives, by psychology, but see their efforts contributing to the whole. They are less susceptible to inner scruples about their family, their colleagues at work, or their personal motivation. Since a career can be a concealed dedication and submission to a myth, it is more difficult for women to grasp the importance of the effort required. "Why should I give up my life for a factory that manufactures machines?" "Why should I trade my current job where I feel good and like the people I work with for a higher position in which my husband and my family would have to suffer?" The human factor carries greater weight for women.

Women's relational orientation may make psychological considerations a major hindrance in career moves. She would not like having to eat lunch at a different restaurant or move to an office on another floor, because of a step on the career ladder. A new position within the same company also would mean a change in the circle of personal acquaintances. In a new and higher position, men look forward to new grandiosity, turning their energy to more important matters, and to coming one step closer to the source of the myth. Women quickly fall prey to the feeling of arrogance and the fear of changes in their relationships. "What will the people I work with think of me?"

In one large corporation, a woman was recommended for the position of department head by the company management. The woman asked for time to consider the offer. She talked to all of the other members of her department to find out how they would feel about her becoming their boss. The company's management promptly interpreted her behavior as "weakness in leadership."

The first thing Ruth Dreyfuss, a new member of the German Parliament, did upon taking office was to make the acquaintance of the people with whom she would be working. It was important for her to get to know everyone from the department heads to the janitorial personnel. She considered her dialogue and relationship with them the basis for her work. Several of the federal employees were taken aback and positively surprised by her action. Until now, they had worked for any number of Members of Parliament without ever meeting them face to face.

Women's emancipation has changed the public sphere. Psychology is pushing its way into the mythical environment, bringing new metaphors from the private realm. We now speak of authenticity, involvement, and relationship and avail ourselves of analogies from private life. This mixing of two soul positions that were previously separate, leads to misunderstandings and difficulties. At the same time, we can see the situation as an opportunity. "Feminine Management," for instance, a less hierarchical,

team-oriented approach, has become a recognized model for
leadership in the United States.

The same holds true for the private sphere. Changes
inevitably result as masculine thinking influences this area of our
lives. A household run by a man looks different than one run by a
woman. Men organize the chores, interact with the children, and
go about their day differently than a woman would. They may
have difficulty in instilling all the thousand details of a home with
soul, in giving them meaning. While a woman experiences the private, immediate areas of life as symbolic of her feminine center, a
man stages myths here as well. He does not want to attend to the
details of the household or the necessities of the daily routine,
rather these things have to conform to him. His idea, his project,
or his plan comprises his focus and not the concrete aspects of the
household or family care. He is after tension and existential challenges. He can get excited about preparing a Chinese dinner, for
example. To clean up the daily chaos in the kitchen, on the other
hand, is a bother if his motivation is only personal. Daily chores
and duties in the household are, naturally, tiresome and boring
for all of us. No one likes to clean the house over and over again
or to be responsible for the daily grocery shopping.

I do not mean to imply that women are predestined for such
tiresome work. Men, however, take on this kind of work out of a
fundamentally different attitude. When men arrange the private
sphere, it changes. They do not focus on details and experience
delight in arranging their personal surroundings. They want to
experience the mythical tension of opposites. They feel their way
around the household looking for challenges requiring them to
mobilize all their strength and imagination.

Women get upset when men install a trellis instead of clear-
ing the supper table or arrange the wine cellar instead of running
the vacuum cleaner or discuss the professional possibilities of a
career in education with a daughter instead of helping her with
her homework. They naturally suspect men of shirking their duty.
Men are only operating out of their mythical orientation in the
private sphere. They want to mark positions, introduce rules, distribute chores and duties. They are only looking for the opportunity to experience their activity in a larger context.

Combining the two realms in life, striving for a gender-neutral
quality for the personal and the public spheres, inevitably brings
conflict. That does not mean we should return to our earlier

gender apartheid. We do need to be open to ways in which the battle between the sexes, the interaction between the psychological and the mythological positions, can be carried out without one or the other being repressed.

## CONCLUSION: NEW RITUALS

The first consequence of the difficulty in combining the two spheres has to do with the attitude men and women assume toward one another. They must learn to recognize and honor their respective uniqueness. Although the areas of agreement between the two are immense, they still encounter each other as alien beings. When a man meets a woman and vice versa, each experiences another perception of the world. For men the emphasis upon the private and personal is not always understandable, but it must be respected. Perhaps men could try to understand women by referring to their own feminine side, by exploring their personal involvement or biography. Women expect men to develop greater sensitivity toward personal feelings and to take feminine communication patterns seriously when they enter "men's domains." They expect men not to dismiss their greater need for personal interaction as uncertainty or a lack of conviction, but to accept it as a specific form of feminine behavior.

It is vital for women to recognize the masculine way of thinking and perceiving. Many women are secretly inclined to proselytize. They do not accept that a man might sense, perceive, and think differently. They are convinced that he could conform if he only wanted to and attempt to force him into the feminine orientation. Generally, women accuse men of dogmatism, one-sidedness, trying to dominate, aggressive behavior, and a lack of understanding. They would do better, both in public discussions and private interactions, to relate to men as myth bearers. As a rule, it is not men, personally, who speak, but myths that speak through them. In the mythical context, the expectation of psychological authenticity and personal involvement is of secondary significance. Women, therefore, must acknowledge men's right to distance from themselves as private beings and to play the roles of public celebrities.

Women should recognize men's need to dedicate themselves to a myth, an object, a passion, or a theme and to forget about the

personal, private realm of relationship. Otherwise, the expectation of authenticity and personal connection robs men of the
strength and the will to invest themselves in something. Life
becomes meaningless for them when it has to be lived exclusively
in terms of the private realm.

It might be some help for women to accept the tension of
opposites, the search for dissent, as a fundamental masculine
characteristic and to hold that tension, themselves. When a
woman's partner divides the world into categories and complains
about the "rednecks," the "money-hungry corporate types," or the
"ivory-tower academics," he is not talking about the nice families
that live next door or across the street. He is talking in metaphors,
images from the public realm, as a way of experiencing the mythical tension of opposites.

The second consequence of the difficulty in combining the
two spheres will occur in different areas of life. Men as well as
women need territories that convey the respective masculine or
feminine qualities. They need places to which they can withdraw to
regenerate themselves as men and women. A woman requires a
personal, psychological place in which she can sense her femininity. A man needs his territory to experience himself as a man.
These "retreat zones" might be concrete places: meeting centers
for women, women's bars or women's groups, men's groups, football, ice hockey, military organizations, or jazz. They might be fig-
urative, arrived at by mutual arrangement in public and private
life. After a social dinner, for instance, men and women might separate into two groups for a short time. The women would spend
time with each other while the men carried on some discussion in
another room. In England, women traditionally have withdrawn
after a meal to the "powder rooms." It may be helpful for women
as well as men to take trips by themselves from time to time when
they would not have to concern themselves with the expectations
and demands of the other sex. For men, this need is frequently met
by business trips, while many housewives spend their days in the
feminine world of personal relationships.

The greater the mixing of the different realms becomes, the
more we will hear the demand for areas just for men or just for
women. We need "zones" where men can act according to their
mythical orientation. I am not thinking just about men's groups
that listen to myths in the wilderness to awaken the "wild man" or
those that, through exchanges with others, become aware of their

masculinity. I mean places that are integrated into our civilization. Even our coeducational school system must again separate out classes only for boys and only for girls.

The third consequence is a greater recognition of the soul orientation of the opposite sex. Men are learning psychology through women; women are becoming more familiar with mythology through men. Women sense the power of the myths "out there" through their relationship with a man, be it their father, brother, or partner. They are defining themselves mythologically through a personal relationship. The myth in which a man participates is often a criterion for the beginning of a relationship.

> When I met my husband for the first time, he had just returned from Africa. He had been working in Tanzania in a developing nations project and, in his spare time, had studied the behavior of apes. His stories fascinated me and opened possibilities for me. I felt the desire to set out with him for those places.

Just as women find their way to the myths through men, men will experience the value of psychology from women. Only psychology can free a man from his prevailing one-sidedness. A man must, therefore, discover the value of relationships, of his personal biography, of personal "space," as well as authenticity, without losing or denying his sense of himself. Usually, this occurs in an encounter with a woman. The danger, though, is that he will subsequently delegate the personal to his partner, wife, or girl friend and only acknowledge it for himself in his relationship with her.

Men also find their way to psychology through personal crises, severe illness, traumas, or a woman's dependence on them. It requires such occurrences to make a man realize that the world is also ruled by psychology. Through a public defeat or a painful separation from a partner, psychology forces its way into a man's life. His private side appears and demands that it also be taken into consideration. We should understand these crises as opportunities to discover our own psychology. Numerous differentiated men have taken this step, not allowing themselves to be blinded by the grandiose myths in which they participate. Instead, they also attempt to attend to the psychological counterpole.

> I was driving my car from Stuttgart to Frankfurt. I suddenly felt very uncomfortable. It felt like I was outside my body. I began to get scared. I trembled and had to stop at the next exit. After this experience, I realized that I had

lost my inner self. I had succumbed to workaholism, had only my business
in mind, and had neglected everything personal and private.

The fourth consequence involves the rituals that we will have
to develop so that interaction between the sexes can become possible. We need social patterns to facilitate men's and women's
learning to listen to and to intellectually understand each other.
These rituals should not be understood too narrowly, but more as
the intention of making interaction easier. Since there is always
the danger in direct confrontation that the sexes will misunder-
stand and blame each other, these encounters should be mediated by a third. Men and women should try to connect with one
another by way of a common activity, theme, or experience.

Long-lasting, direct confrontation requires too much effort.
Feelings of alienation, hate, or resistance will set in when the primary fascination has vanished or the erotic attraction becomes
weaker. In the face of the banality of everyday life, communication shrinks to the familiar seven-minute average. The woman will
interpret any theme from a feminine perspective, while the man
approaches it mythically. Being focused on the same object, the
same task, or the same theme, however, makes a shared solution
possible—provided that the differentness of the other is
respected. In this way, common arrangement of the personal as
well as the public realm can become possible.

When members of a school board have to arrive at decisions
regarding the construction of a new school, they do not just study
various plans, discuss the advantages and disadvantages of air conditioning, or debate the pro's and con's of large expanses of lawn.
They visit other school buildings together, make reference to their
individual experience in school, and consider the opinions and
ideas of their sons and daughters attending school. They do not
base their decision solely on theoretical excursions or the examination of various documentation, but also on reflection about
their personal experience. The personal and psychological has to
take its place beside the public, mythical thinking. Masculine and
feminine thinking should both enter the discussion, be identified
as such, and receive respect and courtesy. Social rituals are indis-
pensable values in this situation. Interactions like this increase the
chances for a *common will.*

Cooperation between men and women can make reference
to the rituals that our culture has already developed as a way of

overcoming opposition. One example is the common meal, a ritual that constellates a space in which difference is acknowledged. The wine, table manners, and food, all provide an opportunity to present oneself as man or woman to the opposite sex. In western cultures in which men and women eat together, meals have become established as rituals of joining. Two, alien beings can come together and study each other.

Travel is another ritual in which we can experience a coming together. Trips to other countries comprise one of the chief occupations for the summer vacation months. By traveling to a foreign country, we distance ourselves from the personal environment as well as from the mythical realm in which we normally participate. The traveler places him- or herself in a kind of soul isolation, even when the foreign culture, landscape, or local customs are interesting or fascinating. This solitude provides an opportunity for a man to discover psychology and a woman mythology.

Traveling together makes possible a more profound exchange between a man and a woman. The strange surroundings allow women and men to engage each other according to their respective soul orientation. While the couple seems to focus primarily on the strange culture, in reality they use it as a tool to help them both realize their own soul images. In the unknown, strange, or fascinating environment, a vessel presents itself that can be filled mythologically as well as psychologically.

We must, however, develop further rituals that promote a more civilized battle between the sexes. We have to pose questions of the changes needed in our political culture, in representative government, in the administrative structure, and in the economic system. In politics, we must arrive at a different language, find another way of reaching decisions, and alter the overall structure to make masculine and feminine discourse possible. In management, whether in business or in politics, we must create new forms of thinking and of ritual interactions between the sexes. We must have these new rituals so that the opposites of gender can play themselves out without our having to revert to gender apartheid, assigned gender roles, or to a privileged status of one gender over another.

# ALSO PUBLISHED BY CONTINUUM

Christine Downing
***THE GODDESS***
*New Continuum Edition*

"A must for those concerned with an experiential approach to religious studies, depth psychology, and above all the Goddess/es." — *Religious Studies Review*

Christine Downing
***MYTHS AND MYSTERIES OF SAME-SEX LOVE***
*New Continuum Edition*

"A massive work of remarkable scholarship, which reads as easily as a historical novel, and draws together depth psychology and classical mythology, Freud and Plato's *Phaedrus.*" — *Journal of Psychology and Christianity*

Verena Kast
***FAIRY TALES FOR THE PSYCHE***
*"Ali Baba and the Forty Thieves" and the Myth of Sisyphus*

"Eminent Jungian analyst Kast utilizes these two myths from different cultures to explore therapeutic themes and archetypes . . . . For anyone interested in the ways stories inhabit our lives, this is an erudite and readable volume." — *NAPRA ReView*

Verena Kast
***LETTING GO AND FINDING YOURSELF***
*Separating from Your Children*

"Separation for parents is often considered a stage of young-adult development, but Kast points out that early in life — from birth, actually — children enter into necessary stages of separation from their parents
. . . . Kast points out how this separation is also an opportunity for redefining oneself and the marital relationship." — *Booklist*

---

Daniel C. Noel
***THE SOUL OF SHAMANISM***
*Western Fantasies, Imaginal Realities*

"This sophisticated book, which reads like a good story, gives a shamanic dimension to psychology and the best psychological analysis to the notion of shamanism . . . . Before reading anything else on shamans or 'spirituality,' read this book." — Thomas Moore

---

Patricia Reis
***DAUGHTERS OF SATURN***
*From Father's Daughter to Creative Woman*

"A brilliant analysis of the father–daughter relationship." — Linda Leonard

---

Patricia Reis
**THROUGH THE GODDESS**
*A Woman's Way of Healing*

"This book is a must for any woman who wants to connect with her deepest resources for empowerment and healing." — Marija Gimbutas

Murray Stein
**PRACTICING WHOLENESS**
*Analytical Psychology and Jungian Thought*

Murray Stein argues that we need to practice wholeness and engage in the endeavor intentionally. It is a daily activity, one performed to deepen our lives and broaden our expression.

Lawrence E. Sullivan, Editor
**THE PARABOLA BOOK OF HEALING**

"A rich melody of wise voices — a haunting tone poem whose golden beat is the age-old search for the elusive and hidden powers of sickness and cure."
— *Whole Earth Review*

Edward C. Whitmont
**RETURN OF THE GODDESS**
*New Revised Continuum Edition*

"A seminal work . . . . This will undoubtedly become a watershed volume in the history of our culture, as well as our consciousness." — *Journal of Psychology and Christianity*

*At your bookstore or from* **The Continuum Publishing Company, 370 Lexington Avenue, New York, NY 10017**